JZ1308 .K46 2009

Ken

The
co

The Sociology of Cosmopolitanism

Also by Gavin Kendall

STATE, DEMOCRACY AND GLOBALIZATION (*with Roger King*)

UNDERSTANDING CULTURE
Culture, Order, Ordering (*with Gary Wickham*)

USING FOUCAULT'S METHODS (*with Gary Wickham*)

Also by Ian Woodward

UNDERSTANDING MATERIAL CULTURE

Also by Zlatko Skrbis

CONSTRUCTING SINGAPORE (*with Michael Barr*)

LONG-DISTANCE NATIONALISM

The Sociology of Cosmopolitanism

Globalization, Identity, Culture and Government

Gavin Kendall
Queensland University of Technology, Australia

Ian Woodward
Griffith University, Australia

and

Zlatko Skrbis
The University of Queensland, Australia

© Gavin Kendall, Ian Woodward and Zlatko Skrbis 2009

All rights reserved. No reproduction, copy or transmission of this publication may be made without written permission.

No portion of this publication may be reproduced, copied or transmitted save with written permission or in accordance with the provisions of the Copyright, Designs and Patents Act 1988, or under the terms of any licence permitting limited copying issued by the Copyright Licensing Agency, Saffron House, 6–10 Kirby Street, London EC1N 8TS.

Any person who does any unauthorized act in relation to this publication may be liable to criminal prosecution and civil claims for damages.

The authors have asserted their rights to be identified as the authors of this work in accordance with the Copyright, Designs and Patents Act 1988.

First published 2009 by
PALGRAVE MACMILLAN

Palgrave Macmillan in the UK is an imprint of Macmillan Publishers Limited, registered in England, company number 785998, of Houndmills, Basingstoke, Hampshire RG21 6XS.

Palgrave Macmillan in the US is a division of St Martin's Press LLC, 175 Fifth Avenue, New York, NY 10010.

Palgrave Macmillan is the global academic imprint of the above companies and has companies and representatives throughout the world.

Palgrave® and Macmillan® are registered trademarks in the United States, the United Kingdom, Europe and other countries

ISBN-13: 978-0-230-00868-7   hardback
ISBN-10: 0-230-00868-2   hardback

This book is printed on paper suitable for recycling and made from fully managed and sustained forest sources. Logging, pulping and manufacturing processes are expected to conform to the environmental regulations of the country of origin.

A catalogue record for this book is available from the British Library.

A catalogue record for this book is available from the Library of Congress.

10   9   8   7   6   5   4   3   2   1
18   17   16   15   14   13   12   11   10   09

Printed and bound in Great Britain by
CPI Antony Rowe, Chippenham and Eastbourne

Contents

Notes on the Authors　vii

Acknowledgements　viii

Introduction　1
　Cosmopolitanism: a brief definition　1
　Distinguishing globalization and cosmopolitanism　1
　The structure of the book　3

1 Problems in the Field of Cosmopolitanism　12
　Introduction　12
　Conceptualizing cosmopolitanism: four problems　14
　　The problem of indeterminacy　14
　　The problem of identification　15
　　The problem of attribution　18
　　Globalization, cosmopolitanism and the problem of government　19
　The cosmopolitan disposition　22
　The sociology of cosmopolitanism: the major themes of the book　27

2 The Question of Belonging: The Nation State and Beyond　33
　Introduction　33
　Local vs cosmopolitan　36
　The cosmopolitan project, the nation state and beyond　40
　The politics of imaginative realism: towards cosmopolitan democracy　44
　The cosmopolitan project and the question of Europe　51

3 Cosmopolitanism and the Political Realm　54
　Introduction　54
　Is classical sociology methodologically nationalist?　56
　Establishing the utility and relevance of classical sociology for analysing contemporary global politics　65
　　The usefulness of Simmel: the city, colonialism and the triumph of the exchange economy　65
　　The usefulness of Max Weber's *Verstehende Soziologie*　67
　From the political to a theory of cosmopolitanism　70
　Concluding remarks　73

vi Contents

4 Cosmopolitanism as a Political Lifestyle: Morality, Technology and Style — 76
Introduction — 76
Cosmopolitan ethics — 80
The problem of hyper-rationality: destroying the cosmopolitan — 83
   Bad technology: impeding cosmopolitanism — 85
   Balancing security and freedom? — 86
   Societies of control — 88
Sociation: reclaiming style — 89
   Organic sociation: authenticity and de-differentiation — 95

5 Thinking, Feeling and Acting Cosmopolitan: The Ideal Types and their Expression in Everyday Cultural Fields — 99
Introduction — 99
Locating the cosmopolitans: some issues — 101
What is cosmopolitanism? Dispositions of openness performed — 103
The cosmopolitan as an ideal type of symbolic specialist — 109
Dimensions of the cosmopolitan disposition: mobilities, competencies and openness — 110
   Mobilities — 110
   Cultural-symbolic competencies — 111
   Inclusivity — 112
   Openness — 113
Cosmopolitanism: some fundamental types — 114
   Type 1: the sampling style of cosmopolitanism — 115
   Type 2: the immersive style of cosmopolitanism — 119
   Type 3: the reflexive style of cosmopolitanism — 121

6 The Cosmopolitan Symbolic Universe and Communities of Sentiment — 124
Introduction — 124
Cosmoscapes and commodity networks — 128
Global commodities: *bonnes à penser* — 140
Exchange and cultural diffusion — 140
Status changes and the demand for culturally novel goods and experiences — 142

Conclusion: Cosmopolitanism as an Intellectual and Political Project — 149

References — 158

Index — 170

Notes on the Authors

Gavin Kendall is Professor of Sociology at Queensland University of Technology. His research interests include social theory, social order and the relationship between culture and socio-technical problems. His previous books include *Using Foucault's Methods* (1999, with Gary Wickham), *Understanding Culture* (2001, with Gary Wickham) and *State Democracy and Globalization* (2004, with Roger King).

Ian Woodward is Senior Lecturer in Cultural Sociology at Griffith University and a Faculty Fellow of Yale University's Center for Cultural Sociology. In addition to publishing many papers on the cultural aspects of cosmopolitanism, he has written extensively on consumption practices, subject-object relations and material culture. He is the author of *Understanding Material Culture* (2007).

Zlatko Skrbis is Professor of Sociology at The University of Queensland. His research interests are located in the intersecting area of migration, nationalism, and globalization. He is the author of *Long-Distance Nationalism* (1999) and *Constructing Singapore* (2008, with Michael Barr). He is a lead investigator on a longitudinal study of Australian young people and their life trajectories.

Acknowledgements

Many colleagues have helped us gather and synthesize our ideas for this book, but we especially wish to acknowledge David Ellison, Mike Michael, Philip Smith and Gary Wickham, whose thoughts and comments were invaluable, and whose commitment to fruitful dialogue inspired us as we falteringly tried to make sense of otherness.

A number of colleagues helped us with the research for this book. Our sincere thanks go to Lyn Calcutt, Jennifer Gearing, Carissa Hoareau and Nick Osbaldiston.

The support of our families has been crucial: our biggest debt is to Trisha, Leanne and Marta, without whom this book could never have seen the light of day.

Finally, our editorial team at Palgrave provided all the advice and support we could ask for. We especially thank Olivia Middleton, Philippa Grand and Jill Lake.

Introduction

Cosmopolitanism: a brief definition

What is cosmopolitanism? Derived from an ancient Greek term meaning a 'citizen of the world', the word captures a receptive and open attitude towards the other. It is, then, an ethical stance, in which the individual tries to go beyond the strong psychological and evolutionary pressures to privilege those nearest to him or her (family, tribe or nation, depending on the scale of the example under examination), and endeavours to see the value of the other, and to work towards the possibility of connection and dialogue with the other. It is a denunciation of the popular saying 'charity begins at home': in bracketing the appeal of the local and the familiar, the cosmopolitan looks outward to see differences as an opportunity for connection rather than as a pretext for separation. Cosmopolitanism is not, however, purely an individualistic state of mind; we also understand it as having a social – processual and contextual – dimension. It is a behavioural repertoire which can only emerge under certain material conditions, and thus is something like Marcel Mauss's or Pierre Bourdieu's notion of the 'habitus' – habits of body and mind that are available in and activated by particular settings. In joining together the idea of an ethical stance with a material context in which this ethics can be activated, we suggest that cosmopolitanism is not possible in all times and all places, through an act of individual will. The cosmopolitan is a product of social and political history, and requires a certain *assembling* of the material culture with which s/he coexists.

Distinguishing globalization and cosmopolitanism

The literature on globalization typically breaks discussion and analysis down into four interrelated fields: the economic, the political, the technological and the cultural. All of these fields focus on the growing

2 The Sociology of Cosmopolitanism

interdependence of world society, which is generally taken to have a long history – stretching back at least 400 years to the beginnings of European colonialism (see Wallerstein 1979) – as well as a more recent phase of rapid acceleration (see Giddens 1990). For example, in the economic field, the emphasis is on how trade has become a global or a transnational rather than a local or a national phenomenon; in the political realm, there are studies and theories of how governmental problems – as well as the political mechanisms needed to deal with those problems – have become less and less local and more and more global;[1] new technologies, such as the television, the telephone, the internet and air travel increasingly connect up distant times and places, and 'shrink' the globe so that it becomes increasingly accessible through a 'networked' or virtual society (Castells 2000); and in the cultural field, the new connections between different parts of the world allow for the possibility of either cultural imperialism (e.g. the Americanization of culture, as seen for example in Ritzer's (2004) McDonaldization thesis) or the undermining of cultural homogeneity (e.g. many parts of the world now feature a variety of cuisines that either come from or directly reference a variety of 'other' places). In all of these fields, as we have suggested, it is usual to analyse how the four forms of globalization have both a long-term history, as well as undergoing rapid change in more recent times and for the foreseeable future.

While scholars of globalization are divided on its moral value – some seeing globalization as a corrosive force (e.g. Chossudovsky 1998), others regarding it as a potentially positive means to spread wealth and freedom around the globe (e.g. Hirst and Thompson (1999), who, though sceptical about the reality of globalization, suggest that we could do with more of it), and still others suggesting its effects are mixed, with definite winners and losers (e.g. Stiglitz 2003) – it is hard to find a similar ambivalence about cosmopolitanism. In fact, cosmopolitanism is often understood as the positive face of globalization – a theme that recurs in Anthony Giddens's work (e.g. Giddens 2000). For Giddens, globalization generates a ground upon which new forms of democratic activity can be built. In this vision, globalization may be understood as a necessary precondition of

---

[1] This is not to deny a renewed interest in problems of local government and the associated impulse to devolve power from the centre; rather it emphasizes the increasing impact of global interconnectedness in the political realm. Issues may have to be played out at local and global levels; for example, local recycling initiatives cannot be divorced from awareness of global problems of global climate change, global resource management, etc.

cosmopolitanism: in particular, cosmopolitan law (Held 1995; Held *et al.* 1999) and cosmopolitan democracy (Held 1996, 2002; Delanty 2000) are held up as morally positive innovations that, while sometimes admitted to be utopian, nevertheless should come to play an increasingly important role on our increasingly interconnected planet. Both cosmopolitan law and cosmopolitan democracy are closely connected to the *political* face of globalization. Clearly, in this context, discussions of cosmopolitanism imply questions of citizenship, rights and responsibilities in a globalized world.

The other face of globalization where the concept of cosmopolitanism emerges strongly is the *cultural*. Appadurai (1986: 27), for example, understands cosmopolitanism as a transcultural phenomenon, where the production and consumption of particular goods across cultures is the major process by which the other is experienced. Though much of the thinking about cosmopolitanism has been in the context of globalization processes, in this work we take a somewhat wider perspective. Frequently, the lay public and scholars alike consider cosmopolitanization to be analogous to globalization; or, they imagine that cosmopolitanization occurs as a result of globalization processes. In a cultural sense, this is only partly correct. Cosmopolitanization does indeed rely on certain types of mobilities; and these mobilities (Urry 2007) are crucial for pushing individuals into spaces and transcultural interactions which promote cosmopolitan outcomes. However, mobility alone does not guarantee cosmopolitanism: mobilities may promote *un*cosmopolitan sentiments and practices. Moreover, it is misleading to think that mobilities have to be global in nature for cosmopolitanization to occur. For example, moving through different parts of the same city might constitute a type of cosmopolitan experience.

There are, of course, clearly also technological and economic elements to this transcultural mixing (goods have to be produced, transported, advertised, sold, downloaded); and so, therefore, as with globalization, it is important to be aware of the constant interaction between the four fields, a point that we develop in the rest of the book. Nonetheless, in most of the literature, cosmopolitanism is understood as primarily a political and cultural manifestation of processes of globalization. These various themes are developed in the following six chapters, as we summarize below.

The structure of the book

We begin the book in Chapter 1 by reprising our arguments (see Skrbis *et al.* 2004) about the nature of recent research on cosmopolitanism.

Establishing the key trajectories and themes of this oeuvre, we highlight four key issues related to the configuration of writing and research in this field. We then progress to outline a synthesis of six major themes in our work.

The question of belonging, which we address in Chapter 2, pervades the history of cosmopolitan thought and is central to Diogenes', Kant's and Habermas's projects of cosmopolitanism. There are countless ways of being- and belonging-in-the-world, and the importance of the concept of cosmopolitanism is that it not only helps us understand the historically conditioned context of our existence but it also gives us tools for thinking beyond its limitations. There are two questions relating to belonging that are of particular interest to us.

The first concerns the age-old difficulty poignantly expressed in Diogenes' statement 'I am a citizen of the world'. Here, Diogenes points to the significance of the tension between local, and more abstract, less tangible ties to humanity or a planetary/global community of humankind. This tension is usually seen as leading to different kinds of loyalty, identity and responsibility. We see it as critical because it problematizes the significance and 'naturalness' of links that an individual forms with the local community. Can humanity inspire as strongly and effortlessly as the local, tangible and intimately familiar features of the social? Can humanity ever compete with the powerful force of what Nussbaum (1996: 15) calls 'the absorbing drama of pride in oneself and one's own'? This is not a trivial dilemma, given that most of us appear to display stronger feelings of empathy with and recognition of those who are close, familiar and recognizable than towards the abstract, the distant, strangers and humanity. The effectiveness of cosmopolitan sentiments is caught up in this dialectical tension between local and non-local, familiar and foreign, concrete and abstract. In sharp contrast to the effective pulling power of the local and familiar, much scholarship in the cosmopolitan tradition privileges the abstract and the universal over locally-defined realities. How do we bridge this gap? How do we make cosmopolitanism a useful concept given that it advocates something that is counter-intuitive, and stands against the accessible, concrete and local in people's lives? We side with Appiah (2005) and Calhoun (2003b), who see cosmopolitanism not as a disparaging dismissal of the local, singular and familiar; rather, the local, singular and familiar are necessary preconditions of an effective – and indeed, affective – cosmopolitanism.

These dilemmas bring us to our second question. In discussions on cosmopolitanism, there is one particular institution that serves as a mediator between local identities and cosmopolitan aspirations: the (nation) state. It is not unusual to see writers on cosmopolitanism avoid discussion of the state. For them, the state is commonly seen as an unsuitable – or, at the very least, unpredictable – companion in any cosmopolitan vision and this is largely because of state's reputation as a key imposer of limitations on cosmopolitan possibilities. Our view of the state is more sanguine; in contrast to these views, we see the state as an institution that can be productively coopted into the cosmopolitan project. There are two reasons for this. The first is that the state's contemporary power and influence are so pervasive that no social project can completely escape its grasp. The second is that the modern democratic state is demonstrably capable of radical innovation and renewal, particular when it engages regional, non-state and global institutions of governance. We do not lionize the institution of the state but we recognize it as an unavoidable point of reference in any project that involves a redefinition of belonging.

Our treatment of the state reveals our position towards cosmopolitanism, which we describe as one of imaginative realism. We enjoy the promise which the cosmopolitan project entails but this promise will necessarily unfold against the backdrop of conditions that are not of our choosing. We follow in the footsteps taken by Held (1995), Archibugi and Held (1995), Habermas (2001b) and Calhoun (2002a) because, the limitations of their contributions notwithstanding, they engage with cosmopolitanism by deploying key social science concepts such as state, public sphere and law. Their work contains an impulse that we consider worth nurturing: it combines social imagination with anti-utopian and sociologically and politically informed commentary.

Behind these debates there are some enduring and important sociological concerns that need addressing. One of them is Calhoun's critique of Habermas's model of constitutional patriotism, which in itself is closely aligned with debates around cosmopolitanism. How could we account for social solidarity in a system that is rooted in legal instead of more traditional sources of solidarity associated with the nation state? Can cosmopolitan be sustained and can effective mechanisms of belonging be generated through largely abstract models of solidarity? These are critical, yet profoundly sociological questions. Calhoun is particularly vocal in his criticisms of Habermas, suggesting that 'Citizens need to be motivated by solidarity, not merely included by law' (Calhoun 2002a: 153). While we appreciate Calhoun's criticism of Habermas, we nevertheless find ourselves defending Habermas by drawing on the debates and emotional responses surrounding the ratification of the European Constitution. In short, legal frameworks and proceduralisms may have a relatively limited capacity to generate bonds of solidarity, but their key significance is not in strength but in legitimacy. Our interest here is not limited to structures and proceduralisms; we are equally concerned with the functionality of everyday reflexive actors as a precondition for a successful cosmopolitan project. In discussing these questions we are drawn into discussing the European Union – which many European social theorists see as a quintessentially cosmopolitan venture. The European project is an experiment with no parallel in history: formerly powerful and self-sufficient nation-states willingly elect to sacrifice degrees of autonomy, transferring their sovereignty to new civic structures.

Chapter 3 begins with an extended critique of Ulrich Beck's assertion that classical sociology is ill equipped to deal with the analysis of cosmopolitanism because it falls prey to what Beck calls 'methodological nationalism' (*cf.* Fine 2007). By this, Beck means that classical sociology's horizons are limited to the national frame, and consequently cosmopolitanism is rendered theoretically invisible. We contrast this reading of classical sociology by suggesting that the horizon of classical sociology was not so much the nation state as the rather complex concept of 'the social'. This understanding is central to our argument that classical sociology has the appropriate tools for the analysis of our contemporary period. We suggest that 'the social' is a concept easily extendable from the local to the cosmopolitan, and that Beck exaggerates a problem of scale which does not exist: 'the social' works at the level of local and global relationships, and anywhere on the continuum between them.

The rest of Chapter 3 develops this notion of the classical concept of the social as the keystone of modern cosmopolitanism. Georg Simmel's work on the triumph of the exchange economy is used to understand the way in which global exchange relationships can be understood as simultaneously economic, political, ethical and psychological: for us, this provides an insight into how a multi-dimensional sociology of cosmopolitanism might begin to think about – and through – the complex network of the social. Following on from this, Max Weber's work is used to see how far an interpretive sociology might be able to throw light on the cosmopolitan social. Our Weberian approach suggests a sociology of cosmopolitanism which must be a moral science; we use Weber to arrive at the idea of cosmopolitanism as a system of ethics derived from the analysis and evaluation of the actions of self and of others. We add to this a sense of the ethical personage as historically located to emphasize that the ethical figure of the cosmopolitan is a political and cultural fiction: an entity that does not stand outside of history. We suggest that this particular type of person – the cosmopolitan – is the ironist, an individual who is 'cold' rather than 'hot' in terms of loyalties, and who finds ambiguity and uncertainty challenging and interesting.

Chapter 4 goes more deeply into the questions surrounding the type of person – the ethical figure – the cosmopolitan can be. We argue that it is helpful to understand cosmopolitanism as a lifestyle; just as forms of personal comportment, such as neo-Stoicism and neo-Epicureanism, were crucial to the formation of the type of person who emerged as the 'new citizen' of the post-Westphalian settlement, and the Stoicism of the Classical period provided a way of life that grounded Diogenes' enunciation of cosmopolitanism, so we think contemporary cosmopolitanism requires a certain type of ironic person; it is not a natural comportment, but is one that emerges from a particular political conjuncture. In this chapter, then, the argument is made that cosmopolitanism is not simply assumed, but is a form of self or person that is slowly constructed, over hundreds of years, in specific historical settings. We think of this form of self or lifestyle in Weberian terms as a 'status'. By following Weber, we can see that there is unlikely to be a one-way relationship between political structures and forms of personal comportment, with the former driving the latter, as seems to be implied in the work of Beck and Giddens. Rather, these forms of ethics can be seen as ways in which political and cultural groups make sense of themselves and are able to generate an 'ideological' justification of their own value. This form of self can then feed back reflexively into developing political structures: the cosmopolitan and cosmopolitanism exist in a mutually nourishing relationship.

To take this argument forward, we make use of Foucault's distinction between morals and ethics; for Foucault, the former represent external and usually rigid codes of behaviour, while the latter are more flexible and less reliant on external justifications. Cosmopolitanism represents an attempt to generate an ethics rather than a moral code. We suggest, following Stephen Toulmin (1990), that this ethical stance requires a commitment to rationality; while it would seem that this rational, ethical type of person would straightforwardly become cosmopolitan, the situation is confused by a widespread erosion of trust in rationality, a tendency strongly marked in the work of Lyotard, for example, but also foregrounded in Giddens's notion of reflexivity. Two possible consequences flow from this. First, in the dystopian vision of writers such as Giorgio Agamben and Christopher Lasch, one can see the emergence of a type of hyper-rationality – a pathological reaction against the crisis in rationality – which threatens and extinguishes cosmopolitanism; increased surveillance and control lead to a closing down of cosmopolitan impulses (international travel, for example, becomes less pleasant and straightforward, and fear of the other is ramped up), and the cosmopolitan is merely a synonym for an ever more elite and individualized character who disconnects from any sense of citizenship and fellow feeling, except to other members of his or her privileged class. In this reading, the in-group/out-group dichotomy is reinvoked, and the cosmopolitan is a member of an international elite. The second consequence is that the rejection of rationality can lead to a privileging of irony and style: as Scott Lash argues, a new type of hybrid, de-differentiated lifestyle can emerge. We suggest that this type of person is fundamentally a result of political processes, but comes to find its clearest expression in cultural realms, especially through consumption practices which mark out its status.

Chapter 5 investigates the cultural formations which compose modern cosmopolitanism. The chapter reviews historical and contemporary studies of globality and considers these literatures in the context of studies of cultural consumption and social status. When one positions these otherwise diverse bodies of literature against one another, it becomes clear that the possibility of *widespread* cosmopolitan cultural formations is largely unpromising. This is because theories of global object networks fail to consider questions of reception and consumption by audiences and users of these objects; while researchers in the field of cultural consumption generally ignore the nature of the global flows which disseminate and enrol consumers. In the global cultural economy there is an apparent confluence between global networks of capitalist exchange and the growth of cosmopolitan habits in a range of everyday fields. On the demand side, shifting and ever more complex status systems, fluid forms of identity that increasingly embrace cultural difference and the search for novelty in consumption habits all point to continued demand for cosmopolitan goods. On the supply side, producers are increasingly aware that cultural difference, exoticism and novelty offer powerful framing devices for goods in globally networked markets. The sourcing of objectified cosmopolitan difference by consumers becomes a means of social differentiation and status acquisition underpinned by cultural appropriation.

The global cultural architecture is characterized by increasingly diffuse networks of human and non-human innovators, carriers and icons of exotic and polyethnic cosmopolitan difference. This is a fact of contemporary global life, which we define as a form of globally spatialized, material-symbolic exchange. These structures are both material and symbolic, objectual and interpretive in nature. Yet, this material diffusion, while putatively global and potentially cosmopolitan in nature, can frequently have the unintended consequence of promoting social status systems and cultural relations founded on *un*cosmopolitan values such as cultural appropriation and status-based social exclusion. What this means is that the objectual, material constitution of cosmopolitan objects in things like food, music, dress or habits is susceptible (and, indeed, by its very nature open) to acts of interpretation which render the objects neutral, or even uncosmopolitan in nature.

Despite the apparent cosmpolitanness of global cultural capitalism, which circulates these containers of cosmopolitan meaning, there is in fact no such thing as a 'cosmopolitan object' *per se*. All such things gain their meaning through acts of interpretation; and there is no guarantee about how such objects are to be interpreted by different social actors. Chapter 5 argues that this fundamental contradiction defines the structural composition of contemporary cosmopolitanization.

The extent of this circulation of objects through global networks creates what we might call, after Appadurai, 'cosmoscapes'. These are spaces, objects, images and practices which afford and construct the possibility of cosmopolitan engagements. Yet, this global field of apparent cosmopolitanness is not given, but has to be reconstructed symbolically and performatively in particular sites and situations. It is thus represented, performed and interpreted as having cosmopolitan qualities, emphasizing interconnectedness and post-national orientations in a range of everyday fields. But crucially there must be an active process of interpreting cultural difference by social agents: a frame which actively identifies the character of 'otherness' as applying and which invokes the cosmopolitan impulse. For this to happen, the elements of social location, cultural capital, symbolic competencies and personal motivation must be fused. In other words, social location fosters forms of cultural capital that can operate in perverse ways to exclude and appropriate when we might imagine them – in line with the cosmopolitanization thesis – to include and connect. There is therefore no assumed connection between cosmoscapes and the fostering of cosmopolitan individuals.

Chapter 6 addresses the question of cosmopolitanism as a thing thought, felt and practised by social actors in a range of everyday settings. If cosmoscapes create fields of objectified, visualized difference, in what ways do actors relate to such material-symbolic constructs? To be a useful sociological concept, we argue that cosmopolitanism must be observable in objects, settings and spaces, and indeed written into bodies, their movements and practices. As part of the expression of cosmopolitan sentiments within spheres of everyday life, we suggest that there should be identifiable carriers of the cosmopolitan – humans and non-humans alike – which act as symbolic containers of cultural difference, and which we can track and map, talk and listen to, observe and interpret. These are mobile, portable symbolic tokens of cosmopolitan sentiments, interacted with and observed by social actors and social scientists alike in everyday settings. Indeed, we think it a fair test of the concept's relevance that there should be identifiable forms of actually existing cosmopolitanism (Robbins 1998). Yet we are also careful to take a critical, realist look at this imaginative and practical capacity, since we cannot assume these forms to be pure or ideal in any way. Like any major social shift, the alleged cosmopolitanization of culture is slow, discrepant and highly variable in terms of its uptake.

As a related issue, Chapter 6 also examines the problems and issues associated with defining and measuring cosmopolitanism. Clearly, the concept is currently very attractive and highly normatively charged, not least because it promises the emergence of cultural values that are reflexive, open and dynamically attuned to humanity and globality. The idea thus has a capacity to energize and attract theoretical energies which are in tune with this laudable promise. But importantly, it is also a complex, multidimensional concept which at its heart is associated with the promotion of fluidity and the multiplicity of attachments and cultural capacities. Such attributes do not lend themselves easily or directly to sociological operationalization and interpretation, despite the lists of research indicators that might be generated in favour of empirical measurements.

In this chapter, we note that definitions of cosmopolitanism have rested upon two major conceptual distinctions which have been both productive and limiting. These are the banal versus authentic (or reflexive) distinction and the accidental and strategic dimensions. Both of these theoretical discourses have structured discussion of cosmopolitan outlooks and practices. Our argument is that cosmopolitan values involve a set of cultural competencies which enable individuals to see things, participate in or with them, and use them in such ways that they are identified and identifiable as cosmopolitan. Such a perspective is broadly drawn from Bourdieu, but expressed through contemporary literatures on cultural enablement, entitlement and performativity. Crucially, to be cosmopolitan involves the power to label and then appropriate cultural objects as markers of cultural difference, cultivation or exoticism; it is thus a type of moral attribution (Skeggs 2004) which begins from a position of privilege and legitimacy, and, as a moral attribution which allows actors to be self-confident, it forms a kind of 'ideology'. We develop this by arguing that such cosmopolitan social actions need to be performed in particular contexts and settings as required, but of course actors must also be competent in understanding and drawing repertoires and schemas from the available cosmopolitan fields. Thus there may be various indicators of cosmopolitanism that sociologists might propose to be clustered into a cosmopolitan schema defined generally by the attitudinal construct of openness, but cosmopolitan sentiments surface and retreat depending on context and the capacity of actors to identify, appreciate and relate to cultural difference in ways which render it as 'cosmopolitan'. There may not be ideal types of cosmopolitans or a pure type of cosmopolitanism, but merely fleeting, unstable and transient manifestations of it. Cosmopolitanism is less an unfolding global certainty, and more an aspirational ideal that certain social groups bring to life for their own purposes. We argue that this desire is expressed through certain 'styles' of engaging with cosmopolitan things, which we characterize as sampling, immersive and reflexive. These styles bring their own ways of constructing, dealing with and engaging cosmopolitan difference. On the basis of our characterization of these types of cosmopolitan practice, we conclude that cosmopolitan traits and habits are gradually and discrepantly infiltrating fields of everyday practice. Taking a more modest approach to observing styles of cosmopolitan practice, we suggest the extent and durability of cosmopolitan change remains an open and ongoing question.

1
Problems in the Field of Cosmopolitanism

Introduction[1]

The recent resurgence of interest in the area owes much to the debate sparked by Nussbaum's (1994) polemical essay on patriotism and cosmopolitanism. An ensuing debate (Nussbaum and Cohen 1996) reinvigorated the concept of cosmopolitanism but also reminded us of its inherent limitations and contradictions: while it commonly represents a tool for radical social imagination through projections of cosmopolitan democracy, law and citizenship (Archibugi and Held 1995; Held 1995; Hutchings and Dannreuther 1999), it is also in danger of being an almost meaningless and glib catchphrase (Pollock et al. 2000).

The idea of cosmopolitanism has 'a nice, high-minded ring to it', as Himmelfarb (1996: 77) notes, but while the inherently abstract utopian value of the term makes a good promise, it does not necessarily make a good analytical tool. We concur with Holton (2002: 154) that the notion of cosmopolitanism 'raises questions about the coherence of this increasingly diffuse and somewhat vague concept for purposes of social enquiry'. Our approach engages with the current literature on cosmopolitanism, but refutes excessively abstract theorizations. We prefer to speak about cosmopolitanism as a progressive humanistic ideal which continues to be embedded in the structural conditions of modernity. We make a case for a more rigorous conceptualization of cosmopolitanism that recognizes the validity of two enduring characteristics of the modern era: the nation state and citizenship (Boli and Thomas 1999).

---

[1]Parts of this chapter are developed from Skrbis et al. (2004).

By understanding cosmopolitanism as embedded in structural conditions defined by citizenship and the nation state, we should be able to better understand not only the possibility of the transcendence of the present, but also the limits of the social. Therefore, we are steadfastly against a cosmopolitanism that fatally accepts the erosion of the nation state; we are against a cosmopolitanism that allows researchers, with good conscience, to ignore questions of the government of internationally mobile individuals; and, finally, we do not see cosmopolitan scholarship advanced when the world is seen as caught up in a Manichean dialectic between Kantian, cosmopolitan perpetual peace and a brutish Hobbesian order (Kagan 2003).

People (or at least *some* people) work, love, marry and live internationally and combine multiple loyalties and identities in their lives. Chernobyl, the AIDS virus, terrorism and CNN make a potent and far-reaching combination of pollution, death, fear and indoctrination precisely because of the permeability of borders. These new global interdependencies give rise to new kinds of human sociability (Beck 2002a: 30). For Appadurai (1990) the new dynamics of time-space compression give rise to new dimensions that are captured in terms such as ethnoscapes, technoscapes, financescapes, mediascapes and ideoscapes. These various scapes are indicative of the power of international flows, which show little regard for notions of a national boundary. Thinking 'ourselves beyond the nation' (Appadurai 1993: 411), beyond citizenship (Soysal 1994), and beyond the fixities of time and space is becoming not only easier, but also increasingly vital.

Not surprisingly, rootlessness, movement, homelessness and nomadism have become the motifs of the analyst of cosmopolitanism. Bauman (1996) likens modern individuals and life to pilgrims and pilgrimage, as identity and individuality shun fixity at any cost. Said (1979: 18–19) talks about a generalized condition of homelessness, an idea that has made its way into many sociological and anthropological texts. Deleuze and Guattari (1987) dwell on the nomad, whose only real place of belonging is movement itself. Similarly, Melucci (1989) likens members of modern social movements to nomads because of their lack of long-term commitments. The metaphor of nomadism is one of the most common ways in which the tension between fixity and fluidity, sedentarianism and dispersion is thematized.

Most contemporary commentators concur that cosmopolitanism – as a subjective outlook, attitude or practice–is associated with a conscious openness to the world and to cultural differences (Beck and Sznaider 2006; Hall 2002; Hannerz 1996; Held 2002; Tomlinson 1999; Urry

2000b; Vertovec and Cohen 2002). Our present times, in which many people have a shared sense of a world as a whole, and experience this through travel, work and exposure to the media, are thus perfectly suited to the proliferation of the idea of cosmopolitanism. The new cosmopolitan subject suffers from 'place polygamy' (Beck 2002b: 24).

Conceptualizing cosmopolitanism: four problems

There are four major problems in the contemporary literature on cosmopolitanism. The first is a problem of *indeterminacy*: cosmopolitanism as an empty signifier that can stand for almost any given reality and aspiration. The second is a problem of *identification*, and targets the pressing question, 'who is cosmopolitan?' The third grows directly from the first two and we call it the problem of *attribution*: what exactly are the determinants of cosmopolitan disposition and culture? While we turn to these three questions in the next section, the fourth issue of *government* goes to the heart of the problematic associated with the contemporary deliberations of cosmopolitanism. It is through the exploration of this last question that we can see cosmopolitanism as rooted in historical, political, social and economic realities of the modern era.

The problem of indeterminacy

We take the problem of indeterminacy to be the ultimate collapse of meaning of the concept of cosmopolitanism. This problem is best illustrated in Pollock *et al.* (2000), who suggest that the best way to deal with the nascent possibilities of cosmopolitanism is to eschew definition or specification of what cosmopolitanism involves, or who 'cosmopolitans' might be. According to this argument, while the problem of cosmopolitanism comprises some of the most pressing contemporary questions related to globalization, nationalism, ethnicity and identity, by their nature the practices and attitudes of the cosmopolitan are unknowable. This type of intellectual strategy is apparently designed to serve the purpose of leaving the category of the cosmopolitan entirely open, free of foreclosure by any set of academic, ethnic or meta-national discourses. Such a position is predicated on the notion that the political possibilities of cosmopolitanism are promising and potentially open to damage by significant attempts at academic territorialization. For Pollock *et al.* (2000: 577):

> cosmopolitanism may indeed be a project whose conceptual content and pragmatic character are not only as yet unspecified but

also must always escape positive and definite specification, precisely because specifying cosmopolitanism positively and definitely is an uncosmopolitan thing to do.

If we do not know what cosmopolitanism stands for, how can we trust these authors, for example, when they affirm that Sarajevo's cosmopolitanism has been destroyed in the 1990s? How can we know that it was truly cosmopolitan before then? What exactly would make it cosmopolitan again? While we are open to the idea that there may be various ways of being cosmopolitan and various possible cosmopolitanisms (Pollock *et al.* 2000: 458), we do not recognize that this is something that logically follows from Pollock *et al.*'s anti-empirical premises.

When Beck defines cosmopolitan society as 'a new way of doing business and of working, a new kind of identity and politics as well as a new kind of everyday space-time experience and of human sociability', he concludes that 'It is impossible to even outline this claim here' (2002b: 30). This is precisely the kind of impotence that is inherent to current discussions on cosmopolitanism. And to make helplessness contradictory, Beck manages to clearly identify the 'enemies' of cosmopolitan societies (2002b: 37).

Related to this idea of 'indeterminable cosmopolitanism' is the suggestion that cosmopolitanism represents the intersection of new historical styles of social and national relations that defy social-structural grounding. This literature constructs cosmopolitanism as a myth by imagining cosmopolitan spaces as free havens of cultural exchange, where 'groups of different religious and ethnic backgrounds intermingl[e] and exchange[e] ideas and lifestyles' (Meijer 1999: 1). Yet despite performing this mythologizing function, these creeds fail to capture the specific set of economic, cultural and social changes that facilitate the development of cosmopolitanization. As Calhoun (2002b: 108) has reminded us, we need to 'recognize the extent to which the cosmopolitan appreciation of global diversity is based on the privileges of wealth and perhaps, especially, citizenship in certain states'. The fantasy of cosmopolitanism is so appealing and effective that it discourages the attempt to tie down any real cosmopolitans; but we must resist the lure of this fantasy if we wish to make cosmopolitanism a valuable analytical concept.

The problem of identification

We are not suggesting that the solution to the problem of indeterminacy is necessarily in painstaking attempts to identify cosmopolitan subjects. Such an ambition would give rise to a new set of problems that we associate with the problem of identification. In the literature we find three populations that have been represented as archetypal cosmopolitans: global business elites, refugees and expatriates. Kanter (1995) tags the cosmopolitans as members of a 'world class' global business elite who possess the knowledge and skills that currently fit productively with economic transformations engendered by rounds of globalization across cutting-edge, emerging industries. For Kanter, the cosmopolitans are 'card carrying members of the world class' who are rich in the 'three C's' (1995: 22–3): concepts, competence, and connections. She argues that this gives them access to the latest and most marketable knowledge, the intellectual and social ability to operate at superior standards anywhere in the world, and the ability to forge global networks. Kanter's emphasis is on the business elites of the cosmopolitan class, which she defines as 'a social class defined by its ability to command resources and operate beyond borders and across wide territories' (Kanter 1995: 22). Although Kanter focuses too heavily on those who make up the über-cosmopolitan class, by summarizing the key cosmopolitan asset as a unique 'mindset' (1995: 23), a useful aspect of Kanter's argument emerges: cosmopolitan classes possess forms of intellectual, social and cultural capital highly valued in the global economy. The Triple Cs are somewhat similar to Kirwan-Taylor's (2002) cosmocrats, the people with MBAs and law degrees, along with a rather snobbish attitude towards those not belonging to their class and with a patronizing attitude towards the cultural other. They are closer to Calhoun's 'frequent travellers' than Kanter's über-citizens, but they certainly see themselves as cosmopolitans. These über-citizens are invariably from first-world countries or the privileged classes whose identification is largely with Western ideals. Under the cosmopolitan identity lurks the recognizable citizen of an advanced liberal democratic 'national' state or the monied and privileged individual from elsewhere, who just happens to be mobile.

At the other extreme to Kanter's world-class citizens are the

> victims of modernity, failed by capitalism's upward mobility, and bereft of those comforts and customs of national belonging. Refugees, peoples of the diaspora, and migrants and exiles represent the spirit of the cosmopolitical community (Pollock *et al.* 2000: 582).

Although these two radically different approaches base cosmopolitan identity on mobility across space and time, they present us with an interesting dilemma. Kanter's definition is more in accordance with traditional understandings of cosmopolitanism because the members of her cosmopolitan class have made a choice on the basis of positive, conscious effort. Refugees, by contrast, not only lack the free will to move but may even consciously prefer to be locals and parochials – anything rather than suffering the tragedy of their enforced cosmopolitanism. And if elite cosmopolitans are part of 'a high order political game' (Kanter 1995: 25), refugees are usually reduced to being the silent pawns in the games of others. In both definitions, human movement in itself is seen as a key determinant of cosmopolitanism. Refugees have no other destiny but to move until they find themselves – if ever – on the receiving end of the principle of hospitality (Derrida 2001). Both Kanter (1995) and Pollock et al. (2000) also assume that cosmopolitanism is a position of epistemological privilege *per se* without acknowledging the limitations of so-defined cosmopolitan positions.

In a quite different way, Hannerz (1990: 243) carefully asserts that the expatriate may be most readily associated with cosmopolitanism. Expatriates have chosen to live abroad, but they also can go back when they choose to. Volition and opportunity to return home is what makes them different from refugees. They are also different from the business elite in the sense that their mobility is not predicated on high status. Hannerz refuses to grant expatriates an epistemological privilege, for they may in fact be profoundly parochial and refuse to engage with the host environment: 'Cosmopolitans can be dilettantes as well as connoisseurs' (Hannerz 1992: 253). Expatriates may stand a good chance of turning into cosmopolitans but nothing guarantees this outcome.

Looking for subject positions taken up by either the elites or the disenfranchised is not the best way to proceed. We do not find much comfort in attempts to add new life to cosmopolitanism by adding colourful adjectives to it. However, we find useful the recent contributions which endorse the plurality and variability of cosmopolitanisms by linking them to fields of social engagement, such as Lamont and Aksartova's (2002) call for a study of 'everyday, practical cosmopolitanisms', or Werbner's (1999) assertion – which goes directly against Kanter's 'elitist' approach – of cosmopolitanism among working-class labour migrants. Our philosophical ideals must not cloud our ability to notice what Malcomson (1998: 238) calls 'the actually existing cosmopolitanisms'. In short, our understanding of cosmopolitanism should not be constructed from a series of imaginary, utopian or ideal types; the fluidity and complexity of cosmopolitanism is only likely to be revealed by the study of its mundane reality.

The problem of attribution

It is not easy to discern agreement in the literature as to what are the attributes of cosmopolitanism. In contrast to Kant's Eurocentric vision of cosmopolitanism (Mignolo 2000: 735), most contemporary authors subscribe to the idea of cosmopolitanism as a form of 'planetary conviviality' (Mignolo 2000: 721), a commercially driven 'end of insularity' (Nava 1998) and a series of multiple mobilities (Hannerz 1992; Urry 2000a). Although there appears to be unequivocal agreement between authors of various persuasions to associate cosmopolitanism with positive values (such as 'openness'), this was not always so. If anything, cosmopolitanism was used in the not-so-distant past to label anyone who did not fit or conform, including intellectuals, Jews, homosexuals and aristocrats (Brennan 1997). Stalin, for example, used the term as an accusation against 'reactionary' elements in Soviet society.

Apart from agreement among contemporary authors that cosmopolitanism designates positive, inclusive values and principles, there is a great deal of diversity when we examine other attributes ascribed to cosmopolitans. For Hannerz (1990), the relevant characteristics of cosmopolitanism include being willing to engage with the cultural Other (both in an aesthetic and intellectual sense), developing dynamic and interdependent relationships with locals ('there are no cosmopolitans without locals'), having a degree of competence and sense of home, or even better, a consciousness of a point of departure. Rabinow (1986: 258) puts it similarly: cosmopolitanism is an 'ethos of macro-interdependencies, with an acute consciousness (often forced upon people) of the inescapabilities and particularities of places, characters, historical trajectories, and fates'. Beck (2002c: 79–80) lists 13 different 'empirical indicators of *cosmopolitization*' that range from international travel to questions of political representation and manifestations of ecological crises. He acknowledges that these indicators lack both 'comprehensiveness and systematic exposition'. However, these 13 indicators are perhaps the closest we get to a systematic explanation that could form the basis for an agreed upon characterization of cosmopolitanism in the field. Unfortunately, his attempt stops short of this possibility primarily because he fails to distinguish between commodities, processes (travel, mobility), legal ascriptions (citizenship) and collective loyalties (national identity).

Urry (2000b) and Held (2002) are more selective and precise in their listing of cosmopolitan practices and dispositions. In Held's reasoning, there are three requirements of cultural cosmopolitanism: the recognition of the interconnectedness of political communities, an understanding of overlapping collective fortunes, and an ability to empathize with others and to celebrate difference, diversity and hybridity. For Urry, the cosmopolitan is characterized by an ability to be mobile, the capacity to consume diverse cultural symbols and goods, a willingness to take risks by virtue of encountering the 'other', the ability to reflexively observe and judge different cultures, the possession of semiotic skills to interpret images of others, and general openness to other people and cultures. Similarly, Lamont and Aksartova (2002: 1) define cosmopolitanism in terms of a practice 'used by ordinary people to bridge boundaries with people who are different from them'. Lamont and Aksartova understand cosmopolitanism as a cultural repertoire of 'particular universalisms' by which individuals understand human similarities (2002: 2–3). Thus they report that the sorts of strategies used by French workers differ from those used by American workers in that the former deploy unique historical and collective referents, yet both base their practices on similar universalistic discourses. While they do not specify cosmopolitan categories, they usefully encourage us to think beyond the limitations of current ways of conceptualizing cosmopolitan practices. Unfortunately, the regular assumption that cosmopolitanism is a form of (Kantian) universalism has condemned many scholars to believe that it can only be understood as an ideal type (Hollinger 1995). However, cosmopolitanism is a lived experience, and one which does not necessarily shy away from particular, local forms (Nava 2007).

Globalization, cosmopolitanism and the problem of government

Beck (2000) discusses cosmopolitan society as 'a second age of modernity', representing a paradigmatic shift from societies operating within the nation state framework. For him, cosmopolitan society not only enforces solidarity with strangers, but also creates conditions for a legally-binding world society of individuals. In line with the essays assembled in Cheah and Robbins (1998), we also take the view that there are different ways in which such an open orientation may emerge, rather than a single liberal Western pathway. In this sense, there are cosmopolitanisms rather than one single form of cosmopolitanism; resistances and blockages to cosmopolitanism are countered and stimulated by the accelerational dynamics of economic, cultural and symbolic capital (Beck 2000).

There is some tension between the idea of cosmopolitanism as a pluralist concept (there are different cosmopolitanisms and people are cosmopolitan in different ways) and the purported origin of cosmopolitanism in Western philosophical thought (Vertovec and Cohen 2002: 14–16). Is the cosmopolitan worldview a view from nowhere, as van der Veer (2002: 165) provocatively puts it, or is it a view of the world from a particular, Western angle? For Calhoun (2002b: 90), there appears little doubt that cosmopolitanism is 'a discourse centred in a Western view of the world', while van der Veer (2002: 166) calls it a Western and profoundly colonial engagement with 'the rest of the world'. There is some productive tension in this West vs. the Rest dilemma (Featherstone 2002: 3), although we see it as largely superseded by existing research on non-Western cosmopolitanisms (e.g. Werbner 1999; Zubaida 2002). What matters most in this context is not whether cosmopolitanism is a Western invention but, rather, whether it can serve as a shared universal value, applicable across different cultural contexts (see the important analysis of this in Calhoun 2007).

For commentators such as David Held, cosmopolitanism holds out the hope of a new type of citizenship. In this scheme, the old political order, which was closely tied to nation states, has its individual analogue in the citizen, who participates in politics at a variety of levels (borough, city, nation). But a new political order needs a new type of transnational citizen, a cosmopolitan who is no longer 'anchored in fixed borders and territories' but instead pursues 'basic democratic arrangements' at the level of cities or regions – and especially transnationally (Hirst and Held 2002). The cosmopolitan, then, becomes the micro-unit, or the agent of change, in a move to a new form of global government. One form of this has been sketched out by George Monbiot (2000), who argues that new forms of global government can be built up from a grass roots level. Now, while it does seem to be the case that new forms of international government are being invented, the basic unit of accountability is still the nation state, and thus the intervention-point of government must remain the citizen of the nation state, rather than the *cosmopolites*. As Hirst and Held (2002) argue, it is notoriously difficult to keep multilevel government accountable; at least in the case of the nation state, there are already mechanisms in place to remove failing (or failed) political actors. At the governmental level, then, it seems that there are strong pressures at work to keep political actors local/national rather than to foster cosmopolitan sentiments. A key question would seem to be: is it possible to build a global democracy, and if so, are our cosmopolitans the key? As an ideal, it sounds laudable, but we should remain sceptical about the possibility of the development of cosmopolitan global democracy.

Hirst and Held, again, deflate the cosmopolitan optimist by arguing that modern democracy developed on the basis of 'sovereign territorial states that had made a huge effort to homogenize their populations, create national languages, common traditions and shared institutions'. In short, democracy requires cultural homogeneity to function and this homogeneity – in its civic and ethno-national versions – is provided by nation state governments (Hirst and Held 2002). However, it is important that we draw attention to a certain 'mythic' element to the homogeneity of the nation state. Any such homogenization came, not infrequently, at the cost of the oppression of minorities (religious, ethnic and indigenous). The homogeneity of the nation state is often an effect of the triumph of its ruling elites.

The existing debates on cosmopolitanism, particularly those that emanate from a cultural studies' perspective, take precious little notice of these structural realities. But there have been a number of notable interventions made in recent times in relation to this issue. Beck (2002b: 34) talks about 'the limits of transnationality [that] continue to be drawn within national spaces' and Bryan Turner (2002: 56) critiques Nussbaum's call to create the new 'citizens of the world' without discussing that such new subjects would 'require a global government to enforce the rights and obligations of citizens. While I can in principle vote in a democratic government as a citizen of a state, I cannot currently enjoy many or any rights as a "global citizen"'. Appiah (1996: 28) similarly emphasizes that we cannot 'think away' the state – after all, the existing 'cultural variability that cosmopolitanism celebrates has come to depend on the existence of a plurality of states'. For Appiah, one of the most important tasks of any cosmopolitan agenda would be to 'defend the right of others to live in democratic states with rich possibilities of association within and across their borders' (1996: 29).

However, there are fields of intellectual inquiry in which the 'modernist' state system has undergone various kinds of marginalization and even repudiation. For example, John Rawls (1993, 1999) has outlined the vision of a modern global peace – a cosmopolitan age – in which moral rational individuals will attain international justice. In similar vein, multicultural theory outlines a new postmodern politics in which the democratic state will directly represent its moral communities (Bader 1999; Taylor 1994) in a system that breaks free from the shackles of the nation state. Beck expresses this possibility: 'Just as the a-religious state finally made possible the peaceful coexistence of multiple religions side by side', he writes, 'the cosmopolitan state could provide the conditions for multiple national and religious identities to coexist through the principle of constitutional tolerance' (2002b: 50).

The cosmopolitan disposition

The term 'disposition' has gained currency in the cosmopolitanism field (eg. Vertovec and Cohen 2002: 14; Featherstone 2002: 1), bearing the marks of Bourdieu's (1977) concept of the habitus. Bourdieu understands the habitus to be a set of principles and procedures which people use in their relations with objects and others. It is a set of dispositions for use in practice, which individuals use for self-orientation. The habitus is formed in individuals through historically and socially situated conditions, and while a person's habitus will direct them towards particular choices, it does not amount to obedience to rules. In defining the habitus, in shorthand, as 'a system of dispositions' (Bourdieu 1977: 214), Bourdieu clarifies three aspects of what he means by disposition, with the most particular component being that it is a 'predisposition, tendency, propensity or inclination' (Bourdieu 1977: 214). As we have specified, commentators commonly suggest that in terms of 'disposition', cosmopolitanism should be understood principally as an attitude of 'openness' towards others cultures (Hannerz 1996; Tomlinson 1999; Urry 2000b; Vertovec and Cohen 2002).

The notion of openness, however, is rather vague and diffuse (Skrbis and Woodward 2007). How is such openness manifested, and what are the sentiments that are embedded within the general attitudinal category of openness? 'Cultural openness' can be manifested in various ways, including, as Urry (2000b) points out, in both intellectual and aesthetic domains. But it must also involve emotional and moral/ethical commitments. Emotional commitment is demonstrated by an empathy with and interest in other cultures, which fuses intellectual outlooks with dispositions centred on such things as pleasurable personal experiences or exposure to media that predispose one to react positively to the idea of contact with other cultures. Closely related to this is a recognition that much openness to other cultures and places derives from a strong ethical commitment to universalist values and ideas that are expected to reach beyond the local (Bauböck 2002: 112). Cosmopolitanism, in other words, entails a distinct ethical orientation towards selflessness, worldliness, and communitarianism. The close connection between ethical commitment and cosmopolitan disposition has been one of the key characteristics of cosmopolitanism since the Stoics, but it has become pronounced in the modern era. Distinctly ethical commitments drive much of the contemporary environmental, anti-war and anti-globalization movements.

In sociological research, there have been few attempts to operationalize and understand empirically what these engagements are and how they might be identified. Using focus group research and content analysis, Urry (2000b) has made progress towards establishing aspects of the everyday reception and interpretation of cosmopolitan texts in the media. Urry's exploration of understandings of cosmopolitanism revealed that media representations have effectively created, via the production and dissemination of cultural symbols through advertising, music, and television, a substantial foundation for the consumption of banal cosmopolitan images. On the basis of this, Urry finds that consumption of such visual and narrative 'stagings of contemporary global life', and the understandings of globalism they engender, may lay the groundwork for the emergence of a cosmopolitan civil society. In this sense, Urry is close to Giddens, except the former emphasizes the cultural basis for cosmopolitanism, while the latter emphasizes the political basis. In an analysis of Australian survey data on popular attitudes to globalization, Holton and Phillips' (2001) study effectively operationalizes the economic and political dimensions of the concept, including attitudes towards protectionism, policies of the United Nations, and foreign economic investment. In terms of cultural, emotional and ethical attitudes and dispositions, which we see as forming a crucial component of the cosmopolitan outlook, Holton and Phillips' conceptualization is less useful, telling us few things about the cultural dimensions of change, the reasons behind it, and the ways individuals adopt and adapt cosmopolitan or global outlooks, manners and consumption styles. Yet their data do tell us who is more likely to be positively disposed to accepting globalization: those who have travelled or lived in another country, those who have used the Internet and made overseas phone calls, those with higher levels of education, and (to a lesser extent) men rather than women and younger rather than older respondents. In contrast, Lamont and Aksartova's (2002) approach is decidedly culturalist, using in-depth interviews to study cultural practices and repertoires used among working class men. They reject the elitist assumptions of the literature that focuses on cosmopolitanism as a strategy of the upper-middle classes. Their interview data shows how cultural groups use particular universalistic discourses to bridge boundaries of difference. Rather than a cosmopolitanism grounded in the consumption-based celebration of multicultural identities, Lamont and Aksartova find references to universal principles of human nature which 'enable people to resist racism' (2002: 18) as evidence of ordinary cosmopolitanism.

In socio-political research, the idea of cosmopolitan dispositions has had some salience over a longer period of time. Robinson and Zill (1997) have defined cultural cosmopolitanism as an openness to cultural products free of local or national prejudices. They find a strong positive correlation between cosmopolitanism and the level of educational attainment, especially for those who studied social sciences and humanities courses. Further, women scored higher than men, as did black respondents and younger people. Interestingly, cosmopolitans were also found to have a more positive and optimistic outlook and to be more satisfied with their lives generally. In attempting to distinguish between locals and cosmopolitans as political actors, Dye (1963) defined cosmopolitans in terms of having an interest in non-local happenings, taking a non-parochial attitude towards local events and issues, and rejecting 'big city' values. Likewise, Jennings (1966, cited in Robinson *et al.* 1993) defined cosmopolitanism as an outlook beyond the local, particularly in relation to national and international events. Even earlier, in his study of influence in a small town, Merton (1957) distinguished between locals and cosmopolitans on a similar basis – cosmopolitans were those whose outlook was national rather than local. As Hannerz (1990: 237) points out, such a distinction now seems rather parochial given levels of international integration.

In addition to this, our review of the literature shows that the cosmopolitan attitude is defined by a series of beliefs, attitudes and personal qualities. The notion that there can be 'banal' or 'mundane' versions of the cosmopolitan attitude as well as 'authentic' versions is useful as a preliminary distinction. Billig (1995) has highlighted how forms of banal or vernacular nationalism such as flag waving, singing national anthems, or engaging in ersatz re-enactments of key moments in a nation's history can serve to reinforce collective national sentiments, despite their apparently trivial or inconsequential nature. Urry (2000b) applies this distinction to a discussion of banal globalism in his empirical study of the reception of cosmopolitan media images, and Hebdige (1990) has called attention to how people can be mundane cosmopolitans simply through consuming media images. Thus any measure of cosmopolitan attitudes must differentiate between these mundane or 'unreflexive' forms of cosmopolitanism and authentic or 'reflexive' cosmopolitanism. Indicators of the mundane or unreflexive forms of cosmopolitanism include: the types of food one consumes, consumption of heavily packaged or mediated cultural and tourist experiences, and the unreflexive consumption of ethnic 'styles' in dress or music. In his critique of the class basis of cosmopolitan elites, Calhoun cautions similarly: 'food, tourism, music, literature and clothes are all easy faces of cosmopolitanism, but they are not hard tests for the relationship between local solidarity and international civil society' (Calhoun 2002b: 105). Nava's (1998, 2007) historical account illustrates how cosmopolitan discourses were incorporated into commercial promotions by Selfridges Department store in early twentieth-century London. While Selfridges was 'founded at the height of British Imperialism' it promoted a 'cosmopolitanism which was modern, urban and cultured' (Nava 1998: 166) by its demonstration of intellectual and aesthetic openness through advertising, store facilities and layout and promotions. While this was a deployment of cosmopolitanism that was related to the growth of modern consumer cultures, representations of luxury and display, and the display of conspicuous signifiers of identity, Nava argues this does not necessarily diminish its critical or transformative efficacy as a cultural text. Indeed, she suggests that the selling of these 'mundane' or 'domesticated' (Nava 2002: 94) forms of cosmopolitan styles goes hand-in-hand with more fundamental and progressive social structural changes. They may, in fact, be the harbingers of wider social changes.

The sociological literature suggests that cosmopolitan attitudes are typically linked to a number of social-structural characteristics. Chaney (2002) has described how shifting aesthetic and cultural economies, coupled with the rising importance of cultural citizenship, have generated the possibility of deploying cosmopolitan symbols as signs of distinction, at least for select groups within a population. He defines the cosmopolitan cultural citizen as having heterogeneous tastes, and the ability to transcend native culture by adopting a learned indifference to local goods (Chaney 2002: 158). Regev (2007a) makes a similar point in relation to what he calls aesthetic cosmopolitanism which emerges at the intersections of global field of art and fields of national culture.

Cosmopolitans are geographically and culturally mobile. As Hall (2002: 26) has recently put it, cosmopolitanism requires the ability to draw upon and enact vocabularies and discourses from a variety of cultural repertoires. The cosmopolitan has the technical and intellectual resources or 'capital' to gain employment across national boundaries, and typically has an ability to traverse, consume, appreciate and empathize with cultural symbols and practices that originate outside their home country. In this sense, we could think of cosmopolitans as similar to the cultural omnivore identified in recent literature on aesthetic tastes, who has an ability to appreciate and discern rules and repertoires associated with cultural symbols or forms that originate across cultural boundaries (Peterson 1992; Peterson and Kern 1996). These consumers, assumed to be part of a new middle class, have an openness and 'desire to participate in or "sample" other social and cultural worlds' (Wynne and O'Connor 1998: 858). Whether they are best understood as a class, a category, or even 'tribe' of cosmopolitan consumers who actively and conspicuously consume global cultural goods or whether such consumption is merely circumstantial, ordinary or 'unreflexive' is something further empirical research could usefully address (see for example, Edmunds and Turner 2001). Whatever the conclusion, the patterns of consumption of these emerging omnivores suggests affinities between them and what we term 'cosmopolitan consumers'.

It is from Peterson's research on cultural consumption that the groundwork has emerged for an understanding of the emergence of the omnivorous, cosmopolitan consumer. Peterson (1990) asserts that the World Music genre, defined as incorporating music of non-Western origin, is likely to be the preferred music of the affluent baby-boomers, and predicts that it may replace classical music as the music of the intellectual classes into the twenty-first century. Van Eijck (2000: 216) speculates that one attraction of these forms of music 'lies in the musical experiment and the juxtaposition of diverse musical elements'. But more than this, such cosmopolitan omnivorousness becomes a symbol of social status and moral worthiness. More broadly, it is a particular type of cultural capital that demonstrates one is able to appreciate the cultural products and practices of others, suggesting openness and flexibility, which are 'important resources in a society that requires social and geographical mobility, "employability", and "social networking"' (Van Eijck 2000: 221). Such a credential is an important emergent form of capital, argue Peterson and Kern (1996: 906):

> While snobbish exclusion was an effective marker of status in a relatively homogeneous and circumscribed WASP-ish world that could enforce its dominance over all others by force if necessary, omnivorous inclusion seems better adapted to an increasingly global world managed by those who make their way, in part, by showing respect for the cultural expressions of others.

The sociology of cosmopolitanism: the major themes of the book

Much of the chapters that follow concern themselves with a dialogue with the major sociological thinkers about cosmopolitanism; consequently, the reader will find arguments with and appreciations of Nussbaum, Habermas, Beck and Appadurai, among others, and will see what we regard as crucial points of agreement and disagreement. In addition, there are a number of threads that run through this book, which, while they are developed more fully as they are canvassed, are worth bringing together and briefly introduced here. This list can serve as an orientation of our major themes for the reader, as well as a summary of our major claims to make an original contribution to the literature.

First, we wish to situate ourselves within 'classical sociology' (Alexander 1987; Calhoun *et al.* 2002; B. Turner 1999, 2006) – the various approaches to sociology developed by the beginning of the twentieth century and associated with Marx, Weber, Durkheim and Simmel. We wish to reclaim classical sociology as a powerful approach to understanding cosmopolitanism. Cosmopolitanism has often been captured as a subject matter by those by whom classical sociology is seen as irrelevant to today's concerns; consequently, an emphasis on the total reconstruction of social theory for totally new times is the leitmotif of thinkers for whom the classical tradition has outlived its usefulness. Such reconstructive efforts may adopt a relativistic stance to systems of thought, and are often content to engage with cosmopolitanism as a system of ideas, as we discussed above. By contrast, our classical cast of mind suggests to us two protocols. The first is that we regard empirical research as crucial to finding out what cosmopolitanism is; we are not so jaundiced that we regard empirical data with contempt, and consequently some of our own research on cosmopolitan attitudes and practices can be found in Chapter 5. The second classical protocol is that we are quite happy to use 'modernist' sociological theory to make sense of our chosen topic. It has become fashionable to suggest that because the world has changed so much in the last hundred years, it is constantly necessary to invent new theories to make sense of these new times. We regard this claim as exaggerated; the newly industrialized world that impelled Marx, Weber and Durkheim to generate their theories was, we think, a genuine moment of discontinuity with what went before, but we who inhabit the early years of the twenty-first century also still inhabit their world. The wisdom of the classical sociologists is still necessary for our ability to make sense of such social arrangements. As Stephen Turner (2004) argues, much recent sociological theory does not so much reinvent the theoretical terrain as move the furniture around a bit; we grant there is a need for some moving of the furniture to accommodate some new aspects of the modern world, but it is our contention that most of the self-consciously radical social theory of the last few years does, in the main, two things: it reinvents the wheel, and it makes careers for its inventors. By contrast, in seeing cosmopolitanism as part of the modern world recognizable to the nineteenth- and early twentieth-century sociologists, we think it is possible to use those tried and tested theories that have served sociology well for a hundred years. We shall also 'move the furniture' a little, but we are adamant that there is no need to go to the store to start all over again. Our adherence to classical social theory, then, is a rejection of armchair philosophy (to continue the furniture metaphor) and the embrace of empirical social science, as well as a refusal to accept the hyperbole of massive social change at the expense of studying continuity.

Our second major theme concerns the relationship between cosmopolitanism and the modern nation state. For many cosmopolitan theorists, the nation state is to some extent the term on the 'problem' side of the ledger, while cosmopolitanism offers itself to the 'solution' side. We should say from the start that we recognize the importance of the modern democratic Western nation state, and do not think it would be possible or desirable to get rid of it: it is a utopian belief that postnational entities, such as the European Union, are up to the job *on their own* of maintaining global or local peace. The nation state remains critically important because it invented a way of maintaining peace and order, and it did this in spite of the enormous difficulties that stood – and continue to stand – in its way. These difficulties at one point made it seem unlikely that it would ever be able to generate its secular authority, and wrest away control from religiously dogmatic warring factions. The Treaties of Westphalia of 1648 signalled a moment when the 'necessary compromise' of the nation state could guarantee peace; although the Westphalian principle of *cuius regio, eius religio* appeared to cement particular confessional practices in particular states, crucially it decoupled religious dissent from citizenship, and by relegating private conviction to the private margins of society, disconnected it from statecraft. This compromise, the deconfessionalization of the Western nation state, is the foundation upon which Western freedom and democracy are built.

However, our enthusiasm for the achievements of the modern democratic Western nation state needs to be finessed. First of all, we see modern cosmopolitanism as not completely contradictory to the nation state and nationalism (*cf.* Delanty and Rumford 2005: 192; Cheah and Robbins 1998). We do not believe that cosmopolitanism is a replacement for the nation state; it is, rather, a development of some of the principles of the nation state that must live alongside it. So, to return to the question of the European Union, and the other (mostly still nascent) supra-state entities: while we are enthusiastic about the possibilities for cosmopolitanism that these afford, we recognize that the nation state is still currently the only game in town, and as such will remain the principal governmental mechanism ensuring social peace and social order. Supra-state entities may be built on top of the nation state, but will have to learn to complement the nation state, not replace it.

The nation state can play two possible roles in the development of cosmopolitanism, as it can in the development of the supra-states: it can play an enabling role, or it can play a corrosive role. Broadly, the enabling role is one played by the secular nation state, and the corrosive role is the only one that the confessional or non-democratic state can play. We make this distinction because it is only secular states that can truly achieve the sort of moral universalism combined with toleration of difference that is both the ground for cosmopolitanism and the structure of civil society which cosmopolitanism can extend. Only a state which understands its role as a *governmental mechanism*, rather than as having claims to particular truths, is likely to be able to play the enabling role that cosmopolitanism needs. To give a concrete example, Islamic states will always struggle to be characterized as cosmopolitan. First of all, when they look outward towards other states, their approach is not to appreciate the other, but understand it as that which must be kept separate, subsumed or destroyed. A corollary of this is that the internal affairs of Islamic states are also uncosmopolitan, because of the way in which difference is coded as and subsequently enacted through inequality (and here we gesture towards the position of women and the widespread use of slavery – for example, in Sudan and Mauritania – in Islamic societies). Furthermore, one can look with some concern at the Universal Islamic Declaration of Human Rights, conceived as a kind of competitor to the United Nation's Universal Declaration of Human Rights: the former document privileges the *shari'ah* as a legitimate limit to human rights, which of course means that rights can be secondary to religious orthodoxy and thus erased by it. And of course, one must make the same point about those totalitarian states, such as North Korea or the former Soviet Union, which view themselves in quasi-confessional terms as privileged centres of truth. By contrast, the secular states, which have given up the idea of a divinely guaranteed *raison d'être* (whether the 'divinity' is Christ, Mohammed, Stalin or Kim Il-sung), become less concerned with the boundaries between themselves and others, and become receptive to experiences of otherness. Of course, increasing secularity is no guarantee of this process; Durkheim (1992: 72–3), for example, was horrified by the growth of secular patriotism in his lifetime, which he saw as a threat to global brotherhood. Nationalism is often dangerous and corrosive to the idea of embracing the other; nationalistic sentiments may lead to what social identity theorists like Henri Tajfel (e.g. 1981) have described as in-group/out-group behaviour, where strong identification with the national group leads to antipathy towards those of other nations. While, then, we are not arguing that secular nation states are sufficient conditions of the cosmopolitan cast of mind, they are in all probability necessary conditions: it is only in such conditions that the ironic self can flourish, and the average citizen, disembedded from 'hot' loyalties, can begin to look outward and see the value of engaging with otherness.

Our third major theme is a concerted effort to reject relativistic modes of thinking when it comes to cosmopolitanism. It is not unusual to see social theory anxious about value judgements, and to move, implicitly or explicitly, to an intellectual terrain where all ideas, cultures, and forms of social life are of equal moral value. However, if all cultures are equal in value, then cosmopolitanism will collapse, because there is nothing any one culture can learn (or have any interest in learning) from another. Bryan Turner (2006) talks of a 'critical recognition ethics' – inspired by Max Weber's work – which can guide a process of cosmopolitanization. In essence, critical recognition ethics amounts to a strong commitment to the work of understanding the other, but it does not shy away from making a judgement of the practices of the other (so, for example, a critical recognition ethics would have no squeamishness in condemning the Taliban destruction of Hindu icons in Afghanistan). Our cosmopolitanism, then, is a kind of *Verstehen* sociology – a serious attempt to understand what the other understands – which does not shy away from the idea of cosmopolitanism as necessarily connected to universalist principles such as freedom of speech, human rights, and so forth, and which must then be viewed as a decidedly *ethical* approach. However, we should not attempt to defend this universalism in terms of a Kantian, rationalistic, Enlightenment position, but rather in terms of a Hobbesian understanding that certain sorts of agreements have to be negotiated, and certain rights and practices given up, if cosmopolitanism is to work. If there are any new stirrings in the intellectual terrain of social theory and in our political consciousness, perhaps it is in the gradual acceptance that 'giving up rights and practices' is not necessarily a loss of freedom, but may be required to guarantee the survival of self and other, and to guarantee freedom. So, for example, the growth of a global comprehension of the problem of climate change has become accompanied by an understanding that what may have previously been seen as a series of rights (to travel and to consume without limit) is in fact more clearly seen as a series of responsibilities to the other and to the ecosystem; it therefore may be that giving up apparent freedoms is required for the continued health of self, other and the planet. We see cosmopolitanism as a negotiated settlement, but a settlement invested with values.

This leads to a fourth point. It is our contention that the various flowerings of cosmopolitanism throughout history – and here we think of the milieux surrounding Diogenes and Kant, as well as the period after the fall of the Berlin Wall – have been rare, and require an unusual set of historical conjunctures. The in-group/out-group attitude is our default social identity. However, we are now at a historical moment where cosmopolitanism is not a choice, but is forced upon us. The global nature of some aspects of our society – especially global risk – means that phenomena like climate change force us into dialogue with others, and force us to understand that our sense of solidarity and belonging is now compelled to be global rather than local. It would certainly be a mistake to imagine that this global interconnection is a purely modern phenomenon, and that the premodern world was a collection of homogeneous cultures which were never mixed. It is not difficult to dispute this myth: one good example is Jack Goody's (2004) work on the constant cultural exchanges between Europe and the Islamic world from at least the eighth century. To this extent, then, cosmopolitanism is not exactly a new problem, since all cultures have always had to deal with the other. But today, our ability to ignore the other is rapidly diminishing. We are becoming cosmopolitan whether we choose to or not.

Our fifth point of emphasis is on the notion of cosmopolitanism as a global exchange relationship. As Bryan Turner (2006) points out, a recurring idea in the sociology of Durkheim, Simmel and Parsons was the emphasis on 'the social' as defined by social exchange (and for both Simmel and Parsons, money is a key exchange mechanism). Turner goes on to suggest that while money may be the major mechanism of exchange in the economic subsystem of society, trust is the mechanism of exchange in the social subsystem. Whether or not one agrees with this emphasis on trust, it is clear to us that Turner has hit upon something important in seeing exchange as fundamental to the social; our development of this idea leads to our emphasis on cosmopolitanism as an exchange relationship in a global social context.

Our sixth theme concerns the emphasis we place on material culture in our theorization of cosmopolitanism. It has become common in sociology to emphasize the role of objects and other nonhumans in the construction of networks in which human social life is but one element. For us, cosmopolitanism can never simply be understood as a mental phenomenon; it is a description of a network in which humans and nonhumans are aligned in such a way as to produce behavioural repertoires recognizable as cosmopolitan.

2
The Question of Belonging: The Nation State and Beyond

Introduction

The question of belonging underpins the notion of cosmopolitanism both historically and philosophically. Diogenes of Sinope's lapidary claim that he is 'a citizen of the world' (*kosmopolitês*) is a profound statement about a sense of belonging and location. These notions of belonging and location do not refer merely to one's relationship with a particular place or community, but also imply broader questions about disposition and openness towards, and potentially participation in, communities outside the field of immediacy. A sense of belonging is central to the experience and performance of elementary human sociality and it is derived from the capacity and the need of people to form meaningful attachments. Attachments can vary in both intensity and focus but they are constitutive of even most elementary and fleeting human relationships.

One could argue that the history of human social systems is a history of continuous articulation and re-articulation of the question of belonging. As we demonstrate in Chapter 6, meaningful belonging is not reducible to human-focused social interaction but – consistent with our approach to the larger question of csomopolitanization – can be derived from relationships with *places, objects* and *ideas*. As for places, Hegel could be forgiven for famously commenting on the Swiss Alps that they represent nothing more than an uninspiring pile of matter. In stark contrast to his genius, however, most of us develop highly intricate, meaningful and emotionally coloured relationships with places and landscapes as attested in landscape poetry (e.g. in the work of the Australian writer Henry Lawson) or nationalist discourses (e.g. Shils and Young 1975; White 2000; Whyte 2002). Similarly, studies of contemporary consumerism demonstrate the importance of material objects for the formation and affirmation of human identities and status (Woodward 2007). Moreover, ties of belonging do not necessarily require tangible and material artefacts of real life but can be generated through engagement with ideas and ideals: feminism may give rise to a sense of belonging to a feminist movement and provide an impetus for action just as communist ideas may generate a strong sense of class belonging and identity.

In their comprehensive review of the literature on the 'belongingness hypothesis' Baumeister and Leary (1995: 497) argue that 'a need to belong is a fundamental human motivation' and that humans 'have a pervasive drive to form and maintain at least a minimum quantity of lasting, positive, and significant interpersonal relationships'. There are important psychological and evolutionary explanations for the need of humans to establish a sense of belonging across the spectrum of life experiences (Buss 1990; Tajfel 1981) but there are also strong social universals that turn humans into belonging-seekers. One of these universals is captured in Giddens's (1991) claim that humans share a universal desire for certainty and ontological security in a world of risk, uncertainty and unpredictability. An ontologically secure existence is one that is fulfilled by multiple and meaningful attachments and a personally rewarding sense of belonging.

Belonging is not only an elementary social need but a culturally conditioned mechanism governing all aspects of social participation and communication. As such, it is an enduring human concern, it is something that is – to paraphrase E.P. Thompson's famous dictum on class – 'happens in human relationships'. Like everything in real life, belonging is a messy affair with no guaranteed outcomes. It is always troubled by the possibility of estrangement and denial of belonging. We see belonging as an active and reflexive process because, to follow Appiah (2005: 212), belonging is about being proactive and about taking responsibility for a common destiny.

The idea of cosmopolitanism has historically been a way of addressing the complexities surrounding the question of belonging: in particular, the tension between belonging to a local community as opposed to a wider world. This tension, imbued with normative meanings and moral aspirations, remains as relevant today as it was at the time of Diogenes' provocative utterance. Yet the need to deploy this concept seems to increase at times when, due to radical breaks in the social and the political fabric, new opportunities for re-thinking the limits of belonging present themselves. Any discussion of cosmopolitanism is always historically conditioned and somewhat a prisoner of its era. Clearly, the world limited by the boundaries of the Greek polis, the emergent modern European state, or the modern system of complex regional, national and international bodies and networks create in turn distinct cosmopolitan possibilities. However, each of the periods in which these thinkers lived presented a threshold of a whole new era, allowing for the re-conceptualization of belonging. The most recent renaissance of interest in cosmopolitanism is partly a consequence of the dramatic events of the late 1980s, particularly the fall of the Berlin Wall in 1989, which created an opportunity to engage the social imagination without the constraints of the global bipolarity associated with the Cold War (Fine 2003: 452). As the divide within Europe of two opposing and occasionally antagonistic powers was erased, the new European arena which replaced it – and within which the Eastern European nations began to think of their future – offered a common destiny in which the sum of the parts might be greater than the whole.

This key idea behind this chapter is our concern about the relationship between the structural conditions of social life and cosmopolitan opportunities which are coded or accessed through belonging. Calhoun (2003b: 2) makes a crucial point in asserting that belonging is not limited to a 'subjective state of mind' but it is also a key feature of social organization. Appiah (1996: 25) is correct in reminding us that cosmopolitanism is more than just 'the feeling that everybody matters'. This is a view shared by Calhoun (2003a: 532) who critiques cosmopolitan liberals for their failure to 'recognise the conditions of their own discourse, presenting it as freedom from social belonging rather than a special sort of belonging, a view from nowhere or everywhere rather than from particular social spaces'. This emphasis on the significance of the social context and opportunity structures that allow cosmopolitanism is consistent with our claim that the concept of cosmopolitanism has no sociological usefulness – no reality – if it can not be linked to empirically observable processes. A more cosmopolitan social order can not be created by fiat; adopting a cosmopolitan posture is not an effortless position to take. It takes both an intellectual effort and a solid grounding in the real world of social action in order to transcend the constraints of the immediate. This is not to deny the significance of normative and aspirational aspects of the cosmopolitan project – they are in many ways essential – but it is our way of imposing discipline on the study of the subject. To concretize this point somewhat: it has been common to think of cosmopolitanism as a type of social integration – a type of belonging – which is guaranteed by values. However, values are never enough: as Beck (2006: 35) argues, forms of interconnectivity may not just emerge from universal rational principles, but may rather be an unintended consequence of new political and ecological developments. In Beck's discussion, cosmopolitanism emerges as reaction to dangers and risks, and the necessity to avoid them. Beck has in mind here ecological risks, and so we can see how external structural issues (political/ ecological) turn into an obligation to engage with otherness.

In addition to this overarching concern of this chapter, we discuss the dialectic between particular and universal, local and cosmopolitan. From this point, we move on to examine the decisive role of the nation state in the growth and articulation of the cosmopolitan project. The question of the modern state and the possibilities emerging from new supra-national structures will be of central importance; and much of our focus here will be on the work of Calhoun, Held and Habermas. We argue that the modern democratic state, rather than being seen with suspicion as an agent of anti-cosmopolitanism, can be productively harnessed into a cosmopolitan project; it can facilitate the formation of new forms of solidarity that can in turn sustain it. We see the idea of cosmopolitan citizenship as having sustainable qualities because of its foundations in what we call 'imaginative realism': it is imaginative (as opposed to utopian) because it pushes beyond the existing social order; and it is realist because it understands the importance of social institutions, particularly the role of the state, and it recognizes the critical role that reflexive, socially located actors play in the process of cosmopolitanization. In short, there is a role for ideals in this process; nonetheless, an assemblage of laws, spaces, institutions and so forth form a background upon which such ideals can play. The ideals and the assemblage enter into a mutually conditioning relationship: in this way, feelings of belonging and political realities can be described by a recursive algorithm. We conclude the chapter with a short case study which reflects on the European Union project and the extent to which it connects to a cosmopolitan vision.

Local vs cosmopolitan

Nussbaum (1996: 15) admits that being a citizen of the world could be a '... a kind of exile – from the comfort of local truths, from the warm, nestling feeling of patriotism, from the absorbing drama of pride in oneself and one's own'. Barber (1996: 24) seizes on Nussbaum's acknowledgement of this weakness of the cosmopolitan imagination by emphasizing that people actually tend to develop attachments and a sense of belonging to specific and tangible things, rather than the abstract: 'we live in this particular neighbourhood of the world, that block, this valley, that seashore, this family. Our attachments start parochially and only then grow outward'. The significance of Barber's criticism is in its emphasis that a capacity to develop immediacy-transcending values must not be severed from our capacity to feel comfortable in a particular place. We can see here the suggestion, which we develop in the rest of this chapter, that cosmopolitanism and the local are not mutually exclusive, either/or propositions. Barber's position echoes Hannerz's (1990: 239) eloquently expressed claim that 'there can be no cosmopolitans without locals'. And this point is not without its historical precedents. When Cheah discusses D'Alembert's entry on 'cosmopolitan' in the eighteenth-century *Encyclopédie*, he reminds us that D'Alembert's reference to universality in cosmopolitanism does not necessarily imply rootlessness or the elimination of the local. Instead, cosmopolitanism entails 'a universal circle of belonging that involves the transcendence of the particularistic and blindly given ties of kinship and country' (Cheah 2006: 478). D'Alembert's position is illuminating because it reminds us that the cosmopolitan ideal – at least in its Enlightenment version – does not necessarily require a radical counter-positioning of particular and universal (i.e. national and cosmopolitan). Instead, it views particular and cosmopolitan as two complementary and dialectically entangled dimensions of the social, while recognizing the inherent transcendental capacity of the cosmopolitan.

Appiah's emphasis on rooted cosmopolitans is perhaps the most well-known antidote to Nussbaum's advocacy of cosmopolitan universalism and the refusal of the local. For Appiah (2005: 241) cosmopolitanism can only be imagined from a particular place and its impact can only be secured through local participation: 'A citizen of the world can make the world better by making some local place better'. Consequently, celebrating roots, points of departure, or origin are not a radical negation of cosmopolitanism but rather represent its alternatives. Appiah's argument is driven by the recognition of that type of universalism which is 'sensitive to the ways in which historical context may shape the significance of a practice' (Appiah 2005: 256). Cosmopolitanism, as Calhoun (2003b: 21) puts it, 'is not wrong, but by itself it is inadequate'. In other words, there is an inherent incompleteness residing in the assumption that cosmopolitanism is simply a value.

The cosmopolitan project is not incompatible with particularist, local, limited and limiting ties which constitute us as social beings in our concreteness. Belonging, then, from the cosmopolitan point of view, comes to be seen as something based on multiple and overlapping levels. One's sense of where and with whom one belongs can be connected at a variety of scales, some of which reflect core sociological concerns with class and status groups, and others of which may connect to more nebulous senses of shared identity. Thus a list of sites of belonging might include: profession, sense of class position, ethnicity, nationality and religion; but it would also include such connections as social clubs, friendship circles, support for a sports team, or adoption of certain fashions. All of these statuses have the potential to be either open or closed. While Max Weber (1948a) regarded status groups as performing the role of social closure, we might think of some status groups as more inclined to open themselves up to the outside, and these senses of belonging are then potentially cosmopolitan.

On the other hand, the rigid and competitive counter-positioning of the cosmopolitan *vis-à-vis* the local or parochial may have a heuristic use (it can help with the articulation of arguments and standpoints in the context of debate). These benefits notwithstanding, such counter-positioning obfuscates the complexities that need to be negotiated by an individual who wishes to reach beyond the local and immediate but who is steeped in the realities of the local. No element of the population, not even cosmopolitans, should be seen as free-floating monads, but rather as inevitably linked to (if not rooted in) localities, embedded in some sense in social structures and institutions of the immediate environment. Cosmopolitanism, after all, 'is a presence not an absence, an occupation of particular positions in the world, not a view from nowhere or everywhere' (Calhoun 2003b: 18). In social life, local and global impacts are of equal significance although of different scale. It is salutary to remind ourselves of Dickens' (1956) novel *Bleak House* where he describes people who are dedicated to 'telescopic philanthropy' in far away places and express beautiful sentiments about the 'brotherhood of humanity' but who have little time or talent to recognize the needs of those around them.

The idea that cosmopolitans, in their enthusiastic embracing of universalism, are (or should be) somehow averse to local attachments has received considerable traction in the literature. We find this position, painted in the colours of abstract universalism, problematic and also one of the greatest impediments to making cosmopolitanism a useful tool of social analysis. Despite the significance of Nussbaum's contribution to contemporary debates on cosmopolitanism, she does radically privilege world citizenship over local attachments and emphasizes the moral superiority of the cosmopolitan over the local – for this, we feel, she rightly earned Scheffler's (2001) charge of 'extreme cosmopolitanism'. Rather than merely extreme, however, we see her position as sociologically uninformed and neglectful of the social groundedness which should accompany the cosmopolitan perspective.

This concern over the power and relevance of local attachments in the context of cosmopolitanism is, of course, nothing new. We tend to be sympathetic to approaches which view local and cosmopolitan as complementary poles of the same field of the social. Being local does not preclude anyone from holding a cosmopolitan vision or engaging in cosmopolitan practices. Cosmopolitans ought not to be expected to dwell in towers of abstract ideals but should acknowledge a sense of location and point of departure. Instead of a priori privileging of cosmopolitan or local, we should acknowledge their fruitful interdependency, constantly lubricated by the reflexive capacity of individuals to move between them. By constructing cosmopolitans and locals as good and bad, open and closed, progressive and conservative respectively, one is potentially failing to understand the complex linkages and interdependencies between them. Our conciliatory ambition draws on a deep commitment of classical sociological theorists to universalism but one which is not oblivious to particularity. As Chernilo (2006: 21) argues, Marx, Weber, Simmel and Durkheim share 'the claim that the modern society is local in origins, national in organization and universal in impact'. Cosmopolitan belonging, then, is built on top of local belonging, and the subsequent rejection and derogation of those local origins is the equivalent of climbing a stepladder, pulling it out from beneath oneself, and expecting to hover unsupported above the ground.

Our attention in the next section will turn towards the key institution that currently serves as a mediator between the local and the cosmopolitan: the (nation) state. Here we refer to the 'nation state', since the state in the modern era has traditionally been forged in a nationalized form, even though the pathways of this formation might differ across time and geo-political space (Habermas 1998). The question of the nation state is critical in the context of this discussion because it is revealing of the existing ambivalence surrounding the role of the state in cosmopolitanism. It is also indicative of the confusion surrounding discussions about the viability and possible success of the cosmopolitan project. There are those who see the state as something that can be harnessed in the process of cosmopolitanization (Held 1995; Habermas 2001b) – and we largely subscribe to this position. The state is not a brick wall against which the cosmopolitan project collides. In contrast, there are others who see cosmopolitanism as something that happens largely outside, and despite, the state framework. This latter position is perhaps best exemplified in the work of Pollock *et al.* (2000: 528), who portray the statelessness and rootlessness of exiles, migrants, refugees and the like as some exemplary embodiments of cosmopolitan virtue (for a critique see Skrbis *et al.* 2004). Such a position ignores the fact that life *within* the state framework is the reality for vast majority of people on this planet, that migrants can be also be exemplary parochials, and that refugees in large part prefer the firm and secure grip of a state (albeit almost certainly not of the one from which they are refugees). The point to make is that we need to differentiate between quixotic fantasies and an empirically engaged sociological imagination which allows us to appreciate the constraints of social structure and the powerful impact of human agency.

The cosmopolitan project, the nation state and beyond

In his insightful paper, Chernilo (2008) explores classical sociologists' conceptualization of the nation. He begins by drawing attention to Anthony D. Smith's (1983) article in which he accuses classical sociologists of 'methodological nationalism', an accusation that has current mileage (see Beck 2006, and our fuller discussion of this issue in Chapter 3). Because classical sociology, Chernilo (2008: 29) argues, 'was able to grasp the *historical elusiveness* (Marx), *sociological equivocations* (Weber) and *normative ambiguity* (Durkheim) of the nation state, it can now help us understand the *opacity* of the nation-state's position in modernity'. Durkheim's (1992) position in *Professional Ethics and Civic Morals* is particularly revealing as it not only adopts a Kantian emphasis on pacifism and internationalism but emphasizes a degree of complementarity between the nation state and cosmopolitan ambition. Although Durkheim's (1973) cosmopolitanism is a 'moral sentiment', it needs to 'find sociological expression within nation-states' (Chernilo 2006: 28).

Whether we think of the nation state as something that needs to be developed and eventually superseded or something that provides direct grounding for cosmopolitan sentiments, the sociological classics have undoubtedly dealt thoroughly with the state and saw it as enabling and constraining at the same time. In the contemporary era, the idea that the state plays a constraining role in social relations, imposing limits on the flows of goods, people, ideas and political goodwill needs to be counterbalanced. Rather, we might take an optimistic account of the role of the state in the context of the cosmopolitan project. This does not mean that we see the state as 'good' or 'necessary', but we believe that we need to *account for* the state given that it has been, and continues to be, the dominant institutional form and organizational principle of social and political life at least since the Treaties of Osnabrück and Münster in 1648. This is not to say that we wish to sing praises to the state, nor do we argue that this dependent framing of social life around the state is necessarily a good thing. Nevertheless, the existence of the state does provide an undeniable point of reference for thinking about belonging.

'Extreme cosmopolitans', such as Nussbaum, fail to account for the institution of the state. Nussbaum's position is consistent with two underlying normative assumptions: that there are moral bases for politics and that each individual should feel primary loyalty to humanity rather than the local (Calhoun 2003a: 538–9). The problem with such an account is that it never engages in any analysis of that large and unmediated space between the concrete individual on the one hand and an abstract category of humanity on the other. Nussbaum avoids direct engagement with this question by implying the moral and logical necessity of cosmopolitan transcendence. This necessity is logically contingent on a normative framework but it is also non-sociological: so, for example, it does not explain how people's judgements (about good and evil) are generated, how people engage in practices (both selfish and altruistic), and how and why they perform their identities within the context of the messiness of social life. The formation of judgements and the politics of practice are inevitably encumbered by the very nature of a particular individual's location in the context of groups and institutions, but it is also dependent on identities that are performed by, or attributed to, persons. One does not become cosmopolitan in a vacuum.

The 'extreme cosmopolitan' position, therefore, suffers from two key omissions. First, it does not explain how love for humanity actually comes into being, apart from emphasizing that this should happen with some help from a good education (Nussbaum 1996: 15). Second, it neglects to explain the complexities of local/universal attachments except by the gesture of privileging the universal over the local. Furthermore, the humanity to which extreme cosmopolitans want to pledge allegiance is an elusive category at the best of times. Having special regard for humanity is commendable, but the actual effectiveness of this love is unpredictable for it largely draws on moral universals and philosophical aspirations. In real life, even one of the most celebrated humanists, Jean-Jacques Rousseau, was preoccupied with his declarations of love for humanity but sent his own children to orphanages (Burke 1985: 300). Carl Schmitt identifies humanity as a dangerously loose concept that is easy prey to manipulation, and we share an unease with the vagueness of the concept. 'Humanity is not a political concept, and no political entity or society and no status corresponds to it', Schmitt (1996: 55) states.

The nation state has been under intense scrutiny in recent discussions about methodological nationalism. Beck (2002b: 19) defines methodological nationalism as a set of 'explicit or implicit assumptions about the nation state being the power container of social processes and the national being the key-order for studying major social, economic and political processes'. There is a large chorus of contemporary scholars who have contributed to the discussion of methodological nationalism and addressed the limitations of the concept (e.g. Wimmer and Schiller 2003; Brubaker 2004; Chernilo 2006, 2008). Beck acknowledges the significance of the nation state, but refuses to confine the cosmopolitan outlook within the horizon of this institution. He recognizes the state's continuing relevance and significance in the affairs of the global citizenry, warning that the denial of its continuing centrality could lead to the dangers of 'a philosophical never-never land' (Beck 2006: 49). While himself a victim of this mistake on more than one occasion, as we discuss in more detail in Chapter 3, Beck's point is important because it alerts us to the superficial divisions separating the local/national and cosmopolitan (indeed, cosmopolitan literature often treats the nation state as the outer boundary of the local). Beck, forever a creative wordsmith, invented the notion of 'cosmopolitan realism' as a compromise between the two, understanding cosmopolitanism as something that nationalism can actually help stabilize. In this ambition he echoes Roudometof's (2005: 122) point that 'cosmopolitanism should not be confused with the negation of national identity'. Cosmopolitan realism 'should not be understood and developed in opposition to universalism, relativism, nationalism and ethnicism, but as their summation and synthesis' (Beck 2006: 57). He lists the EU, UN and NATO as examples of realistic cosmopolitanism. This view is shared by Guibernau (2004: 164), who sees a *democratic* form of nationalism – one which rejects territorial expansionism and respects internal diversity – as providing cosmopolitan orientation to its citizenry.

Two comments are in order at this point – and both derive from the largely symbiotic relationship between nation and state in the modern era. First, given that nationalism and cosmopolitanism are often seen as natural antidotes it may seem surprising to try to develop a conciliatory position between the two. The antithetic nature of cosmopolitanism and nationalism has been referred to, following Turner's (2000b: 27–9) adaptation of McLuhan's terminology, as a distinction between cold and hot loyalty to a community (*cf.* Nash 2003). Nationalism's association with hot emotions is not surprising given its well-established reputation for mobilizing people, emotionalizing collectivities and unashamedly asking for sacrifices in the name of the nation, territory, historical memory or simply in the name of nationalist imagination. In contrast, cosmopolitanism, the heir of Enlightenment reason, is seen as suitably dry, cool and largely bereft of any capacity to emotionalize and lead people into action. We feel that the alleged impossibility of cosmopolitanism to generate hot emotions may have been pronounced too early and we shall return to this point later in this chapter. What can easily escape our attention, however, is the fact that nationalism and cosmopolitanism both require 'quite a loftily abstract level of allegiance – a vast, encompassing project that extends far beyond ourselves and our families' (Appiah 2005: 239). Clearly, the key issue in terms of the relationship between nationalism and cosmopolitanism are not the things that separate them but various continuities that can be drawn between them. Habermas's project of constitutional cosmopolitanism is useful to bring into this discussion precisely because of its underlining ambition to harmonize cosmopolitan institutions while simultaneously re-affirming national identity (*cf.* Fine 2003: 462; 2007: 41–4; Calhoun 2007).

The second point relates to the changing nature of the state as a social institution and the consequent changes in the relationship between nation and state. David McCrone is correct to emphasize the historical, even contingent, nature of the state. The classical nation state, the one created by classical nationalism, 'is losing its *raison d'être*' (McCrone 2001: 186) and it appears that the link between the nation and the state is weakening (Keating 2001). For example, Scottish, Breton and Catalan nationalists are just as likely to discuss their ambitions for autonomy with Brussels as they are with the political elites in their respective states (*cf.* Keating 1988; McCrone 2001; Guibernau 2004). In the last decades we have seen an overwhelming increase in commitment to participation in shared institutional frameworks at the regional, continental and global levels. The contemporary democratic state, with national sovereignty progressively undermined (Habermas 1998: 106–7), is increasingly likely to be a willing player in the 'civilisational community of fate' (Beck 2006: 7). This is the kind of change that is not only making the previous characterizations of the state obsolete but it also provides a framework for rethinking of the nation state both in terms of its internal legitimacy (i.e. the extent to which it represents its citizens as bearers of civic or ethnic attributes) and its capacity to cosmopolitanize its presence in the context of global affairs.

Even as we see an ever-more globally integrated socio-economic system, issues of social and political integration always tend to lag behind. In other words, there is a 'lack of fit between the material interconnectedness brought about by global capitalism and the degree of formation of global solidarities' (Cheah 2006: 491). Similarly, increasing levels of transnationalization do not directly translate into higher corresponding levels of cosmopolitanization. Roudometof (2005: 121) usefully decouples the cosmopolitan outlook from transnational experiences, reminding us that people can be exposed to other cultures on a daily basis through the media without actually being mobile (he calls this internal globalization) and may encounter people from different cultures by simply walking the streets of their own neighbourhoods. This echoes what Beck (2002b) calls 'banal cosmopolitanism', Szerszynski and Urry (2002) 'banal globalism' and Pieterse (2006) 'Wal-Mart cosmopolitanism'. The more basic point, however, is that 'the degree to which cosmopolitanism is related to the presence or absence of transnational experience is a relationship that can be (and should be) considered an open-ended question' (Roudometof 2005: 121). These cautionary comments notwithstanding, the globalizing tendencies and the new transnationalization of the social have generated and expanded the communicative horizons of social interaction, allowing social actors across the globe to participate in an ever expanding and diversifying 'international public sphere' (*cf.* Dryzek 2006: 109). This emergent international public sphere has an important effect on the modern state, which finds itself 'increasingly trapped within webs of global interconnectedness permeated by quasi-supranational, intergovernmental and transnational forces' (Held 1995: 92). Simultaneously, these new circumstances provide new opportunities for democratic growth and association beyond the nation state: for more cosmopolitan forms of existence.

The politics of imaginative realism: towards cosmopolitan democracy

Research surrounding the concepts of cosmopolitan democracy (Held 1995; Archibugi and Held 1995), constitutional patriotism and the public sphere (Habermas 2001a; Calhoun 2002a) can best assist in navigating these dilemmas. This research utilizes the social science concepts of democracy, state, public sphere, and law to ground cosmopolitanism within the context of existing social structures. Although this approach is imaginative, its ambition is anti-utopian and sociologically and politically realistic because it engages with key suppositions that we believe are essential for a sociologically grounded cosmopolitan project. The cosmopolitanism project is only possible if it does not deny the significance of the local/national; if it does not pit rooted identities against a sense of cosmopolitan belonging; if it recognizes that universalism and particularism are closely intertwined and that cosmopolitan association with abstract universalism should be avoided; if it accepts the nation state as a powerful ally in any ambition to advance cosmopolitan agendas.

In their work on cosmopolitan democracy, Archibugi and Held (1995) draw attention to the new realities surrounding contemporary states and governments forcibly enmeshed in international and regional networks. The state is integrated into, but also increasingly dependent on, the external environment; at the same time, the previously strong and proscriptive relationships between citizens and the state, although still significant, are now increasingly impacted by regulatory mechanisms outside the aegis of the state. Habermas (2006: 77–8) articulates this problem as the erosion of the nation state's traditional prerogatives. These include lost autonomy (it can no longer effectively protect its citizens from processes beyond its borders), emerging deficits in democratic legitimation (in cases where there is a clash between the state and international agreements), and restrictions on the capacity for intervention (the state cannot intervene in global markets). Yet while this erosion of nation state prerogatives is real, governments are expected and obligated to take into account international conventions and edicts. This in turn changes the established institutional pathways of state-citizen relationships and the nature of state sovereignty. The consequences of these developments are not simply procedural but also substantive. Cosmopolitan democracy is about the development of democracy 'both within states and among states' which requires the emergence 'of authoritative global institutions able to monitor the political regimes of member countries and to influence the domestic affairs of states where necessary' (Archibugi and Held 1995: 14). Elsewhere, Held (1995: 233) articulates this idea through the notion of the multilayered democracy of regional and global parliaments. Individuals are no longer seen as simply citizens of their respective states but as persons enjoying multiple citizenships and having a sense of belonging to a multitude of communities.

Cosmopolitan democracy is predicated neither on the relegation of the state to a secondary actor in societal affairs nor on the complete reinvention of democratic political processes and institutional frameworks. Archibugi (2000) reinforces this point by calling not for the abolition of states, but for a global civil society that will monitor the system of states. As we write, the state remains the only widely accepted 'coercive negotiator [which] presides over a community' (Brennan 2001: 82). Given that the state is an historically contingent way of organizing people into political communities (Fine 2003: 453), rather than a universal and necessary institution, we may see this change at some point in the future. Nevertheless, whatever might eventually replace it will have to fulfil exactly the same role of the 'legitimate manager' of the communities, groups and individuals under its jurisdiction. In this way, the project of cosmopolitan democracy coopts and harnesses the state to the project of cosmopolitan democracy, using it as an enabler rather than an adversary. Held takes for granted that people are first of all citizens of national states who have the capacity to exert influence on global affairs through mechanisms of democratic governance, and 'gives ontological priority to the state as a locus of membership and political agency' (Shah 2006: 403).

Habermas takes an equally measured view of the role of the modern democratic state, emphasizing its capacity to create constitutionally binding communities. Habermas (2001a), arguing in favour of the idea of a European constitution, says that the challenge is not the invention of a new type of state but the conservation of the existing achievements of the state combined with the necessity to think about the state beyond its own limits. The nation state and democracy have a capacity to stabilize each other and have 'jointly produced the striking innovation of a civic solidarity that provides the cement of national societies' (Habermas 2001a: 16). He credits the constitutional state with a particularly important civilizing mission, through its capacity legally to tame 'political power on the basis of the recognition of the sovereignty of the collective subjects of international law' (Habermas 2006: 24). Habermas's model relies on established mechanisms of interaction between the state and its citizenry and the ability of the state to promulgate a sense of participatory political culture, secured by laws and workable systems of representative democratic government. The reliance on a legally framed capacity for deliberative politics and the assumption of the primacy of rational actions of social actors makes Habermas one of the staunchest and most consistent defenders of the centrality of rationalist discourse among contemporary social commentators.

There are many important and useful critiques of Habermas's approach, but here we wish to limit ourselves to criticisms concerning the weak account of solidarity in his model, particularly as developed in the work of Craig Calhoun. The question of solidarity is critical because it represents an essential component of any social model and it serves as a critical mechanism for the reproduction of norms, values, practices and routines of social life. The question of solidarity is one of the foundational puzzles of contemporary social thought, stretching back to the Hobbesian question of social order through to the work of Durkheim and latter-day functionalists such as Shils and Parsons. Durkheim's extensive work on social solidarity is particularly instructive. He knew that the modern nation can only survive if it can forge meaningful ties of solidarity between individual and the state. However, he also knew that the state is too distant to an individual, which is why ties of solidarity and meaning are actually created through a range of secondary groups with which individuals can identify (*cf.* Isin and Wood 1999: 97). The theme of solidarity and the question of the strength of social ties have constantly entered and re-entered social and political science vocabularies under different names, most recently as social capital (Putnam 2000).

Accounting for social solidarity and its sources is crucial when considering the possibilities of cosmopolitanism because, in contrast to more traditional sources of solidarity associated with the nation state, the cosmopolitan model presupposes the ability to integrate individuals into a much more intangible community than a national society. While national society can readily call on its citizenry, reminding them of commonalities based on tradition, memory, ethnicity, shared language, religion or racialized prejudice (giving rise to 'hot' emotions), the cosmopolitan model relies on more abstract points of identification. Heinrich Laube captures this point in his contrast between 'practical, useful, joyous and comforting' patriotism with cosmopolitanism which, although 'splendid', it is almost too large for a human being: 'the idea is beautiful, but the result in this life is inner anguish' (quoted in Beck 2006: 1). The key challenge for cosmopolitan thought is the generation of ongoing source(s) of social solidarity and a sense of belonging. There can be no cosmopolitanism without effective solidarity mechanisms.

Calhoun's charge against Habermas's model goes to the heart of the latter's emphasis on deliberatively-derived constitutional arrangements and a resulting constitutional patriotism. In Calhoun's view, Habermas relies too heavily on the assumption that the public's sense of belonging and solidarity will result from the strength of an adherence to a legal framework. For Calhoun, this suggestion is insufficient because it places too much emphasis on a bare inclusion into the legal-political framework afforded by the constitution: 'Citizens need to be motivated by solidarity, not merely included by law' (Calhoun 2002a: 153). The problem is not the centrality of constitutionality itself but Habermas's failure to complement it 'by the notion of *constitution as the creation of concrete social relationships*: of bonds of mutual commitment forged in shared action, of institutions, and of shared modalities of practical action' (*ibid.*: 152–3). Habermas's cosmopolitan liberalism displays the weaknesses of classical liberalism: what is absent is a 'strong account of social solidarity or of the role of culture in constituting human life' (Calhoun 2003b: 5). Furthermore, cosmopolitan liberals of Habermas's ilk, while privileging rationality, remain highly suspicious of ethnicity, communities or nations (*ibid.*: 7). We accept Calhoun's point that cosmopolitan theories 'offer an abstract normative structure which, however much occasioned by real-world social change, can only have the standing of "abstract ought" with all the potential tyranny over the immanent projects of social improvement that implies' (Calhoun 2003a: 532).

We shall discuss this further in Chapter 4 when we deal in more detail with Christopher Lasch (1995) and Stephen Toulmin (1990), but another problem with Habermas's emphasis on rationality is that not all commentators are so sanguine about the power of rationality to deliver us from evil. Lasch and Toulmin share a cynical view of how the ramping up of rationality may lead to the 'iron cage', which in turn leads to an increasing lack of faith in rationality. This is a key problem for Habermas, for whom the public's 'in good faith' participation in decision making is vital for their acceptance of the results of those decisions. Similarly, Bruno Latour diagnoses that the Habermasian split between instrumental rationality and communicative action – between means and ends – results in giving too much power to reason, and too little to humans, ultimately silencing the latter (Latour 2004a: 262, 266). Of course, this is the complete opposite of Habermas's intention:

> As soon as we conceive intentional social relations as communicatively mediated... we are no longer dealing with disembodied, omniscient beings... Rather, we are concerned with finite, embodied actors who are socialized in concrete forms of life, situated in histor-

ical time and social space, and caught up in networks of communicative action (Habermas 1996: 324).

Calhoun's emphasis on something additional – solidarity and belonging – is thus a vital additional element to add to the Habermasian approach, and a rejection of the idea that norms can really mediate between facts and values; following Calhoun, it would seem that all Habermas's insistence on this moment of mediation does is keep facts and values separate; the task, rather, is to theorize their indissolubility and understand their mutually conditioning effect. Once again, to paraphrase Calhoun, the solution is the introduction of culture.

Habermas's vision of a constitutionally bound citizenry may not provide a 'strong account of social solidarity', and he argues that such a strong account is not necessary. He points out that 'The strength of the democratic constitutional state lies precisely in its ability to close the holes of social integration through the political participation of its citizens' (2001a: 76). What he means here is that there is nothing in democratic participatory mechanisms that should predispose us to think of them as generating weak ties. The heated debates surrounding the ratification of the European Constitution may be used to prove the point about legal proceduralism's ability to generate emotional responses. Nonetheless, although it seems unlikely that procedural rationality has a capacity to generate emotionalized bonds of solidarity, we should note that once these participatory processes are embedded in the mechanisms of democratic life, and are distinguished by their *legitimacy* rather than any 'hot' emotions, they may become part of a recursive process of building solidarity as they begin to become enmeshed in culture.

The need for a strong account of social solidarity is, especially relevant for a nation state preoccupied with internal legitimacy crises rather than its place in a broader global community, desirous of maintaining outcome-oriented communicative processes. This does not mean that cosmopolitan arrangements do not require solidarity ties; rather, the very nature of solidarity has changed. The type of solidarity derived from political participatory processes is derived from two sources. The first source is from horizontal ties of connectivity linked to local and national communities – this source has traditionally been seen as producing strong solidarity ties. It is complimented by mechanisms of vertical integration, which allow national communities to reach into regional and global realms, regulating through legal norms and embedding through rational deliberation principles. Such types of solidarity are distinguished by integrated solidarity mechanisms which do not negate what has traditionally been conceptualized as strong solidarity, but rather stabilize and complement it. There is nothing stopping us from seeing this new type of integrated solidarity as potentially 'strong', but its strength would likely not be derived from a 'schmaltzy' conception of solidarity found in more traditional nationalist projects. Integrated solidarity is of a qualitatively new type and not an extension of a singular nation state's ambition to pit its interests against another. Citizenship as a fundamental legal document is about solidarity and belonging, as Habermas (2006: 100) contends when writing about 'an entirely new, abstract, and legally mediated form of social solidarity'.

Any workable cosmopolitan arrangements require much more than bare institutional rules of engagement – even though, as we have seen, these achieve much more than simply provide 'structure'. What is needed is the recognition that the cosmopolitan outlook is 'a politically ambivalent, *reflexive* outlook' (Beck 2006: 8) which consequently requires a pool of reflexive social actors (a theme we develop in Chapter 4). In speaking of a reflexive actor, we do not refer to a new breed of utopian, cosmo-enlightened social actors. Instead we use the term to refer to an elementary building block of the cosmopolitan vision: the *everyday reflexive actor* who is periodically requested to act as a decision maker and agent of change, as a voter, an engaged citizen, a contributor to local community initiatives, and so forth. By turning our focus to this everyday level, we can more clearly see the incremental development and realization of the cosmopolitan vision through continuing engagements with horizontal and vertical axes of belonging. Everyday reflexive actors are not perfect players in the game of cosmopolitan deliberation, yet they possess two important qualities without which the process of cosmopolitanization can not even begin let alone continue: they are socialized into the rules of a democratic game and they play an active role in this process. In other words, the cosmopolitan vision must accept that the limits of its possibility rest with an individual *cum* reflexive social actor already embedded within the established deliberative institutional mechanisms of the existing nation state. The interaction between the individual and these institutional mechanisms creates a communication space where people can have a 'common conversation about... shared ideas and objects' (Appiah 2005: 258) and where debates are subjected to rational deliberative discourse. This transcendentalizing of the conditions of communication is strategically interesting: nonetheless, to reiterate, the Habermasian insistence on the separation of instrumental rationality and communicative action means that his use in a theory of cosmopolitanism is limited, because culture (especially as accessed through and built out of senses of belonging) is relegated to a minor role. This insistence on rationality and rational society most clearly associated with Habermas has been critically reflected upon by a number of scholars (e.g. Calhoun 2003b, 2007; Cook 2004; Lasch 1995; Toulmin 1990; White 1980). For our discussion, the analysis of the role of rational rules of engagement is important. Bauman (2004: 125–6), in his discussion of Tzvetan Todorov's musings on Europe, stresses the historical and contextual contingency of reason, but emphasizes the key point, that

> all habits and their reaches need to justify themselves in the court of reason was and remains one habit Europe has hardly ever broken. That belief elevated argument and discussion above force – it was a prompt 'to exchange arguments more often than blows'.

The debate about the status of reason in the cosmopolitan project leads us to conclude by drawing on a long-standing debate about the connection between cosmopolitanism and its European roots (Calhoun 2002a: 150). What is the relationship between the European Union project and cosmopolitanism?

The cosmopolitan project and the question of Europe

As argued earlier, the idea of cosmopolitanism owes its existence to Greek and Western philosophical influences, most notably to Enlightenment ideas of rational and contractual social order. Contemporary debates about cosmopolitanism openly link the cosmopolitan project with its European heritage (Delanty and Rumford 2005) and many see modern Europe as an exemplary cosmopolitan effort. Beck (2006: 173) talks about it as an undoing of the 'project of national homogeneity', because the very existence of Europe as a political entity is predicated on unity through diversity, organized through mechanisms of civic, secular and democratic order which, given its decision-making procedures, allows for horizontal and vertical integration within and beyond its boundaries. Europe as a union of nations had to be invented (to use the words of Monnet, its principal architect) but it can only be sustained 'from below – by its citizens and by movements in civil society, and not from above, by the member states and their governments' (Beck and Grande 2007: 81). The European Union can be seen as a cosmopolitan outgrowth emerging from a substratum of existing nations (Beck 2006: 176) and as the latest step in a tradition of democratic achievements (Habermas 2001a: 6), including attempts to democratize the modern territorial nation state (Fraser 2007: 10).

Most contemporary European social theorists and commentators see the European project as a quintessentially cosmopolitan venture and also talk about it with uncontained excitement. Bauman (2004: 40), for instance, claims that 'Europe is well prepared if not to *lead*, then most certainly to *show* the way from the Hobbesian planet to the Kantian "universal unification of the human species"'. A similar sentiment is espoused by Rifkin (2004: 382), who enthusiastically talks about the European Dream and its high moral ground *vis-à-vis* its American counterpart: 'Europeans have laid out a visionary roadmap to a new promised land, one dedicated to re-affirming the life instinct and the Earth's indivisibility'. The future, Rifkin argues, is European rather than American, particularly because of the European propensity to focus on sustainable development, quality of life and interdependence rather than economic growth as an end in itself, and for a conception of freedom which is linked to embeddedness rather than autonomy (*ibid*.: 3–4). Stevenson (2006: 485) similarly talks about 'the sense of Europe's historic mission to protect the values of democracy, pluralism and participation and develop new institutional structures that are adequate for an age that is increasingly defined by globalization'. The European connection with cosmopolitan ideals is specifically strengthened through the evolution and expansion of the European Union, with its unique ambition to build a supranational institutional structure in which a common future, based on common goals, mutual respect and responsibility towards members and outsiders is paramount.

The European project affords cosmopolitan possibilities on a novel scale but it also exemplifies the difficulties and dilemmas associated with its implementation. Despite all its shortcomings and faults, Europe is a social experiment with no historical precedent.[1] It is indeed unprecedented to see the formerly powerful and self-sufficient nation states willingly sacrifice their respective degrees of autonomy, transferring their

---

[1] It is difficult to think of previous associations of nations or city states that have had such an explicitly cosmopolitan rationale as the EU. So, for example, the Delian League of the fifth century BCE had a number of interesting parallels with the EU, given its interests in trade and a reasonably democratic structure. Nonetheless, the League was primarily set up as a military entity, and clearly engaged in the politics of exclusion. See, for example, Hornblower (2002: ch2).

sovereignty to civic structures that are divorced from the language of ethnic politics. The European Union also provides an example of the negotiated building of an institutional framework which follows the ideals of supranational and cosmopolitan governance. Its foundation in secular principles provides mechanisms which are designed to safeguard against excessive intrusion of particularist interests, whether ethnic or religious.

Our enthusiasm for the new European project, however, does not so much lie in the poetic qualities encapsulated in Rifkin's (2004: 382) glowing tribute to the European Dream. Instead, what makes the European project exciting and promising is something much more elementary, and stems from our claim that the cosmopolitan project can only be effective if it is seen as pursuing the agendas of imaginative realism. We see the strength of the European Union's cosmopolitan vision where most perceive its weaknesses: in failures accompanying the ratification of the European constitution, and in squabbling around tariffs and accession of new member states and the slow pace of institutional reforms. While these weaknesses *per se* are nothing to be too excited about they are revelatory of the robustness of the vision and institutional pathways that are required to move the cosmopolitan agenda ahead. It utilizes democratic proceduralisms to generate legitimacy while simultaneously building the bonds of solidarity – however tentative and slowly – across its political realm. It is an illustration of what we called imaginative realism because the building and strengthening of the European agenda is fundamentally about the combination of a cosmopolitan vision in conjunction with the recognition of the need to take this vision through the process of public and institutional deliberation.

In other words, it is a good thing that the European project is bereft of any notable signs of extreme cosmopolitanism. It is sensible that there is little emphasis of the abstract principles of cosmopolitanism as morally superior; it is sensible that there is no forgetting that the project needs to be grounded in social, political and economic realities. As Beck (2006: 57) argues, cosmopolitan realism should not be thought of 'in opposition to universalism, relativism, nationalism and ethnicism, but as their summation and synthesis'. The cosmopolitan project can only proceed, and succeed, if it does not deny the relevance of the local/national, if it is not blinded by abstract universalism, if it does not see contradiction between local and cosmopolitan belonging, and if it recognizes that cosmopolitanism is a project and not a nirvana-like state of social existence and harmony.

3
Cosmopolitanism and the Political Realm

Introduction

By the end of this chapter, we intend to have developed a characterization of cosmopolitanism which can be summarized through three interlocking elements: the notion of a global exchange relationship; the notion of a Weberian critical recognition ethics; and the moral notion of individual worth and equality within a global community. The third theme is one we alluded to in Chapter 1, but the first two have only been mentioned in passing, so they will be built up here. We address these themes as issues of cosmopolitanism within the political realm.

As Hayden (2005: 2ff.) usefully summarizes, we can very roughly characterize political thought about twentieth-century global politics as dominated by two, apparently opposite, conceptual approaches: political realism and liberalism. Political realism focuses on the struggle for power between various nation states, and tends to conceptualize the global political environment in terms of a zero-sum economy: that is to say, the power and influence of individual states comes at the expense of other, competitor states. By contrast, the liberal approach to global politics more strongly emphasizes the moral element, and tends to analyse statecraft in terms of its connection to values such as individual freedom, democracy, principles of international justice, equality, and so forth; in the liberal approach, it is perhaps easier to see an international realm in which all are winners, as democracy and freedom spread around the globe. While these two approaches are in many ways opposed, it was not unusual to see them mixed together in twentieth-century foreign policy, or even in our current conjuncture. So, for example, the USA, particularly after the Second World

War, frequently engaged in *realpolitik* in relation to perceived threats from communist states, and sought to weaken these states as a way of guaranteeing its own power. At the same time, its foreign policy was often suffused with a commitment to the universalistic values of classical liberalism (democracy, individual freedom, etc), and an apparent desire to spread these benefits.

Up until the fall of the Berlin Wall in 1989, both political realism and liberalism were – at least in mainstream political theory – enacted and thought through in relation to the nation state system. Even to the extent that forms of international government, such as the United Nations, were invented, these forms were composed of nation state units, and never really erased the national as the primary unit of meaningful action. However, towards the end of the twentieth century, new forms of international cooperation started to emerge. The end of the massive communist command economies was decisive in triggering these sorts of changes; for example, the European Union became a much more serious post-national governmental agency. In other realms, a growing awareness of the global nature of environmental threats led to the (attempted and occasionally successful) formation of global governmental initiatives, such as the Montreal Protocol to deal with the problem of the hole in the ozone layer, the Kyoto Protocol to deal with global warming, and the Earth Charter; in addition, the growing power of NGOs such as Greenpeace and Friends of the Earth signaled the emergence, perhaps, of a new kind of cosmopolitan law – an attempt to govern post-nationally, or at least in a way in which nation states were no longer seen as the major units of action or the only entities endangered by perceived problems. The world as a whole was affected by such problems as global warming, the hole in the ozone layer, and so forth, and these (primarily environmental) problems were no respecters of national borders.

At first glance, then, it appears that the period from about 1989 can be characterized as post-national: that is to say, the world is no longer meaningfully described using nation states as the sole units of political action, and political theory correspondingly started to move away from its dependence on the state as a first principle. This is certainly Hayden's line, when he argues (2005: 1ff.) that cosmopolitan global politics supplanted the traditions of political realism and liberalism and provided us with a theoretical break with the older traditions. It is also the argument of Beck (2006: 24ff.) when he suggests that we must, and have indeed already begun to, go beyond methodological nationalism. By this, Beck means that our habit – both common sense and social scientific – of imagining the nation state to be the source of all political intelligibility needs to be broken:

> the territorial social ontology of the national outlook is not just 'at home' in the everyday world of political parties, the mass media and politics, but even more so in law and especially in the social sciences. The founding duality of the national outlook – foreigner-native – no longer adequately reflects reality... [Methodologically nationalist approaches] are unprepared for the realities of life in a world that is becoming increasingly transnational and involves plural attachments that transcend the boundaries of countries and nationality (Beck 2006: 26).

Is classical sociology methodologically nationalist?

At this point, it is worth dealing more closely with Beck's objections to 'methodological nationalism', and his allied claim that the social sciences, and especially (political) sociology, are flawed because they are trapped within a mistaken theoretical paradigm. In his analysis of the major principles of methodological nationalism, Beck asserts first that methodological nationalism subordinates society to the state (2006: 27ff.); the world is composed of a variety of societies within nation state 'containers'. While the form of Beck's argument is that the state is seen as a higher-level organizing principle for society, in effect his argument amounts to the state and society being coterminous for the methodological nationalists. Interestingly, he asserts that this principle of methodological nationalism can be found in Durkheim (Beck 2006: 27) and Parsons (although he does not provide any direct references), a mistaken attribution we shall return to shortly.

The second principle, closely tied to the first, is that methodological nationalism operates with the notion of national/international as an exclusive binary relationship, which maps too easily onto inside/outside (2006: 28ff.). Beck's objection here is that the national and the international are not so decisively distinguished, and that each presupposes the other: we might be better off thinking, then, of 'nationalness' and 'internationalness' along a continuum, the extreme ends of which – purely national or purely international – are unlikely to be seen very often.

The third principle of methodological nationalism is the incorrect generalization from particular societies to a universal model of society. Marx, for example, is accused by Beck of generalizing from British capitalist society to a model of modern capitalist society as a whole; Weber is accused of over-generalizing Prussian bureaucracy and turning it into a universal ideal type; and C. Wright Mills is accused of assuming that a specific study of American power elites provided the basis for a conceptualization of power elites throughout a universalized conception of society (Beck 2006: 28). Beck points to the development of a series of comparative studies which sought to deal with this problem of overgeneralization, but asserts that these studies typically partake of methodological nationalism, since any comparisons they make are on the basis of a pre-existing commitment to the nation state as the unit of meaningful analysis. That is to say, even as differences around the globe are uncovered by the comparative sociologists, the differences are reduced to those *between* nation state based societies, while the generalized model still survives, with variants from it becoming a footnote in the continued unquestioning overgeneralizations about the nature of society. The global is reduced to 'the maximum intensification of the national' (2006: 29), and scholars such as Immanuel Wallerstein (1991) and John Meyer and his team (Meyer *et al.* 1997) are found guilty of this mistake by Beck.

The fourth principle moves the target of analysis from society to culture, but is, *mutatis mutandis*, the same criticism as the third principle we saw above. Beck (2006: 29) argues that if culture is seen as organized within nation state containers, then analysis of cultural difference ends up with two, equally 'sterile', possibilities: universal sameness (as, for example, in the McDonaldization literature) or the incommensurability of cultures (cultural relativism). Unfortunately, the humanistic impulse at the heart of many apparently cosmopolitan outlooks (Beck is careful to contrast these interlopers with his own authentic cosmopolitan outlook) means that ultimately they tend towards universalism, or the first of these two theoretical traps; pluralism is slowly eradicated as global society tends towards greater and greater cultural homogeneity. The methodological nationalist alternative, which emphasizes differences between cultures contained within nation state territories, ends up with the impossibility of meaningful dialogue, and eventually gives way to (cultural and political) imperialism and Huntington's (and others') 'Clash of Civilizations' (Beck 2006: 30; Huntington 1996).

Beck's fifth principle (2006: 30–1) centres on methodological nationalism's tendency to try to purify and separate political realities which are interconnected (the example he gives is of the distinction made between the Islamic and the Jewish tradition in terms of our understanding of the limits of the national and of the cultural, a distinction that it is hard to justify historically because of the rich tradition of exchange between these two worlds). For Beck, this tendency is a result of an overextension into the historical consciousness of an idealized version of national boundaries: to the extent that, for example, Israel and Palestine have ever been neatly cordoned off (more in the political imaginary, of course, than in actual borders), the idea can emerge that the history of these two politico-religious traditions can be separated.

Beck continues with more in this vein, but we can leave our summary of him here; he tends to generate tendencies of methodological nationalism rather than principles, or expand upon existing principles (the either/or tendency, as opposed to cosmopolitanism's both/and tendency; so, for example, international relations theory, because it is built up from examining nation state units, is accused of methodological nationalism), and his arguments become repetitive. They tend also to have a flavour of 'straw man' arguments, since entire sub-disciplines are characterized as having a single theoretical impulse. It is worth stressing, however, that Beck does not deny the importance of the nation state as a unit of social scientific analysis – his point is rather that it should be seen as only one of many possible units of analysis.

Much of what Beck says, although undeniably harsh to vast tracts of excellent social scientific work and, as we have suggested above, perhaps prone to over-generalization, is unexceptionable. We would agree that it is important to understand politics as composed of more than just nation state activity. In fact, we argue that this emphasis needs to go further in certain respects than Beck has taken it. Beck occasionally slips into an argument that we especially need to understand the transnational nature of political life in an era of globalization, implying that the nation-centred approach was once appropriate, but has recently become outmoded. For example, when Beck says 'transnational realities and causalities are *becoming* the universal norm' (2006: 28, emphasis added), surely the implication is that they have not always been – and presumably that national realities and causalities, pure and simple, were once the universal norm. Yet surely the idea that nation states were ever able to exist as isolated societies and to shun the transnational is questionable. Jack Goody (2004), for example, clearly shows us that as early as the eighth century C.E. – well before the nation state had become a political reality – the development of European art, culture, literature, science and everyday life was thoroughly suffused with Islamic ideas, and that the development of 'Islamic' and 'European' culture (to the extent that we can talk of these as distinct entities) happened in the context of continual exchange (see also Hodgson 1974).[1] Given that the European nation state only became a meaningful political unit in the early modern period, it is not hard to argue that its development was always in the context of transnational concerns; it is correspondingly difficult to argue that it has ever been possible for a European-style national society to have developed in its own autonomous and purified milieu, and even in those situations where national societies aimed at excluding outsiders, the porosity of their borders was always an obstacle to such dreams of national purity. So we have no problems with Beck wishing to emphasize the dangers of thinking about the political in ways limited by the national; but it may even be that the discontinuity Beck implies exists between a period of nationalism (first modernity) and the current period of globalization and cosmopolitanism (second modernity) is too crude, and that Beck imagines a mythical past of insular nation states.

However, we have another beef with Beck, one that is theoretical rather than historical. Beck is surely mistaken in his argument that the classical sociologists were simply concerned with the analysis of societies as contained within nation states, an argument he makes with the intention of ruling them out as irrelevant to the analysis of the second modernity (and presumably as a way of making his own contribution so much more necessary). Bryan Turner (2006) suggests that the concern of classical sociology was not so much national societies; rather it was 'the social'[2] more generally, and this notion of the social was always

---

[1] This example of the constant interchange between European and Islamic culture is just one of many. The spread of Viking culture, for example, during the period 750 to 1050 AD is another well known instance of widespread cultural exchange beyond the original homelands. Archaeological evidence – the most well known being the L'Anse aux Meadows site in Newfoundland – is now confirming Viking settlements in the Americas 400 years before Columbus.

[2] In attempting to define the social, especially as distinct from 'society', Turner suggests a parallel with Carl Schmitt's (1996) notion of 'the political' as distinct from 'politics'. 'The political' is the emergency in which friend and enemy struggle, and this struggle shapes their world; by contrast 'politics' is merely the management of political affairs. In the same way, 'the social' can be distinguished from the mundane world of society: 'the social' is the moral sphere, separate from egoism. Turner suggests 'trust' might be the core social dimension we need to concentrate on here: trust is the medium of exchange in the social, just as struggle is the medium of exchange in the political. In addition, the social, for Turner, must be composed of patterns of social interaction, characterized by symbolic exchange, which cohere into social institutions (Turner 2006: 135–6).

understood as a transnational phenomenon. Turner (2006: 137ff.) shows, for example, how Parsons's work on the social was never conducted simply through the lens of national societies (although these did matter to Parsons), but ranged through dyadic relationships (e.g. doctor and patient), social groups and their leadership, and the sociology of international relations (Parsons 1937, 1971). Turner's argument here hinges on Parsons's understanding of sociology as answering questions that individualistic disciplines like economics and psychology cannot deal with, in particular the problem of social action. The crucial issue for Parsons became the analysis of social norms and values that guaranteed social order (his analysis, of course, is made through his famous AGIL scheme – see Parsons 1951; Parsons *et al.* 1955). What we must stress here is that Parsons's application of the AGIL (Adaptation; Goal attainment; Integration; Latency) scheme is never simply to society understood *qua* national society, as Beck mistakenly asserts. Parsons is interested in the social, ranging across various 'social systems', and was alive to the idea that these social systems might have a variety of salient 'boundaries' (so, for example, the business firms that he analysed as part of the 'adaptation' functions were well understood by him as operating globally rather than nationally).

Durkheim is the second sociologist whom Beck (2006: 27) accuses, without specific citation, of being fixated on the analysis of national societies, and thus of being guilty of engaging in methodological nationalism. Again, Bryan Turner's defence of Durkheim as an analyst of 'the social', rather than of specific societies, is compelling. In particular, Durkheim's (1992) detailed account of the struggle between the nationalistic-patriotic and the world-patriotic moral viewpoints is one in which Durkheim's cosmopolitan leanings are on display, and in which it is clear as day that Durkheim's notion of society is not one limited by the container of the (French or any other) nation state:

> Now, societies are becoming ever greater in scale an ever more complex: they are made up of circles of increasing diversity, and of manifold agencies, and these already possess in themselves a value to be reckoned. Therefore if it is to fulfil its function, the State, too, must branch out and evolve to the same degree (Durkheim 1992: 65–6).

> No matter how devoted men may be to their native land, they all to-day are aware that beyond the forces of national life there are others, in a higher region and not so transitory, for they are

unrelated to conditions peculiar to any given political group and are not bound up with its fortunes. There is something more universal and enduring... National aims do not lie at the summit of this hierarchy – it is human aims that are destined to be supreme (Durkheim 1992: 72–3).

Further, in his work with Marcel Mauss, Durkheim shows a keen understanding of the necessity to switch in and out of the national frame depending on the objects under investigation:

> not all social phenomena are equally apt to internationalize themselves. Political institutions, juridical institutions, the phenomena of social morphology constitute part of the specific character of each people. On the other hand, the myths, tales, money, commerce, fine arts, techniques, tools, language, words, scientific knowledge, literary forms and ideas – all of these travel and are borrowed (Durkheim and Mauss 1998: 153).

Clearly in these writings Durkheim shows us that his notion of the social connects much more to forms of Kantian universalism – certainly a form of cosmopolitan imagination – rather than to a narrow nationalistic way of thinking. Certainly, Durkheim is adamant that existing national states will have to be the agency for the evolution of world patriotism, or cosmopolitanism; but this does not make him a methodological nationalist, any more than Beck is when he admits that the nation state must remain an indispensable analytic unit in any realistic political analysis ('the cosmopolitan outlook retains a reference to the nation-state but situates and analyses it within a radically different horizon', is how he puts it – Beck 2006: 33). Clearly Durkheim understands that much of the development of culture and civilization must be studied from a global perspective. We should also add that Durkheim's great rival in early French sociology, Gabriel Tarde, while disagreeing fundamentally with Durkheim's Kantian approach (Latour 2001), nonetheless emphasized 'associations' at a variety of scales and levels as the subject-matter of sociology (Tarde 1907).

The more general point we want to pursue here is that classical sociology's analysis of the social is perfectly well equipped to enable us to comprehend changing transnational realities. The classical emphasis was never solely on national societies, and Beck's assertion that it was, while it conveniently allows him to argue that he has invented a much-needed new analysis for new times (and his analysis continues by linking a variety of new and emerging themes, such as cosmopolitan consciousness, risk society, and second modernity), is deeply flawed.

We have already begun to see, then, how classical sociologists like Parsons and Durkheim attempted an analysis of the social, and this social was never understood as simply contained by the practices of the nation state. Parsons's work, as Bryan Turner (2006: 139) has it, is a contribution to the analysis of civilizational processes, and the 'systems' Parsons analysed were never simply national in character. Durkheim's plea for cosmopolitanism – a desire for new forms of universal moral individualism which could be substituted for dangerous forms of national patriotism – clearly emerged from a background understanding of the social as so much more than simply a series of outcrops of national processes. In particular, in seeking to diagnose and cure the moral egoism he associated with the growth of utilitarian thinking, Durkheim's proposed cosmopolitan solution connected to forms of 'universal moral consciousness' – a phrase that we might use as a rough definition of what Durkheim meant by the social (see B. Turner 2006: 140). Interestingly, then, we can begin to see that Durkheim's analysis of the social was always cosmopolitan in character – cosmopolitan thinking was a fundamental component of classical social theory. To expand this point with a further example, in his classic work on suicide, Durkheim is eager to show us how nationality as a variable does not explain suicide rates. Durkheim displays one of the most famous tables in sociology (2002: 22) to show national suicide rates, but this is a prelude to dismissing suicide and nationality as having a simple causal relationship (a crucial piece of evidence against this for Durkheim (2002: 106ff) was the finding that Bavaria – the most Catholic area of Germany – had the lowest suicide rates within the regions of Germany; nationality, then, could not be the crucial variable). For Durkheim, suicide is something which is woven into a complicated notion of the social, and in particular bears a relationship to degrees of social integration, but this social integration must be analysed with an open mind as to scale.

It is hard to see, then, how Beck can sustain his argument that classical sociology was fixated on the nation state. If one examines still more examples of the classical approach – for example, the works of Max Weber and Georg Simmel – Beck's analysis seems still less plausible. For example, Weber's work might reasonably be understood as a contribution to the emergence of culture and cultural values, and even though the term 'cosmopolitanism' does not take centre stage for Weber, his work analyses the constant interconnection between cultures. Take this passage from *The Protestant Ethic*:

> The rationalization of private law... was achieved in the highest hitherto known degree in the Roman Law of late antiquity. But it remained most backward in some of the countries with the highest degree of economic rationalization, notably in England, where the Renaissance of Roman Law was overcome by the power of the great legal corporations, while it has always retained its supremacy in the Catholic countries of Southern Europe.... [I]f under practical rationalism is understood the type of attitude which sees and judges the world consciously in terms of the worldly interests of the individual ego, then this view of life was and is the special peculiarity of the peoples of the *liberum arbitrium*, such as the Italians and French are in very flesh and blood (Weber 2001: 37–8).

In this short section, Weber does not shun a discussion of national characteristics, and the forms of cultural, political and legal life peculiar to England and Southern Europe. In doing so, he does not lose sight how elements of the phenomenon of rationalization might be repeated in different geographical locations. Yet he is able to include in this discussion the transnational phenomenon of Roman Law as well as the role played by sub- and inter-national actors such as legal corporations, and the very localized influence of the Augustinian concept of free will. This is not a passage written by someone for whom the nation state was the limit of his thinking about society: he was thinking beyond through it, but was also alive to the sub-national and the supra-national.

Georg Simmel, another of the major classical sociologists, contributed not so much to our understanding of nationally-limited forms of culture, as to our understanding of how culture circulates around the social, characterized by Simmel, as by Weber, as a complex interweaving of various cosmopolitan entities. Two of the many themes that Simmel develops are, to our eyes, extraordinarily redolent of contemporary cosmopolitan scholarship. First, Simmel (like Tarde) often dwells on the theme of the social as a variety of associations; like Durkheim, Simmel was appalled by the growth of egoistic and individualistic culture, and saw some higher purpose in the various associations individuals enter into (see, for example, Simmel 1949). Second, and relatedly, he develops the theme of exchange as fundamental to modern forms of the social; in Simmel (2004), for example, money is analysed as an exchange mechanism. This exchange mechanism simultaneously erodes some of the forms of individuality of the premodern world, at the same time as it fosters a kind of cosmopolitan culture in which every individual's world becomes 'networked' (to use a currently fashionable term) with more, and further flung, people and objects:

> the money economy makes possible... a specific kind of mutual dependence, which... affords room for a maximum of liberty... [I]t creates a series of previously unknown obligations. Dependency upon third persons has spread into completely new areas... The more the activity and life of people becomes dependent upon objective conditions by virtue of a complicated technology,[3] the greater necessarily is the dependence upon more and more people... The general tendency, however, undoubtedly moves in the direction of making the individual more and more dependent upon the achievements of people, but less and less dependent upon the personalities that lie behind them... Compared with modern man, the member of a traditional or primitive economy is dependent only upon a minimum of other persons (Simmel 2004: 295–8).

Here, Simmel recalls Durkheim's emphasis upon the modern division of labour, but his emphasis is on interconnection and exchange, as well as the more Durkheimian loss of sense of self, or *anomie*. At the same time, Simmel anticipates the Eliasian theme (Elias 1994) of how individual belonging and exclusion are primarily constituted by the nation state and its juridical powers. Simmel certainly does not foreground the role of the state in this process to anything like the extent Elias does (although Simmel does mention – with chilling foresight of what the rest of the twentieth century would look like – how these forms of dependency and the erasure of personality can be seen in forms of state socialism – see Simmel 2004: 297), and so hardly seems to display the sorts of nation-centred perspective Beck claims to see in modernist sociology.

---

[3]We shall return to the theme of technology in the next chapter.

Establishing the utility and relevance of classical sociology for analysing contemporary global politics

The usefulness of Simmel: the city, colonialism and the triumph of the exchange economy

The key text for our purposes is Simmel's 'The Metropolis and Mental Life', originally published in 1903. Simmel draws an illuminating parallel between the development of modern capitalism and the emergence of a global world. For Simmel, the city came to supplant the countryside and provided not only a geographical location for the development of capitalism (a place for factories and other heavy machinery), but it also was a place that fostered the psychological conditions under which humans could accept a capitalist system, especially in terms of two decisive psychological comportments that grew in urban conditions: the blasé attitude, and the acceptance of a society of exchange instead of a society of use. The constant stimulation of the city famously results in this blasé approach, of course (Simmel 2002: 14), but we also should stress that the triumph of the money economy erases the emphasis on the use of things in favour of their exchange value:

> The essence of the blasé attitude is an indifference toward the distinctions between things. Not in the sense that they are not perceived... but rather that the meaning and the value of the distinctions between things, and therewith of the things themselves, are experienced as meaningless... This psychic mood is the correct subjective reflection of a complete money economy to the extent that money takes the place of all the manifoldness of things and expresses all qualitative distinctions between them in the distinction of how much (Simmel 2002: 14).

The city is properly the place *par excellence* of the cosmopolitan attitude. Not least because of its essential anonymity, the life of the city fosters greater amounts of personal freedom than the countryside: 'the citizen of the metropolis is "free" in contrast with the trivialities and prejudices which bind the small town person' (Simmel 2002: 16). This freedom is not without cost for the personality and the intellect, however, which, insulated from wider meaning by the division of labour, decline:

> [f]or it is this [the growing division of labour] which requires from the individual an ever more one-sided type of achievement which,

at its highest point, often permits his personality as a whole to fall into neglect (Simmel 2002: 18).

Simmel takes it for granted that the city (and city life) acts as a colonizing and corrosive force in relation to the countryside and its values, slowly destroying the other (see also Frisby and Featherstone 1997). The city, then, is the source of cosmopolitanism, but it is a corrosive cosmopolitanism, as it continues its reach beyond the confines of the perimetropolitan areas, and slowly colonizes the globe. For Simmel, perfectly well aware of globalization at the end of the nineteenth century, cosmopolitanism was ultimately urbanization – and vice versa. Elsewhere in this book we discuss Simmel as a cultural theorist, but what should be clear here is the political point that Simmel sees cosmopolitanism as a form of colonialism: certainly a form of life that increases freedom, but one which is in many ways intellectually and spiritually impoverished. And to continue this colonization theme, there is also present in Simmel the idea that the movement from a material culture to an informational culture – roughly speaking, the triumph of the money economy, or the loss of value of material things in themselves in favour of the exchange value – creates a situation in which the individual is confronted with massive amounts of cultural information.[4] In confronting this cultural and informational sublime, people are forced to pick and choose from a variety of 'objective cultures', as Simmel puts it, that they find most edifying. What flows from this is that other cultures become colonized and packaged up for our (the West's) use.

Simmel's characterization of cosmopolitanism, then, is not just limited to culture. He also offers us an economic and political understanding of cosmopolitanism where the cultural changes embed, and

---

[4] Just think for a moment, for example, about the huge amount of choice we now have in relation to the music we listen to and buy, in terms of genre, and its temporal and geographical origin, as well as the inevitable hybrid forms it immediately starts to take; it has become quite impossible to deal expertly (and 'authentically') with it all, and so we are forced to filter it to suit our (quite trivial and arbitrary) needs and preferences. One can engage in a number of coping strategies, including the following, which are far from exhaustive: a) only listen to a narrow selection (e.g. one period, composer, group or a narrow genre); b) trust 'experts' (writers, journalists, knowledgeable friends, etc.) to key one in to types of music that are new (or least new to the listener); c) adopt an eclectic and serendipitous attitude, waiting to hear new things that interest and intrigue.

Cosmopolitanism and the Political Realm 67

are embedded by, changes in political and economic systems. Cosmopolitanism must be understood as a vector for the transmission of the values of the centre to the periphery and vice versa, a process of appropriation involving incorporation of the periphery into the centre according to logics established in the centre – a truly colonizing impulse. While Simmel is rather sanguine about this colonization, he is also clear that there is an element of cultural loss in this movement. The expansion of the periphery comes at the cost of the erosion of differences – the triumph of the money economy, which levels everything, helps see to that. While scholars both before and after Simmel prefer to emphasize the ethical character of cosmopolitanism (which of course ends up valorizing cosmopolitanism), Simmel's approach sees the ethical and psychological components of the cosmopolitan temper as the corollaries of cultural imperialism achieved through economic flow. In part it does this because money, even though it flattens out and dulls everything that it supposedly puts a value on, nonetheless extends the circulation of trust from the local arena to the global. In this way, Simmel's work gives us a purchase on cosmopolitanism as an ethical, psychological, economic and political entity. We shall develop this idea of the ethics of cosmopolitanism and their connection to politics in the next section, as we deal with Max Weber.

The usefulness of Max Weber's *Verstehende Soziologie*

As we have already suggested, it is possible to think of Weber as a theorist of cultural or civilizational development, rather than as simply a political or sociological theorist of the nation state (although this is not to deny his enormous contribution in the latter area). Accordingly, Weber's influential ideas about the decisive role of the nation state – built on its capacity for the legitimate use of violence – need to be addressed in the context of the limits of globalization and cosmopolitanism, and we shall deal with this later. However, first we choose to consider Weber's well-known approach to *Verstehende Soziologie*, which, following Bryan Turner (2006), we take to be a fertile ground for understanding the ethical preconditions for cosmopolitanism. Famously, *Verstehende Soziologie* (or 'interpretive sociology') was Weber's (and Dilthey's – see Dilthey 1989) attempt to work out a way to carry out comparative studies. The method sounds deceptively simple: it requires putting oneself in the place of the other, and using the other's concepts to understand, for example, social structures – rather than using one's own concepts as a yardstick. In Weber's work, this practice was linked to the generation of 'ideal types' which could then be used as explanatory categories. Among Weber's 'ideal types' are the famous trio of forms of authority – traditional, charismatic, and rational-legal – which, as is well known, Weber suggested were unlikely to be seen in their pure forms.

Interpretive sociology, then, is about attempting to understand social actions – actions which take account of other people – and being able to relate them back to an explanatory schema. Weber, of course, is one of the people Beck has in mind as a methodological nationalist, as we have discussed above, but Beck is not the first to mount this criticism of Weber's state-centred approach. As Bryan Turner (2006: 141–2) argues, Giddens had also made a similar critique: in developing a fourfold framework of the processes of globalization, Giddens (1990) explicitly develops four elements of Weber's work – 1) the growth and role of capitalism, 2) power, authority and surveillance, 3) state violence, and 4) the extraction and use of natural resources – while simultaneously suggesting that these elements in Weber are ill-suited to an analysis of a globalized world because they emerged from, and are only relevant to, a reading of nation state-based relationships, whether within or between states.

However, there are problems with this Giddensian/Beckian characterization. Weber's goal was not, we think, to generate a series of generalizations or teleological explanations of how Western nation states operated. The point is to move from understanding social action – being able to describe actions, beliefs, and reasons through the interpretive approach, and being able to package these up into explanations – to tentative causal conclusions. Weber was very cautious about the movement to these tentative causal conclusions: from descriptions, and from packaging descriptions into explanations, candidates sometimes emerged for Weber as causes, though the evidence for this had to be strong enough to meet something like the probabilistic standard for a cause in law. Stephen Turner (1986: 163–79) argues that Weber, as a trained lawyer, relied heavily on a probabilistic standard for causes very much like that employed in the law. The candidates for cause should be able to explain the actions, beliefs, and reasons in terms intelligible at the individual level. As Stephen Turner puts it:

> In historical explanation, this commitment to individual explanation implies that such *explanans* and *explananda* as the Protestant ethic and the spirit of capitalism, rational law, rational accounting, the rational organization of labor, and so on must be treated in a particular way: they cannot be treated as 'effective forces'; their

causal and explanatory adequacy depends on the possibility of our 'cashing them in' for individual explanations (Turner 1986: 214).

What follows from this is that when a Weberian cause is offered it should never be taken to be a teleology; it is simply a cause for the particular object under investigation; it cannot serve as a universal, timeless principle (see also Wickham and Kendall 2008). Weber was not interested in posing 'the process of rationalization ', for example, as a teleology. Again, Stephen Turner summarizes this idea well:

> explanation must be a work of tessellation, the composition of a pattern of actions. Ideal-types were a shorthand means of describing the patterns in this mosaic, but no more – not Millian causes made up of institutional facts, and not the immanent universal historical forces of rationalization (Turner 1986: 216).

To summarize the points made above, the Weberian approach is not about isolating any such generalities as 'the workings of Western nation states', 'the rationalization process', or 'the role of religion in social and economic development'. The Weberian approach is about moving from description to tentative causal accounts. It is tempting to understand the role of ideal types in this approach as universal – but they are not at all Platonic in their character. Ideal types are rather convenient descriptions of patterns. If they cannot be cashed out for specific explanations, they are of no use. All of this is built on a description and analysis of actions and beliefs. There is, then, no in principle problem with using a Weberian approach to understand 'global society', for example, even if we accept the Giddensian and Beckian proposition that such forms of the social are radically different from those characteristic of the 'classical' age of modernity.

Bryan Turner's call for a critical recognition ethics (Turner 2006: esp. 141–5) is based on these Weberian principles, and forms the basis of our Weberian-inflected theory of cosmopolitanism. For Turner, there must be four stages to what he terms a 'cosmopolitan hermeneutics': recognition of the other, respect for difference, critical mutual evaluation, and finally care for the other (Turner 2006: 142). Moving through a discussion of Hegel, Nancy Fraser and Charles Taylor, Bryan Turner argues that mutual recognition, whether between individuals or between communities, will always be hard to achieve unless societies commit to social equality (or at least to move nearer to social equality) through a system of rights and obligations. Habermas's work on communicative rationality is brought in at this point to provide the mechanism for meaningful and respectful dialogue between individuals or communities. In particular, through Habermas, Turner argues that recognition ethics can become *critical*: recognition of the other is an important step, but we need to be able to evaluate competing ethical claims and, if necessary, disagree: '[t]he role of judgment distinguishes critical recognition theory from anthropological descriptive relativism and from epistemological disinterest, because these anthropological positions rule out any judgment' (Turner 2006: 144–5). The connection with Weber here in the formation of this cosmopolitan ethics is threefold: first, the Weberian emphasis on understanding and describing values – whether values of our own or of the other – provides the basis for our ethics; second, these values, with the help of ideal types, can be the source for the generation of 'plausible accounts of the actions of others in terms of their own meaning systems' (Turner 2006: 145); third, the Weberian approach to sociology, which understands it primarily as a moral science, directs us to critical judgement of actions and meaning systems. We are in a position, now, to comprehend why Weber is so valuable for advancing cosmopolitanism: first, his work directs us, and gives us a method for, the generation of 'plausible accounts of the actions of others in terms of their own meaning systems' (Turner 2006: 145); second, there is nothing stopping us from making a judgement of these cultures, and nothing tying us to moral relativism.

From the political to a theory of cosmopolitanism

These Weberian moves are crucial for us in developing a theory of cosmopolitanism which emphasizes the generation of a moral account from a political base. By following Weber, we are able to escape the clutches of cultural relativism, and need not be scared to judge actions as good or bad. This is no mean feat, since the historical emergence of cosmopolitanism as a fundamentally Western discourse (an idea we expanded upon in our Introductory chapter) means that applying judgements of cosmopolitanism outside of Western contexts might appear *prima facie* to be an exercise in cultural imperialism. Our Weberian critical recognition ethics compels us to make a strong commitment to the work of understanding the other, but it does not shy away from making a judgement of the practices of the other (so, for example, a critical recognition ethics would have no squeamishness in condemning the Taliban destruction of Hindu icons in Afghanistan). In particular, we can condemn the anti-cosmopolitan: that which makes no attempt to understand the other, that which makes no attempt to engage dialogically with the other, but which moves straight to judgement based on a commitment to non-reflexive principles, such as those of religious dogma.

Our argument here straddles what appears to be quite contradictory territory. We are certainly in favour of a normative approach to cosmopolitanism: what is needed is a series of judgements about what is good and bad, because we regard cosmopolitanism as a *moral* dimension – the moral dimension that has become paramount in a globalized world. For us, then, echoing our earlier definitional work, cosmopolitanism is the moral notion of individual worth and equality in the context of global exchange relationships. It is built out of Weber's *Verstehende Soziologie*, and thus must be a serious attempt to understand what the other understands. We have become used to cosmopolitanism as necessarily connected to some universalist principles like freedom of speech, human rights, and so forth; and our analysis in the Introductory chapter of the Kantian roots of cosmopolitanism discussed why this is the case – why most understandings of cosmopolitanism lean upon universalistic notions founded on rationality. However, what we propose is a cosmopolitanism which is not universalistic in terms of a Kantian, rationalistic, enlightenment position. Our shift of emphasis is necessary because the hidden danger of the dominant, Kantian approach is that other, higher forms of reason may be invoked to revise cosmopolitanism, and ultimately to destroy it. This is exactly what happens when religious viewpoints get invoked – they claim a form of reason higher than earthly reason, and in this way, faith-based actions can claim the highest possible normative ground. The Taliban see nothing wrong in destroying the cultural artefacts of other religions (as we mentioned above, and as infamously happened a few years ago in Afghanistan), because for them, all other religions have succumbed to a false form of reason. Our point here is that to allow cosmopolitanism to emerge from a battle of reason is to leave it hostage to assertions about the character of *specific forms of reason*.

However, it is possible to generate an understanding of cosmopolitanism in the political realm which does not rely on Kantian universal rationality, and the Weberian approach which we have outlined is an important part of this alternative form of normativity. Our version of Weber, however, is not the Parsonian Weber who is known throughout the USA, but the voluntarist, Hobbesian Weber. Against a Kantian, rationalist cosmopolitanism, we champion a politically-focused, voluntarist rival, which has its roots in early modern European thought, when key thinkers like Hobbes and Pufendorf had to confront the reality of religious civil wars threatening entire populations. These wars gave a clear indication that human reason has its limits, and that a strong state under the rule of law would offer a much stronger form of protection, against both internal and external passion-driven excesses, than a reliance on human reason ever could. The Westphalian settlement of 1648, which marked the end of these religious wars, was the moment at which twin concepts – the strong autonomous nation state, and state-based citizenship – came into being as a way of guaranteeing a realm of individual freedom and safety. We need always to remember that this realm of safety is formed by, dependent upon, and never separable from, the realms of politics, law and the state which generated it and continue to generate it today. This idea is developed in Weber (1948b), where he discusses the interplay of politics and the state (although not to Schmitt's 1996 satisfaction – Schmitt wishes to remove some of the circularity he sees in Weber's dual invocation of politics and state) as a foundation for a series of other social associations. We suggest that just as the Westphalian settlement allowed for forms of nationalism dependent – or even parasitical – upon on the political, so a meaningful cosmopolitanism must be rooted in politics, the state, and the rule of law.

It is instructive to analyse the components of the Westphalian solution. There developed a number of mechanisms – some 'external' to nation states, and some 'internal' to them – in order, in the first instance, simply to secure civil peace in times of extreme intercommunal, inter-confessional violence, and simply to limit the flow of blood. First, absolutist sovereignty, as famously described in Hobbes's *Leviathan*, insisted that all judgements about moral worth were taken from every set of hands other than those of a sovereign, whether individual or corporate. Second, a public legal conscience emerged, which was explicitly developed as a direct alternative to private religious conscience; the key notion here was to dispute the possibility that moral judgements born of religious belief, including those judgements which necessitated killing those of different religious faiths, could form a sensible basis for citizenship. Third, public law, or law of the state, was developed to replace and/or supplement private law, and to enforce the state's judgements. Fourth, neo-Stoic and neo-Epicurean personal disciplines, like *decorum* and *constantia*, became understood as part of the moral armoury of the citizen (see Oestreich 1982); these personal disciplines aimed to teach individuals to quell their passions and allow the small dose of reason they were given by nature to do its work. It should be noted that nearly all those who developed the mechanisms on this list were voluntarists; they believed, contrary to the rationalists, that humans do not have enough reason to rule themselves by reason alone, but only enough to necessitate a combination of external and internal governing mechanisms.

Weber, we assert, understood the political base that guaranteed a particular set of moral forms that we can call 'citizenship'. For Weber, the clash of politics was an inevitable aspect of life, but something we should face up to honestly, and out of which we should be able to make our moral choices. Weber, in trying to understand how a person can make such moral choices, suggests that the characteristics required are not natural: they are not the part of the domain of metaphysics, as philosophers such as Leibniz and Kant have been at pains to emphasize. Rather, rigorous judgement emerges from an historically formed persona: a persona that is achieved by training (see especially Weber 1948b). This is a theme that can be seen in a way of thinking about social action that has become rather unfashionable of late, but can be seen in the work of thinkers such as Michael Polanyi, Edward Shils and Michael Oakeshott. Oakeshott, for example, suggests the concept of tradition as the best means of avoiding the problems of metaphysical forms of rationality. A tradition, in his hands, is that which we have received, that which shapes our thinking and may have causal effects – that is, may be the source of subsequent events, in the manner of one thing leading to another in a directly attributable way – but is definitely not the source of a teleology, whereby things lead to things not in a directly attributable way but only in a vague, general, force-beyond-us way. Crucially, a tradition is not something within us, nor is it part of our natural reasoning capacities, nor is it part of our natural morality (see, for example, Oakeshott 1993). In addition, for Oakeshott, as for Shils and Polanyi, tradition is a source of innovation and reinvention – it is not understood as the dead hand of the past.

Concluding remarks

Contemporary cosmopolitanism can learn several lessons from this type of thinking and from the traditions of the Westphalian settlement. First of all, any forms of political cosmopolitanism are likely to be imperfect solutions, built to deal with political emergencies, and built to overcome failed interpersonal relationships. First, cosmopolitanism needs to be built from a political base; more specifically, forms of cosmopolitan law, and the extension of national-based regulation, especially focusing on individual rights and responsibilities, need to be constructing. These elements are already underway in some parts of the world, and be seen in political experiments such as the European Union. However, we must remember that Westphalia would never have worked without inventing guidelines for new forms of personal conduct, and it likely that these are the basis for any actually-existing cosmopolitanism. Quite what these new forms of personal conduct might look like is hard to say, but Bryan Turner (2000a) has some intriguing speculations. For Turner, a sense of irony, of detachment, and of distance might prove useful personal qualities in generating an ethos of toleration. As Turner puts it:

> hot loyalties and thick solidarities are more likely to be points of conflict and violence in post-modern, ethnically diverse labour markets. Indifference and distance may be useful personal strategies in a risk society where ambiguity and uncertainty reign... Because historically we have learned to respect the virtues of loyalty and duty, we find it difficult [to accept this idea]... It was the political environment of loyalty to the state and trust in political leaders which at least contributed to twentieth-century authoritarianism on both the left and the right. The ironic citizen of the global city may hopefully be less likely to give her undivided support to whatever government happens to be in power (Turner 2000a: 142).

Over the course of this chapter, we have been keen to advance the position that classical sociology already has the tools for an analysis of cosmopolitanism. In particular, we have analysed how Weber, Durkheim and Simmel (and, to a lesser extent, Parsons) constructed sociologies which emphasized not so much the nation state as a realm that we can call the social. Whether this realm of the social is understood in terms of more or less local, or more or less global, is not especially relevant. And so we also spent a lot of time attacking the view, quite prevalent in the contemporary social sciences, that we need to reinvent our tools for thinking because we live in such different times. This is a mistaken viewpoint. The challenges of cosmopolitanism are simply an intensification of challenges we have seen throughout human history. The 'intensificatory moment' of the late-nineteenth and early-twentieth century was seen especially clearly by Durkheim – who worried about nationalism – and Simmel – who correctly identified the importance of mechanisms of (global) exchange and the triumph of urban life as decisive for new forms of living. Weber clearly identified sociology as a moral science – he saw that the analysis of social action required a series of judgements, and that these judgements required a certain sort of person formation. The problem of cosmopolitanism, then, is one which connects closely to all these thinkers' concerns. We have emphasized that cosmopolitanism is not, as Beck would have it, the description of a new form of already-existing social arrangements, or the brute fact of 'second modernity'. Rather, cosmopolitanism is a fragile and incomplete political settlement. The key to this settlement is the form of self that it requires, and in the next chapter we shall analyse this form.

4
Cosmopolitanism as a Political Lifestyle: Morality, Technology and Style

Introduction

The classical tradition's emphasis on sociology as a moral science makes it an obvious and resilient resource for understanding cosmopolitanism, which is fundamentally a moral discourse around global exchange relationships. We can start to build on this classical premise by our suggestion that cosmopolitanism – as a moral achievement – can only realistically be understood as built from existing (primarily national state) foundations. These may be political in form, as we shall discuss below, or they may be cultural. Our argument in the previous chapter was that the cultural forms of self are intimately connected to never-quite-fully-achieved political goals. Just as the personal comportments derived from neo-Stoicism and neo-Epicurean forms of discipline connected up to the political settlement of the Treaties of Westphalia (see, for example, Oestreich 1982), so it is likely that forms of cosmopolitan comportment that we need to encourage – an example of which is Bryan Turner's 'ironic' citizen – will be intimately connected to the progress of cosmopolitan law and the emergence of transnational government. This is, of course, a style of arguing familiar to the reader of Max Weber: for Weber, political and cultural innovation emerged from forms of self-understanding.

In terms of the cultural and personal foundations of cosmopolitanism, one potentially instructive example is Habermas's (1989) discussion of the important role of the British coffee houses, the French salons and the German *Tischgesellschaften* in the emergence of a public sphere during the seventeenth and eighteenth centuries. These coffee houses were not only the place for the emergence of a society of letters, but they also promoted and actively fostered a sense of common humanity and equality:

> the authority of the better argument could assert itself against that of social hierarchy and in the end carry the day meant, in the thought of the day, the parity of 'common humanity' (Habermas 1989: 36).

These coffee houses were wedded to – and constructed – the intellectual climate of the day not just because they were an informal venue for discussion, but also because they operated as de facto offices and 'drop zones' for the editors of the increasingly popular periodicals (Habermas 1989: 42). Habermas is concerned here to emphasize how the realm of the public sphere was enabled and strengthened; that is, he is interested in how a national sense of identity could be built from the ground up in these local venues. A 'lifestyle' can be built up in this way, and here we can draw out the connection between Habermas's work and Weber's ideas on status. Habermas shows us how the public sphere emerged from a series of specifically located activities that were associated with particular social roles. These roles were not just jobs or activities, but included certain sorts of prestigious styles of living. For Weber, these types of roles are understood as 'statuses'. A status is understood as that which brings social honour, and is defined by Weber as 'every typical component of the life of men that is determined by a specific, positive or negative, social estimation of honor' (1968: 932). For Weber, statuses are intimately connected to lifestyle – in fact, it is through particular lifestyles and ways of comporting the self that an individual's status can be made evident. Of course, these lifestyles transcend the purely individual level, and become markers of 'community': a community is recognizable to the extent that it has a recognizable style. There are elements of Weber's work here that correspond to Marx's idea of a 'class for itself' (i.e. the moment at which a class attains a form of self-understanding), but for Weber, these forms of community can be wider (or indeed narrower) than a social class (for example, lawyers, academics, or cosmopolitans). Importantly, what Weber's (and Habermas's) work does here is enable us to see the connection between quite local forms of social action, and how they might begin to be transformed into a political identity.[1]

If we take Weber's lead here, we may begin to think of cosmopolitanism as a lifestyle. We do not mean to use this term in any negative or superficial way; instead, we think of cosmopolitanism as a series of ethical understandings that connect closely with a way of life, and this way of life connects to notions of status and social honour. Cosmopolitanism is not an simply attitude that can be taken on or thrown off at will; it is a fundamentally western form of persona, built up from national and pre-national notions of how a certain style of life can be lived and be 'prestigious', to borrow Mauss's (1973) phrase. Ultimately, cosmopolitanism is a way of understanding oneself and others in a (political) framework which is an expansion of notions related to domains such as human rights, human worth and citizenship. These notions have so far been developed to their fullest form in the liberal democracies of the West. While certain academic studies have tended to focus on cosmopolitanism as an attitude, then, our suggestion is that it is better to understand it as a form of self; this emphasis removes cosmopolitanism from the realm of the merely psychological to the politically determined and determining.

There are two further points we wish to make here. The first is that it was clear to Weber that a vital feature of the power of the modern nation state was the ability to generate strong feelings of national identity that could be mobilized at times of crisis. There is a strong link,

---

[1] We concentrate here on Weber's notion of status, which seems to us the most useful for thinking about cosmopolitanism. However, Weber's other ways of understanding stratification should also be mentioned, as they also provide us with useful tools for thinking about cosmopolitanism. First of all, Weber's analysis of class, although chiming with much of the Marxian position, de-emphasizes the notion of community in favour of the decisive importance of market situation. A class is a grouping of people who share economic interests, but Weber (1968: 927) is not especially interested in understanding class as anything more than this. This may be instructive in drawing our attention to the way in which the cosmopolitan 'class' share economic interests, a position which has been argued (although not from an explicitly Weberian position) by scholars such as Kanter (1995). A second term in Weber's analysis of stratification is party. Here, Weber's emphasis is on the way in which access to political power can be achieved through a structure (a party) specifically formed to that end. We are yet to see parties that represent cosmopolitan interests, although this may just be a matter of time.

then, between forms of political organization and forms of personal political identification. This is a theme taken up especially by Edward Shils and Young – see for example Shils and Young (1975). Famously, Shils and Young use the coronation of Elizabeth II as a case study to show the interconnection between the signs, symbols and rituals of a culture and its forms of political life: personal identity, cultural activity and political expression go hand in hand.[2]

Second, and relatedly, the force of what Weber argues for here is that forms of self (we would add, like cosmopolitanism) are not simply the results of individual decision-making and preference. Just as Weber sought to connect forms of self with decisive historical social events, we can connect up the cosmopolitan form of self with developments in nationalism and in international relations. Ulrich Beck (2006) has tried to do this (without, it should be said, much acknowledgement of Weber's lead) by suggesting that globalization induces cosmopolitanism as a necessary side-effect. Beck's argument is rather unidirectional, in that cosmopolitanism is a forced product of globalization; by contrast, we, perhaps more faithful to Weber, suggest there may be a mutually reinforcing relationship between globalization and cosmopolitanization.

The main argument of Beck's (2006) book is for a periodization between the first age of modernity and the second age of modernity. The first age is very much characterized by methodological nationalism, and is in the shadow of a Kantian-based integration of values into everyday life. The second age – very much characterized by Beck's pet notion of a world risk society – can only be understood by eschewing methodological nationalism.

> This is not a matter of values-based integration (as methodological nationalism postulates) but of integration through dangers and their aversion, whose binding power grows with the extent of the perceived danger. Instead of integration through national and universal values, the global character of dangers reflected in a world public

---

[2] Another compelling example concerns the cosmopolitan elite of fifth-century BCE Athens. The most elite group of citizens had a fascination with parties in which their good taste, their cosmopolitanism and their social status were all paraded simultaneously. The goal was to have a party with the best wine, prostitutes, food (but especially fish) from far-flung places. This fashion was so costly that many came close to bankruptcy in this display of cosmopolitan savoir-faire. See Davidson (1998).

entails a new dialectic of conflict and cooperation across borders (Beck 2006: 35).

Methodological nationalism imposes a world-view based on national states and their interaction – an 'either inside or outside' perspective – whereas the cosmopolitan outlook, seen by Beck as appropriate to the second age of modernity, makes use of a 'both inside and outside' (of the nation) perspective. Furthermore, for Beck, the cosmopolitan outlook is a coerced, irreversible side effect of global interdependence. It emerges from a dialectical relation between a number of factors that it always interpenetrates:

> Cosmopolitanization is a non-linear, dialectical process in which the universal and the particular, the similar and the dissimilar, the global and the local are to be conceived, not as cultural polarities, but as interconnected and reciprocally interpenetrating principles. The experience of global interdependence and global risks alter the social and political character of societies within nation states. What is distinctive about cosmopolitanization is that it is internal and that it is internalized from within national societies or local cultures. But it is also a cosmopolitanization of the self and of national consciousness, however deformed (Beck 2006: 73).

What is valuable about Beck's work is the way it clearly connects forms of lifestyle – cosmopolitanism – to political conditions – the various forms of modernity. However, in its insistence on a particular unidirectional analysis of historical development (whereby lifestyles or statuses, to use the Weberian terms, are results of politics) it seems to us to miss the possibility of cosmopolitan statuses as connected to and causative of political change. Yet there is a rich sociological tradition which takes this as an important theme – from Weber and Simmel, through Mauss, Elias and Foucault, and through the 'tradition' thinkers, including Polanyi, Shils and Oakeshott, whom we mentioned in the previous chapter.

Cosmopolitan ethics

What we have argued for so far is that cosmopolitanism is not simply an attitude, but is a moral and ethical form; in particular, it is a form of moral self-understanding characteristic of modernity, and given decisive impetus by the ways in which globalization foregrounds global exchange relationships. In turn, its development gives increasing impetus to globalization and all manner of thinking beyond the local. Cosmopolitanism, then, is the moral or ethical component of these global exchange relationships. In the social sciences, there has been a longstanding interest in these forms of 'moral self', especially in terms of the connection between moral selves and moral regulation. We gave an example earlier of one particular form of this relationship, when we stressed the important role neo-Stoic and neo-Epicurean forms of personal understanding played as they fed into the moral regulation of those who were likely to kill in the name of their religion in sixteenth and seventeenth century Western Europe. Michael Mann (1993) has emphasized how the generation and maintenance of 'morale' – in particular the morale of ruling elites – is a crucial function of ideology; for Mann, then, ideology does not serve a purely negative function of shielding the truth from the oppressed, but it also plays the positive function of providing a sense of self-justification for those who would rule. There is a strong dependence here on the work of Max Weber (as well as that of Norbert Elias, whom we shall discuss below); Weber, as we have suggested, understood ethics as providing a source of self-justification for ruling elites and the fortunate more generally. To build on this idea, it is possible to view moral forms – like cosmopolitanism – as constitutive of subjectivity, rather than as built upon that pre-existing subjectivity. Instead, then, of seeing 'cosmopolitan ethics' as established among a pre-existing group, it might be more useful to analyse the ways in which the particular groups actually manufacture themselves as having a moral authority; these groups' 'cosmopolitanness' allows them to achieve self-understanding, and legitimates their life. The question which this then raises is about the nature and content of those ethical techniques which are put into practice on the self and which form what we term 'cosmopolitan subjectivities'.

At this point, it is useful to flesh out the distinction that Foucault (1986, 1988) makes between morals and ethics, and which informs our argument about forms of ethical comportment. Moral regulation was regarded by Foucault as something which was related to the inculcation of particular moral codes. The codes themselves are external to the individuals who are subjected to them. The other side of this 'external' process is the 'internal' process of ethics: the way in which the self can be fashioned and transformed according to certain techniques. Ethics, then, are internal to the subject, and are thought of by Foucault in terms of the relationship the self has with the self, or the *rapport à soi*.

In times when moral codes are less evident or straightforward, ethical techniques of the self tend to come to the fore. This is, we suggest, the main reason why, in the last phase of his research, Foucault was interested in the ancient Greeks: their society had become one in which morals and moral codes were not particularly strong, and the formation of an 'ethic of the self' became all-important. It is interesting that this was the context for the rise of the first 'wave' of cosmopolitanism: Diogenes' refusal of the bonds of local belonging is an indication that he was living in a society in which morality had given place to ethics. Foucault saw some similarities between ancient Athenian society and our own modern societies, which are, perhaps, becoming less 'moral', in the sense of no longer being governed by strong external codes such as Christianity. As we live in times where less and less is laid down morally, we may turn inward upon ourselves, Foucault suggests, to what he terms techniques of the self.

In the aftermath of the Enlightenment, and the Kantian statement of cosmopolitanism, a nineteenth-century tendency emerged which sought to rebuild ethical life in a secular direction, a tendency that can be seen in Matthew Arnold's (1965) *Culture and Anarchy*. According to Arnold, nineteenth-century life was driven by two ethical tendencies, Hebraism and Hellenism. Both aimed at 'man's perfection or salvation', yet they differed in terms of their spontaneity and their moral/ ethical flexibility. Arnold regarded Hellenism as the appropriate ethics for a new age of intellectual daring. The English had failed to realize that Hebraism should be on the decline and Hellenism in the ascendant. Many followed Arnold in turning to the Greeks for a way of reconceptualizing ethics.

First, to many nineteenth-century commentators, the Greeks were considered as an example of morality at its sternest without the light of the Gospel. A growing interest in the possibilities of secular democracy, fuelled by liberal philosophy and political practice, no doubt made the Greeks seem pertinent for our nineteenth century would-be cosmopolitans. Second, Hegel's reading of the historical development of Greek philosophy was seen as apposite. Many nineteenth-century thinkers accepted his view of the passage from *Sittlichkeit* to *Moralität* in Greek civilization and detected a similar movement in their own age. According to this famous distinction, *Sittlichkeit* constituted the morality residing in the unreflective custom and religion of the ancient community. *Moralität* was the reflective morality that developed as the individual subjective consciousness looked within itself to discover what objective truth would have moral authority over it. In the light of this, the various waves of interest in cosmopolitanism can be understood as connected to those moments when societies are especially concerned with self-understanding, and when external moral codes no longer provide satisfactory questions to such answers. Both the Enlightenment and the mid-nineteenth century revivals of interest in cosmopolitanism make sense in these terms. In the recent social scientific literature, the fall of the Berlin Wall in 1989 signalled a similar revival in cosmopolitanism: it began to furnish individuals with a way of understanding themselves – with a morale, but not with 'morals' – at a time when old certainties (the old moral codes of the Cold War) had suddenly been consigned to the dustbin of history.

It is instructive that the mid-nineteenth-century quest to invent a reflective ethics (what Foucault would call an ethics of the self) imagined the bedrock of this ethics to be Enlightenment rationality. Stephen Toulmin (1990) has suggested that the modern quest to shoehorn life into rationality (a quest begun, according to him, with Newton and Descartes) reaches its apogee in the Cosmopolis – the condition of universal rationality. For Toulmin, however, the rational dream has Weberian unintended consequences: on the one hand, Cosmopolis becomes something like the Weberian iron cage, while on the other, Giddensian processes of reflexivity lead to the erosion of trust in rationality.

The problem of hyper-rationality: destroying the cosmopolitan

These remarks of Toulmin alert us to the danger that an over-reliance on rational systems might lead to a kind of closing down of cosmopolitanism. Christopher Lasch (1995) is one of the most eloquent spokespeople for this idea that a cosmopolitanism fuelled by modern (and we would add Kantian-inspired) rationality might have a dark side. For Lasch, the privileged classes – those who most readily seem to demonstrate the cosmopolitan virtues – are removed from any sense of belonging to their local community and to their nation state. Their connections to their counterparts (the rich business elite) around the world grow stronger than their fellow-feeling for their compatriots. They begin to resent the responsibilities they have to their homeland (especially taxation), as they imagine themselves to be getting nothing back from a state which increasingly expects them to make private arrangements for security, schooling, health care, superannuation, and so forth. They do their best to avoid putting anything into the national treasury, and concentrate instead on 'put[ting] their money into their own self-enclosed enclaves' (Lasch 1995: 47). In Lasch's dystopian vision, then, cosmopolitan connections erode any sense of community, and ultimately play an individualizing function; in this diagnosis, cosmopolitanism is seen clearly as the bastard offspring of individualistic liberalism. Yet these elite cosmopolitans may not just be rejecting the responsibilities of national forms of citizenship; they may also be contributing to the erosion of the rights of citizens, as we discuss in the following case study.

It is common in the literature to suggest that the fruits of cosmopolitanism are reserved for elites (e.g. Calhoun 2002b; Kanter 1995), not least because a number of expensive technologies provide vital enabling factors for cosmopolitan lifestyles. These enabling technologies include, most obviously, transportation technologies, but also media and communications technologies. Only the well-off can afford access to air travel, mobile phones and cable television, for example, and it primarily through these mechanisms that the local or national citizen is understood as becoming imbricated in a global ethos. The now regular global music festivals with an eye to fund- and consciousness-raising, perhaps first seen with 1985's Live Aid and 2006's Live 8, are a case in point: the global elite can enjoy a spectacle that foregrounds their global citizenship aspirations (ending poverty, African debt reduction, world music consumption), while the world's poor are largely unable to consume the spectacle, and are reduced to bit-part players (through the occasional television cross-over to disenfranchised poor) – objects rather than subjects of the intervention. For Lasch, then, an unintended consequence of Enlightenment rationality is a form of disconnected individualism: the cosmopolitanism, although appearing connected to everything, is in fact connected to nothing.

Derrida sums up a common theme in the cosmopolitanism literature: the extent to which the development of science and technology is a spur to the development of cosmopolitanism:

> It goes without saying that the development of sciences and technologies ... breaks open the path, for better or worse, for a cosmopolitical communication (Derrida 1994).

To a great extent, this is because science and technology have allowed an increase in speed, scope and affordability of movement – and movement is one of the keystones of cosmopolitanism (see, for example, Bauman 1996). Similarly, the nomad – whether traveller, refugee, runaway – is the symbolic identity of the cosmopolitan age (Deleuze and Guattari 1987). Similarly, as we have discussed above, Beck regards cosmopolitanism as enforced by the globalization of risk, as technology contributes to new risks (e.g. man-made global warming) and makes us all aware of these risks through global media.

There is a connection between cosmopolitan possibilities and the ways in which technology enables an individual to escape the traditional strictures of the nation state. In other words, those technologies which internationalize the life of the individual may often work to dissolve that individual's connection to their nation state. Lasch's de-nationalized cosmopolitan is only connected globally to his or her 'class' because of such technologies. Of course, many recent technological innovations can work both to encourage and to impede cosmopolitanism – the (biometric) passport, for example, which allows some (but not all) to move freely around the globe (on the passport, see Torpey 2000). However, in general it is reasonable to propose that access to other countries, to the food, music or ideas of other cultures, and so forth, require access to mobility technologies, iPods, (cable) television, computers and the internet, etc.

A brief consideration of the technological connections to global citizenship might be valuable, then, since without technologies, the cosmopolitan is confined to his or her local time and space. However, technology is Janus-faced, because it can also impede cosmopolitanism, reinforce traditional nation state boundaries, and reduce circuits of global movement. In the case study below, we investigate how an almost Orwellian control over nation states in the period after September 11, 2001, threatens the cosmopolitan ethos.

Bad technology: impeding cosmopolitanism

There is also a long history of technology – especially surveillance technology – being used to protect nations against the perils of cosmopolitanism. We might briefly mention three of the greatest surveillance nations ever to have existed, all of whom, by investment in technology, sought to keep themselves 'pure' and to remove the possibility of pollution by foreigners. Nazi Germany, the Soviet Union, and the German Democratic Republic all invested an enormous amount in personnel and surveillance technology to maintain a fiercely nationalistic and anti-cosmopolitan attitude (Stalin even used the term 'cosmopolitan' as a pejorative label against those he saw as 'reactionaries'). As Koehler (1999) reports, the GDR organized perhaps the most impressive surveillance state of all time. 97,000 Stasi officers policed a population of just 17 million; when one takes account of part-time informers, it is thought that the ratio of state police personnel to the general population was an incredible 1:6.5. Nazi Germany, in spite of its best efforts, could only manage a ratio of 1:2000, while the Soviet Union's ratio was 1:5830 (see also Funder 2002). In the surveillance operations of all these three states, the provision of high-tech spying devices to the secret police was the decisive element in how these surveillance states were kept strong. Aside from person-on-person spying, an enormous investment in camera surveillance, bugs, phone tapping, and complicated dossier systems were the foundations for a thorough knowledge of the population and its (dis)loyalty.

The fall of the Berlin Wall spelled the end – or so it seemed – for these sorts of projects of mass surveillance. While writers such as Foucault (1977) drew our attentions to the surveillant elements of the capitalist West, there was a certain amount of hyperbole in the claim that we lived in surveillant societies, and for the most part sociologists understood that surveillance was, in the main, reserved for the underclasses – in prisons, workhouses, and so forth. The triumph of Western-style freedom over communism would, it was thought, be accompanied by a new cosmopolitan outlook. This new cosmopolitanism – the opening up of a global society to Eastern Europe (and vice-versa), and the end of the fortress mentality of the West – was in turn facilitated by techno-scientific innovations that provided the means to enjoy a new existence unbounded by the nation-state. East Germans, for example, now had access to much more than the few Western radio and television stations they could once only access illegally.

Balancing security and freedom?

When we fast forward to the period immediately after the attacks on the Pentagon and the World Trade Center in 2001, however, it is apparent that the efforts to deal with terrorism through technological innovation have had the effect of reducing the cosmopolitan ethos, and strengthening a more inwardly-focused nation-state strategic outlook. The Patriot Act in the USA, for example, allowed quite extreme powers of arrest and detention over non-resident aliens. Giorgio Agamben (1998, 2005) has been perhaps the most strident critic of this shift in global politics, drawing our attention to how attempts to secure the West have led to a diminution of freedoms for all. Agamben makes three important points. First, the sorts of biometric data collection that have started to become customary in the West (for example, fingerprinting and retinal scanning of aliens entering or in transit through the USA) are characteristic of authoritarian states, which always start policing foreigners before imposing such requirements on the population as a whole (Agamben draws out the similarities between modern US biometrics and the tattooing favoured by the Nazi regime, and uses the Nazi experience to predict the spread of biometric 'tattooing'). Second, Agamben notes the revival of the 'camp'; towards the end of *Homo Sacer*, Agamben discusses how Auschwitz or the Gulag represents the 'nomos' of modernity, and we cannot fail to notice how Guantanamo Bay or Port Baxter represent a kind of normalizing of the experience of the camp in the twenty first-century West. The camp has become a rather unexceptional part of our society, and a part that most of our political leaders seem quite comfortable with. Agamben's third point, which to a certain extent encapsulates the other two, concerns what he terms the 'state of exception'. By this, Agamben refers to the way in which exceptional state powers (such as powers of indefinite detention of suspicious non-citizens, or the use of military trials in the place of normal civil criminal proceedings) can de-democratize states, and allow them to become authoritarian. These 'exceptional' powers can quickly become seen as normal, so as a state reacts against external threats, it develops anti-democratic impulses, limits the freedoms of all its citizens, and decries those who speak out against loss of freedom. Such states hide behind the 'war against terror' as the justification for internal policing measures which would once have seemed beyond the pale.

It is only through technological innovation that this 'state of exception' can come into existence. The development of biometrics, for example, holds out the possibility for the nation-state of fixing the identity of citizen, non-citizen, friend and terrorist alike. More generally, the idea of the body as a source of information (especially through DNA) has gained currency outside the realm of crime fighting (Nelkin and Andrews 2003). Elsewhere, CCTV, Intelligent Transportation Systems (ITS) and the use of geographic information systems (including surveillance work around zip codes and other so-called geodemographic systems) have delivered a number of ways to think about and introduce the possibility of a more surveillant society. While there have always been societies who have put a strong emphasis on internal control and strict surveillance (think of the ancient Spartans, for example), the technological innovations of recent times have made such projects relatively easy to accomplish – if the political will to do it is there, and if opposition to the loss of civil liberties can be effectively stifled.

Societies of control

Such technological innovations have allowed us to enter what Deleuze (1992) calls 'Societies of Control'. In this model, societies form a closely woven mesh of various surveillant technologies, which are loosely connected. Deleuze suggests we have moved beyond Foucault's societies of surveillance. The citizen is no longer a *tabula rasa* disciplined by machines; rather, discipline is found in finer and subtler nets, in mundane practices and transactions, which make liberal citizens responsible for their own well-being. In control societies, a range of information sources, databases, etc, form a loose, rhizomic structure, which gradually creeps through the nooks and crannies of society; like a noxious weed, these rhizomic structures, on their own so thin and insubstantial, slowly choke society and grow into a thick, impenetrable configuration. Haggerty and Ericson (2000) call this configuration a 'surveillant assemblage'.

While there is much of interest in the Deleuzian position, as Stalder and Lyon (2003) argue, it is also possible that the surveillant assemblage can suddenly be concentrated in a single surveillant mechanism – a kind of return to the Foucaultian moment. Such a concentration can be seen, according to Stalder and Lyon, in the identity card. The identity card brings together all the databases – driving licence, medical records, fingerprints, retinal scan, and many more possibilities – in an integrated central register. While identity cards have been rejected recently in Australia, they are possibly to be introduced in the UK, have been used in Germany since 1987, and have been established in high-tech manifestations in many of the countries of south-east Asia (Thailand, Malaysia, Singapore and Hong Kong). The debates in the UK are instructive, focusing on familiar discussions of security and freedom; but it is interesting that the fear of terrorism seems to be enabling the introduction of something to which there has been historically great opposition. To a certain extent, the arguments about safeguarding against terrorism are specious, of course: as Stalder and Lyon point out, profiles of terrorists often show that they have no criminal records, and usually have all the paperwork, visas, etc, that they need. None of the September 11 terrorists had criminal records, for example, and, of course, 'there are no repeat suicide bombers' (Stalder and Lyon 2003: 85). While these sorts of schemes are used to mark and secure the internal spaces of the nation-state, it is also worth mentioning how they can be used in external policing (what some might call the work of empire). For example, the 2004 US 'reconstruction' the Iraqi city of Fallujah involved biometrics of the returning refugees, who were all retinally scanned, fingerprinted and given compulsory identity cards to be carried at all times. In this way, the new, rebuilt Fallujah was peopled with a perfectly 'known' population.

In this case study, we have investigated the links between technology innovation and cosmopolitanism. We certainly do not wish to argue for any form of technological determinism, and it seems to us clear that technologies can facilitate or impede cosmopolitanism. Human beings on their own do not achieve much; technologies allow them to extend their actions, to make them last, to make them more powerful. Accordingly, we suggest that technologies such as air travel and cable television facilitated what might come to be seen with hindsight as a high point of the cosmopolitan moment – between 1989 and 2001. And yet technology has also facilitated the current closing down of the cosmopolitan ethos in the period after 2001: identity cards and biometric technologies have been used in a return to the safety of the nation-state, and have promised to protect us from dangerous aliens. The fond hope is that these technologies can protect the nation-state and permit the rapid global movement of the 'legitimate' traveller, for example; such is the goal of machine-readable passports, which, it is hoped, will trap the ne'er-do-well while speeding up the passage of the innocent. What seems more likely is a rather crude sorting based on race, appearance, nationality, religion, will exacerbate the differences between the haves and the have-nots. Unfortunately, if Lasch is right, the cosmopolitan may not care, since s/he no longer understands these rights of freedom of movement or association as of any concern to his/her daily life.

As we have seen in this discussion, there is no simple path from rationality to cosmopolitanism; in particular, there is no necessary path from technology to cosmopolitanism. Both rationality and technology enable cosmopolitanism, but they are also both able to destroy it. In this way, we can see that cosmopolitanism as a political lifestyle is fragile; the very processes that construct can swiftly reverse and destroy it. While rationality and technology (specifically, the technological aspects of globalization) appear to be necessary elements in the cosmopolitan ethos, they are no guarantee of cosmopolitanization.

Sociation: reclaiming style

Cosmopolitanism, then, in the view of Toulmin and Lasch, may erode certain forms of (national) association and culminate in a pathological individualism; an opposite problem is similarly possible, whereby extreme in-group mentalities erode cosmopolitanism at the expense of only the most basic local forms of identification. If we accept such an analysis, it might seem that there is a continuum from local/social to cosmopolitan/individual, and the danger is that the cosmopolitan, in escaping the social bonds of the local, is left with no fate other than extreme individualism. In this dystopian view, only banal cosmopolitanism is possible, with the grasping of global consumption and other cultural opportunities inevitably disconnected from meaningful belonging or any concern for the other. While we agree that this is clearly a danger (or possibly that the insular global business elite may not be best described by the adjective 'cosmopolitan'), it may be possible to think about this problem in slightly different terms. Georg Simmel's work focuses our attention on cosmopolitanism as a form of *sociation*[3] – and here we see a connection to Bryan Turner's (2000a, 2000b) ideas, discussed in the previous chapter, about ironic forms of selfhood that may be cosmopolitan and non-nationalist. Simmel's understanding of sociation was of a realm which could be used to escape the grind and sterility of modern life. There are, of course, elements of cynicism in Simmel's discussion of an almost neurotic response to the pressures of modern life, an attitude nicely captured in his discussion of the taste for Japanese woodcuts in Germany, and his discussion of Kitsch more generally:

> Berlin at last has started to imitate Paris with the taste in Japanese art. But unfortunately we have already arrived too late, for the market is almost exclusively filled with the modern Japanese products which emerged under European influence and which thus represent such a bastardised style of the most impure kind (Simmel 1896: 187, cited in Frisby 1991).

For Simmel, these voyages into 'style' are the way in which individuals (cosmopolitans, we suggest) confront their own isolation, and begin to

---

[3] Sociation, and association, featured much more heavily in the sociology of the late-nineteenth and early-twentieth centuries than they do now. Half-forgotten sociologists, such as Gabriel Tarde, were eager to understand the social as a series of associations rather than as a political foundation reified through the state. See, for example, Tarde (1907).

understand themselves as connected to something bigger than themselves. As Simmel (1991a: 69) puts it:

> Style... is the source of the calming effect, the feeling of security and serenity... Thus we are saved from absolute responsibility, from balancing on the narrowness of mere individuality.
>
> What drives modern man so strongly to style is the unburdening and concealment of the personal, which is the essence of style... It is as if the ego could really no longer carry itself, or at least no longer wished to show itself and thus put on a more general, a more typical, in short, a stylised costume... Finally, style is the aesthetic attempt to solve the great problem of life: an individual work or behaviour, which is closed, a whole, can simultaneously belong to something higher, a unifying encompassing context.

As we have already seen, these attempts at belonging are linked by Simmel to the commodification of the exchange system. He connects world cities, styles and commodification in his discussion of the Berlin Trade Exhibition: a world city is a place where all the products and styles of the world are put on display (Simmel 1991b). Walter Benjamin (1973) echoes this emphasis on a passive uptake of commodified style as a way of making sense of the self, and of building associations with others of the same outlook. Of course, this theme of commodification and consumption as the basis of self-understanding and self-presentation is a common theme in classical sociology. Karl Marx emphasized how the character of the consumer was an inevitable result of the heightened production of the industrial revolution:

> Production is also immediately consumption... The act of production is therefore in all its moments also an act of consumption... The product only obtains its 'last finish' in consumption... Production... produces not only the object but also the manner of consumption, not only objectivity but also subjectivity. Production thus creates the consumer (Marx 1993: 90–2).

In similar vein, Thorstein Veblen stressed how consumption allowed the individual to attain a certain status and to feel a legitimate member of a prestigious group:

> The basis on which good repute in any highly organised industrial community ultimately rests is pecuniary strength; and the means of

showing pecuniary strength, and so of gaining or retaining a good name, are leisure and a conspicuous consumption of goods (Veblen 1991: 70).

And, famously, Simmel (2002) describes how the ironic and detached life of the city dweller (of the cosmopolitan, of course) rests on 'sham individualism'. In these analyses, then, the urbanite is already disconnected from those around him or her. There are echoes of Toulmin and Lasch, in that the hyper-rationalization of modernity leads to pathological individualization. Nonetheless, especially in Simmel, we see the possibility of escaping this individualization through sociation, a moment of escape or adventure. Through adventures in style, the urbanite positions him- or herself among others of similar blasé and ironic mentalities. This connection is something like the status group as described by Weber. But here we take Carl Schmitt's (1996: 38) point that Weber often focused too much on a circular relationship between the state and the political, as if politics could not 'derive its energy... from the religious, economic, moral, and other antitheses'. Cosmopolitans – as status groups with political desires – may indeed emerge, and gain impetus, from such an apparently trivial (but we would say moral) series of problems. In this way, the somewhat neurotic character of sociation – especially as these attempts are articulated through style, over-commodified objects, and display – might not be an obstacle to an important political role.

There is also the figure of a stranger, a concept which has played a central role in sociological theories of group relations at least since the publication of Simmel's (1964) celebrated essay titled 'The Stranger'. Even though the stranger is an abstract category, it is fair to say that in sociological scholarship it has commonly been associated with migrants, foreigners and outsiders – those, in short, who find themselves in unfamiliar territory, confronting the legitimacy of belonging (Bauman 1997; Diken 1998; Elias 1994; Schuetz 1944; Simmel 1964).

While we recognize that a stranger can be seen as a figure of speech – i.e. a way of speaking about issues surrounding accommodation of difference – it can also denote specific categories of population, such as migrants. Ahmed critiques approaches which give the stranger 'the status of a figure which has a referent in a real world... "The stranger" when used in this way, works to conceal differences; it allows different forms of displacement to be gathered in the singularity of a given name' (2000: 5). Migrants embody most of the characteristics associated with the figure of the stranger in social theory. Indeed, discussing migration-related issues brings to the fore some of the key concerns associated with the handling and accommodation of contemporary difference and diversity, much of which derives from ever-increasing and world-wide population mobility. For example, migrants in advanced capitalist economies of the West provide a continuing challenge to socially and culturally embedded assumptions about legitimate belonging, social cohesion and national identity. It is no doubt for these reasons that the fate of some migrants is the camp, as we saw in our discussion of Agamben's work above. Do migrants belong? To what extent are they coopted into the social fabric of society? Who grants them belonging and in the name of which group?

We evoke the figure of the stranger to emphasize some profound continuities in these debates. In particular, the stranger adds to the complexities of modern social life and evokes an image of a different life and culture. The stranger's arrival makes people sit up and notice, evokes envy, jealousy and resentment. The question is not just how one receives and treats the stranger, but rather in what ways are strangers (mis)incorporated into the fabric of the social. This new type of question owes debt to Savage *et al.* (2005) who, in their study of Greater Manchester, show how in a modern city the whole traditional dynamic between locals and newcomers is inverted and requires new conceptual lenses.

Simmel's short essay has been pivotal in the development of an entire sociological opus concerning the figure of the stranger and, by implication, discussion around group membership and belonging. Simmel's stranger is a quintessential creature of modernity, a person propelled into the community by the whirlwind of modern life. The city is the natural milieu for the stranger; Sennett (2002: 43) reminds us of Simmel's letter to his friend: 'As I look out into this teeming square what I understand is that the city is the site of strangeness'. This description of the stranger resonates with the contemporary experience of migration. His stranger is a person 'who comes today and stays tomorrow' and whose position is defined by the virtue of arrival and 'the fact that he has not belonged to [the group] from the beginning, that he imports qualities into it, which do not and cannot stem from the group itself' (Simmel 1964: 402). The stranger is present and visible within the group but is also separated from the community of belonging. Most importantly, 'strangers are not really conceived as individuals, but as strangers of a particular type: the element of distance is no less general in regard to them than the element of nearness' (*ibid*.: 407).

The force of Simmel's observations resonate in the later works of Park (1928), Wood (1934) and Schuetz (1944). In Schuetz (1944: 499), the stranger is exemplified by the figure of an immigrant, always characterized by 'doubtful loyalty': an unwillingness to 'substitute the new cultural pattern entirely for that of the home group' (*ibid.*: 507). In this way, Schuetz argues, the stranger finds him or herself 'on the verge of two different patterns of group life, not knowing to which of them he belongs'. This theme was later taken up by Julie Meyer (1951: 476), who again links the figure of the stranger with that of a migrant. For Meyer, even if the stranger 'settles down, he remains a migrant by background'. The struggle to belong is ongoing, and even if the migrant accepts the values of the host environment this does not provide any guarantees because 'the unknown part of his life differentiates him from that of the people who are rooted' (*ibid.*). This 'unknown' that lurks in the background always threatens to transform a familiar outsider into a stranger.

In recent times the concept of the stranger has undergone a revival of a sort. Most prominent of these recent accounts is Zygmunt Bauman's (1991) depiction of the stranger as a quintessential creature of postmodernity, caught up in the universal experience of rootlessness and strangehood. Stichweh (1997), following the systems approach, argues that a highly differentiated society is impregnated with strangers and that strangehood is a norm. In some ways, this means Stichweh postulates the disappearance of the stranger, a conclusion which sits uncomfortably *vis-à-vis* other commentators (e.g. Tabboni 1995; Marotta 2000). However, our interpretation is that this does not so much represent the disappearance of the stranger as the multivalence of this concept. The stranger is a type of person who emerges from the workings of in-group/out-group mentality; the stranger also becomes a status or lifestyle (not necessarily an envied lifestyle, of course); the stranger is also circumstantially induced by new mobilities, the growth of cities, and the triumph of new types of more abstract exchange economies. The stranger, then, is an indeterminate figure: a fragile concept that can be glamorous or reviled, can be welcomed by the ironic seeker of new experiences, or excluded by the hot loyalties of parochialism.

Just as with Simmel, there is a similarly foreboding and anxious feel to Norbert Elias's (1996) account of the interconnected development of German culture, manners and political identity, which will be is instructive in developing our argument here. As in the rest of his work, Elias is concerned with the connection between forms of self and the development of the modern European state. The concern of *The Germans*, however, is more specifically the possibility of 'decivilizing' spurts in the trajectory of nation states: the possibility that the violent tendencies of humans, which had to be repressed and redirected to allow the development of modern forms of social and political relations, might re-emerge under certain conditions. What this draws to our attention is that we should not necessarily expect the emergence of ethical cosmopolitans to be a matter of historical unfolding. In this respect, Elias is quite unlike Arnold and the other nineteenth-century Hegelians who hoped for the ethical perfection of the human species. After Elias, too, we should not be surprised that 'authentic' cosmopolitanism waxes and wanes. For this trio of thinkers – Elias, Schmitt and Weber – who have in common at least a conception of the importance of violence in the development of politics, the fragility and contingency of the cosmopolitan is evident.

Rationality, then, poses a number of threats to cosmopolitanism. As we have already seen, critics such as Lasch and Toulmin see the unintended consequences of modernity leading to an iron cage. For Simmel, Benjamin and Veblen, the rationalization of capitalism leads to a number of almost neurotic attempts to mark out social status and to avoid the grinding effects of the modern 'machine'. For Elias, Schmitt and Weber, violence is the inescapable variable of politics, constantly threatening destabilization, constantly reminding us of the 'hot' loyalties just below the surface. Finally, in his analysis of the postmodern condition, Jean-François Lyotard (1984) argues that faith in grand narratives seems more and more naïve, and that rationality can no longer be relied upon as foundational for any value system. Yet we suggest in the section below that the concept of sociation can still be used with some optimism.

Organic sociation: authenticity and de-differentiation

Max Weber strongly distinguishes between two types of action;[4] *Wertrational* and *Zweckrational*. The former is driven by ethics, values, and so forth, while the latter is more instrumental, and is driven by efficiency (Weber 1968: 25ff.). For Weber, modernity is characterized

---

[4]For Weber, action is planned and purposive: a behaviour which takes account of others. By contrast, 'behaviour' is simply an unthinking response to a stimulus. Actions, therefore, reveal an individual's social understanding.

by the latter (the sort of technocratic thinking and practices we saw in our discussion of bad technologies above), and the former is slowly squeezed out. Cosmopolitanism, of course, would be a type of *Wertrational* action: a reinstatement of values into an 'efficient' world. It may be, then, that we end up with a more optimistic view of the possibilities of cosmopolitanism than Simmel and Benjamin offer, and it may be that cosmopolitanism could be more than the absence of nationalism that is offered in Bryan Turner's 'ironic' cosmopolitan virtue. In assessing this possibility, we discuss below some ideas of Scott Lash. But first, it is worth dwelling on an important point Philip Smith (2001: 17) makes about the absence of Weber's thinking from cultural theory. For Smith, Weber's analysis suggests modern society has been drained of *Wertrational* action, leaving us merely with an efficient and disenchanted world. This amounts, says Smith, to a Weberian hypothesis about the disappearance of culture from the modern world. This may be true about cultural theory; but it is also possible that Weber overstated the supplantation of *Wertrational* action in modern life, and that it has made something of a comeback, perhaps even made possible by the way in which globalization has put international culture at the forefront of all our attention, while the *Zweckrational* action tendencies of the nation state have been softened and limited. Certainly, the globalization literature seems marked by the extent to which the phenomenon of globalization is either understood as homogeneous and culturally empty (in the approach of thinkers like Ritzer, for example), or as leading to increased hybridization and cultural reinvention. Our own feeling is that these processes and tendencies seem to wax and wane. Our discussion above of the closing down of cosmopolitanism by the 'state of exception' suggests that a disenchanting, *Zweckrational* action process can emerge quite suddenly and have a powerful effect. On the other hand, *Wertrational* action can suddenly allow an injection of morality – through the mechanism of culture, as we discuss in Chapters 5 and 6 – to allow cosmopolitanism to be realized. Bruno Latour (2004b) has a very instructive essay which is mostly a critique of Ulrich Beck's notion of cosmopolitanism. Latour's scathing assessment of Beck is right: Beck merely writes a grander version of Habermas's humanism (Latour cunningly makes the point as he says that this characterization would be unfair to Beck!), and his cosmopolitanism is impossible because he has failed to notice there is no longer a single cosmos to provide a rationally agreed-upon referent. Yet Latour makes the opposite mistake, imagining rationality to be exhausted and the cosmos to be entirely shattered.

Both Latour and Beck are half-right but also, of course, half-wrong; our world snaps in and out of the *Zweckrational* and the *Wertrational*, refusing to be simply and eternally one or other. As we discussed above, a surveillant assemblage can suddenly form, and just as suddenly dissolve: this is why cosmopolitanism is so frequently a victim of fashion. The moral and the cultural can be suddenly overwhelmed by the rational and instrumental, but they can return and be reactivated. This see-sawing is not so much a dialogue as a series of violent replacements.

An interesting take on this idea can be seen in Scott Lash's (1990) work on differentiation and de-differentiation. Differentiation describes the move from the pre-modern to the modern world, where, for example, the aesthetic and the moral are distinguished (and, once again, Kant dominates this landscape), high and low culture are rigorously separated, etc. Lash argues that in the pre-modern world, no real efforts were made to police these boundaries, but modernism is obsessed with these processes of differentiation and categorization (see also Latour 1993). The advent of postmodernism sees these separations become problematic, and for Lash a de-differentiation comes into play. Following Lash, different types of de-differentiated status groups emerge; so what counts as prestigious, what gives status, and so forth, has become a much more complicated matter. The suggestion here is that the breakdown of modernist certainties allows for a much more complex set of lifestyles to emerge: we suggest that cosmopolitanism can be seen as an example of the de-differentiated possibilities for the construction of a hybridized lifestyle. While we do not necessarily want to follow Lash in his periodization of the modern and the postmodern – so there is no need to assume a causal role for some kind of *Zeitgeist* – nonetheless it is interesting to speculate that the cosmopolitan is a good example of a de-differentiated status group. In constructing him- or herself through style, consumption and a knowing engagement with a broad range of cultural markers, the cosmopolitan emerges through the gaps in a disenchanted world.

Lash further suggests that the de-differentiated form of self is one which takes a 'canteen' approach to identity, picking and choosing elements for the self as they seem pleasing and useful. This invites us to speculate once more on the banal vs authentic dimensions of the (cosmopolitan) self; indeed, Lash conceptualizes this very problem, but in slightly different language. Spectral postmodernism is the lens through which Lash frames the more superficial or banal forms of identity, especially those taken up through empty consumerist practices. By contrast, a more authentic type of self – in Lash's discussion, especially the type of self that can be seen in new social movements – emerges out of organic postmodernism. What is valuable about Lash's contribution here is that he avoids a deterministic reading of the consequences of social change. The de-differentiated identity can be banal or authentic, an empty cipher or part of a new social movement, a jejune consumer or a culture aficionado. For us, the cosmopolitan is always the second of that pair, the ironic, ethical self.

In short, we have argued that there is a constant recursive relationship between the political and the cultural. Cosmopolitanism as a cultural style is borne of certain political possibilities; it is the cosmopolitan's capacity to move and look beyond themselves which affords the development of their cosmopolitan lifestyle. But we must remember that this is enabled by certain political settlements; in addition, certain technological means can be used to police and surveil these settlements. These technologies are not in themselves good or bad, but both enabling and constraining depending on the political environment and intent. We develop this theme in the following chapters, where we discuss the idea of flexible cosmopolitan objects – objects which are not cosmopolitan per se, but are made so depending on context and meanings.

In this chapter, we have tried to avoid a simple characterization of the period we live in as modern or postmodern, rationalized or de-rationalized, differentiated or de-differentiated. Rather we suggest that it is possible for the entire assemblage that we can call 'the social' to snap rapidly in and out of different phases. We think that cosmopolitanism – that form of ironic, detached, but fundamentally ethical concern for the other – is very fragile, and is susceptible to threat. Because, as we suggest, it is so heavily reliant on a series of exchanges with the other, it can disappear at those moments when exchange becomes difficult or derogated. So, for example, the state often presents two (or more) possibilities, with different affordances. On the one hand, the withering away of the state under neo-liberalism – especially the removal of duties of citizenship – make cosmopolitanism seem possible (Ong 1998 discusses 'flexible citizenship' in such contexts). On the other hand, the reinvigoration of the state and centralized state control (through such innovations as the Patriot Act and the activation of the exceptional state) close down boundaries and make for a much less fertile ground for cosmopolitanism. Politics does not determine the cultural possibilities we have; rather culture, ethics, politics and technology form an indissoluble assemblage.

5
Thinking, Feeling and Acting Cosmopolitan: The Ideal Types and their Expression in Everyday Cultural Fields

Introduction

As the preceding chapters have discussed, cosmopolitanism is a challenging concept. Our analysis of its political and ethical elements suggests a normative approach, but also draws attention to a difficult balancing act between the fixity and fluidity at its heart. Cosmopolitanism describes a set of emergent contemporary outlooks and practices that are, according to a variety of commentators, becoming increasingly widespread amongst individuals. It also represents a laudable – though not uncomplicated or flawless – set of ethical principles which could guide action in the contemporary world. From an analytical perspective, cosmopolitanism is made up of major elements that are not just dimensions of a larger concept, but significant projects in their own right. These elements consist of a set of outlooks and practices available to individuals, an ethical and political viewpoint that infiltrates and invigorates social institutions and, finally, a set of supranational arrangements and quasi-legal structures that, symbolically at least, bind individuals to the other in various ways. Moreover, as we pointed out in Chapter 4, it is in the historical connections between law, the state and forms of cosmopolitan subjectivity that the concept can be best understood. One consequence of the multidimensionality of the concept is the problem of disentangling what is new about these 'cosmopolitan' outlooks from other values like tolerance, empathy for others, and inclusiveness. For the analyst, this represents a task requiring some precision. More importantly for the context of this chapter, for the modern individual the challenge of becoming cosmopolitan – at least in the ideal ways defined in the literatures – is perhaps even more difficult. The goal of this chapter is to interweave theoretical accounts of cosmopolitanism with an exploration of forms of cosmopolitanism that are practised in everyday contexts by individuals. As suggested by Cheah and Robbins (1998), we wish to investigate the ordinary practices, norms and discourses associated with 'thinking and feeling cosmopolitan', but in addition we wish to weigh up these ways of being cosmopolitan against theoretical literatures.

The expansive nature of the concept of cosmopolitanism demands the application of multiple intellectual and methodological vantage points. From the outset of this work we have emphasized the importance of incorporating and synthesizing a diverse mix of concepts, methods and approaches in understanding cosmopolitanism. Yet, like the concept itself – which is defined by a dynamic, delicate balance of fluidity and anchoring – there must be some buttressing principles. One of the hallmarks of our approach is a commitment to the value of classical sociological theory for understanding the contemporary processes and challenges posed by cosmopolitanism. We have taken up Turner's (2006) argument about the value of the sociological classics in dealing with universal characteristics of 'the social', rather than dealing necessarily with any bounded 'society'. Along similar lines, Chernilo (2007) usefully recommends analysing the universalistic-cosmopolitan tendencies in strands of classical social theory.

Another characteristic of our approach is the value we place on the related principles of empiricism and observability. Here, we urge that there should be forms of 'actually existing' (Robbins 1998) cosmopolitanism, of the everyday or 'ordinary' variety (Lamont and Aksartova 2002). By their nature, these are not necessarily banal or spectral forms of cosmopolitanism, but represent the gradual and sometimes discrepant infiltration and uptake of aspects of cosmopolitanism into the practices and outlooks of everyday citizens. These types of thinking and feeling cosmopolitan (*cf.* Cheah and Robbins 1998) are visible in more modest and mundane ways. We work from the principle that the extent of such cosmopolitan change, its degree and ultimate effects, are something of an open and ongoing question. Although we value the application of a heterogeneous and robust theoretical armoury, we also work from the proposition that cosmopolitanism is something that can be observed in objects, settings and social spaces, and that it is something – to suggest it is a set of values, attitudes and practices is sufficient for the present – that should be identifiable in individuals as forms of cosmopolitan subjectivity. Our reasoning is if cosmopolitanism is held to be a relevant concept to describe emergent global aspects of culture then it must be observable in people's outlooks and practices. We hold to this principle because it seems an important way to explore, develop and, to some degree, test the usefulness of the concept for social inquiry. As part of the emergence of cosmopolitanism within everyday spheres, there should be identifiable 'carriers' who play a role in diffusing or sowing the seeds of cosmopolitanism as they go about their normal business of work, travel and association. These issues are explored in the discussion below.

Likewise, and just as importantly, we should be able to say that certain places or things – for example, a city or a technological object – possess a cosmopolitan character or afford the expression of a cosmopolitan sensibility. Cosmopolitanism is not just about a process of reflexive individualization, but one of 'objectualization' (Knorr-Cetina 1997) – it is accomplished by humans and non-human alike. But, thinking about cosmopolitanism as something felt and thought by individuals, we ask what exactly is the 'sensibility'? Is 'cosmopolitanism' a set of values, a disposition, a repertoire or even something that exists only in particular 'habitats'? Along with addressing this question, the current chapter is an analysis of the major features of cosmopolitanism as it can be observed in individuals. While the discussion is directed by key theoretical literatures it also draws upon multiple data sources to stack up this theoretical picture with available empirical evidence about the qualities – both attitudinal and performative – of such cosmopolitan individuals.

Locating the cosmopolitans: some issues

Starting from the principle of observability raises a range of issues in relation to identifying cosmopolitans, their practices and habits. First, there is the question of whether we can agree upon a definition of cosmopolitanism in order to measure its existence within individuals. Beck (2002c: 79–80) provides a specific list of empirical indicators of cosmopolitanization, as do Szerszynski and Urry (2006: 114–15). Such a list seems a positive way of proceeding, but on the other hand, there are those for whom providing such a closed list of 'indicators' is problematic, misguided or reductivist (e.g. Pollock *et al.* 2000). Moreover, where do the definitional thresholds stand in such a long list? Are some elements more or less important to the definition? Are some elements more basic in the sense they are productive of other peripheral characteristics? For example, international travel and a variety of other mobilities (Beck 2002c) may be seen as a generator of cosmopolitan outlooks – or one of the crucial pathways to cosmopolitanism – rather than a central 'indicator'. There may also be a set of predictors of cosmopolitanness, but a range of other things may drive the tendency for cosmopolitanism to develop in the first instance. Providing a clear definition, rather than an extensive and expanded list, is by no means easy but it is necessary.

A further problem of identification, even when agreement upon a basic definition might be reached, is that there is little progress toward empiricizing any preliminary conceptual discussions that do exist. Some qualitative work which gets to the heart of being and feeling cosmopolitan and its dimensions has been carried out (e.g. Lamont and Aksartova 2002; Savage *et al.* 2005; Skrbis and Woodward 2007; Szerszynski and Urry 2002, 2006). These studies have been valuable in grounding cosmopolitan practices and outlooks in everyday settings and so help to develop understanding of the cosmopolitan outlook from the ground up, but at this stage very few large scale, multivariate quantitative studies have been published (see Woodward *et al.* 2008). Further studies in this vein will clearly be important in progressing socio-political studies of cosmopolitan actors, their outlooks and practices by sifting through the possible indicators and generators of cosmopolitan outlooks.

The second implication of our principle of observability is that cosmopolitanism is amenable to measurement in the first instance. How valid are survey measures of cosmopolitanism? Undoubtedly globality is an important emergent process in all of the debates about cosmopolitanism, but this in no way guarantees the uptake and expression of cosmopolitanism. How can we be sure we are identifying genuine 'cosmopolitanness', rather than the by-products of globalization? For example, an indication of the desire for travel tells us nothing about how and why such travel takes place, or indeed the type of travel experiences undertaken. Likewise, an expressed agreement on the pleasure of experiencing other cultures tells us little about the forms and basis of such of such experience, which might in the end be judged shallow or even exploitative. On the other hand, frequent travellers may become less interested in the so-called pleasures of cultural exploration and more committed to the comforts and certainties of home (our own discussions of these issues with international airline staff and elite business travellers backs up this idea – repetition breeds ennui, and too much travel means that the comfort of hotels and lounges, rather than the joys of experiencing otherness, becomes paramount). Such a problem throws into question the nature of cosmopolitanism as a characteristic that 'floats' through individuals, media, objects and society. How exactly is it diffused and how does it impact on outlooks and practices? Given the static and snapshot nature of survey research, and the local and contextualized nature of interview and historical research, how can we make any universal claims about the nature or practice of cosmopolitanism?

There is a substantial point of difference here between those who believe survey items could possibly validly measure cosmopolitanism, and those who believe that the very nature of the concept eludes survey measurement. If we accept that cosmopolitanism can be quantitatively measured, then a further question arises regarding a broader agenda, one that might be identified as a cosmopolitan paradigm (Delanty 2006). That is, how do our observations fit into a broader theoretical and schematic agenda? What do they tell us about cultural processes of inclusivity, belonging and valuing beyond the existence of values held, or practices admitted? A more processual, subtle approach to the performativity and contextual expression of cosmopolitanism is required here. Ethnographic and observational data in known contexts may be necessary to adjudicate on the nature of cultural judgements and appropriations made by cosmopolitans. Here, questions of cultural capital, authority and legitimacy, symbolic manipulation and cultural boundaries seem appropriate.

Finally, in terms of giving a full account of cosmopolitanism, we do not wish to rule out the possibility that cosmopolitanism is observable within *non-human* actors and processes. Can objects, places and settings possess cosmopolitan traits or characteristics? What is the relationship between human and non-human in the facilitation of cosmopolitanism? Is it possible that an 'object-centered sociality' (Knorr-Cetina 1997) cultivates or affords cosmopolitan practice, rather than the spontaneous stirring of universal sentiments within the minds of social actors? A first response must be 'yes', it is possible for objects to both symbolize and facilitate cosmopolitanness, and that in reality both humans and objects play a part in its construction. Before we can progress further in untangling these questions we must be clear about what this thing called 'cosmopolitanism' is and how it can be defined in sociological terms.

What is cosmopolitanism? Dispositions of openness performed

What is the best way to think about cosmopolitanism analytically? Put another way, what is cosmopolitanism and how is it 'made'? There are two primary dimensions of the concept that come into play here. Firstly, there is a distinction between *accidental* and *strategic* cosmopolitanism. That is, do we conceptualize cosmopolitanism as something individuals come to possess passively, perhaps accidentally, by absorption; or a symbolic field of practices increasingly available to social actors – though differentially adopted – for use in multiple fields? Secondly, a further dimension relates to the distinction between *reflexive* and *banal*[1] forms of cosmopolitanism, the first supposedly related to the capacity for inclusive ethical practice, and the latter to the sampling and enjoyment of cosmopolitan opportunities in a variety of settings (e.g. as a tourist), but not much more. The identification of these dimensions raises some basic questions that go to the heart of how we imagine the power and reach of the concept of cosmopolitanism.

The suggestion that cosmopolitanism is a circumstantially induced tendency picks up on the proliferation of global flows and mobilities as a context for the uptake of some aspects of the cosmopolitan disposition, but in the end is a weak account of cosmopolitanness because it fails to identify the cultural location and capacities of cosmopolitan subjectivities. If cosmopolitanism is a body of cultural practices then it must also rest on a particular set of cultural competencies, which in turn rely on structured culturally meaningful fields for the uptake and expression of cultural capital. In acknowledging this, we come to see that being cosmopolitan is itself a cultural location that affords individuals the capacity to see, and to 'consume' otherness, in ways which reproduce patterns of cultural power. It is a particular style of selfhood. In identifying strands of research that theorize cosmopolitanism as a characteristic within and of individuals, Vertovec and Cohen (2002: 13) identify the cosmopolitan individual as having a distinctive set of attitudes, and a discernible corpus of practices. In distinguishing between attitudes and practices as two components of the cosmopolitan individual, Vertovec and Cohen usefully append practices to attitudes, suggesting that to be cosmopolitan involves a mode of acting or performing, as much as it does thinking and feeling – in other words, they gesture towards a performative definition of cosmopolitanism. We understand attitudes to broadly encompass beliefs, values and outlooks, while we take practices to refer to coordinated sets of learned cultural competencies which must be applied in particular

---

[1] In Chapter 4, following Lash (1990), we made a similar distinction between the organic and the spectral.

social situations, akin to a cultural repertoire or mode of behaviour. Hannerz (1990: 239) also highlights this discursive feature of cosmopolitan orientations, referring to cosmopolitanness as a body of cultural skills required to manoeuvre within 'a particular system of meanings and meaningful forms'.

So, part of the preliminary answer is that cosmopolitanism is a tendency to view otherness and cultural difference as something desirable, and that cosmopolitanism always involves a cultural mode of seeing and valuing difference based on a moral attribution. The very fact that something or someone can be called cosmopolitan implies the adoption of a regime of value, a discourse that rests on *a way of seeing*, with its associated inclusions and exclusions, which paradoxically is antithetical to the nature of the concept itself. This is a contradiction and tension that is considered in further detail throughout this chapter.

As something identifiable in individuals, cosmopolitanism has both ideal and pragmatic dimensions, attitudinal and behavioural aspects. People bring these outlooks to bear on objects, other humans and non-humans, and events within particular spatio-temporal locations. Cosmopolitanism therefore involves the knowledge, performance and command of symbolic resources for the purpose of highlighting and valuing cultural difference. While claiming to be a universal position of cultural inclusiveness and generosity, it is in fact, a culturally located view which is itself based in a regime of value-attribution.

In outlining the dimensions of cosmopolitanism as a culturally located disposition we proceed with at least two related principles in mind. First, we need to agree on the types of attitudes and values that distinguish cosmopolitans from non-cosmopolitans. Relatedly, we should identify the structural conditions within the spheres of cultural production and consumption which tend to nurture these cosmopolitan dispositions. The first set of conditions relates to the identification of individuals with particular attitudinal characteristics (encompassing beliefs, attitudes and values) which can be identified as cosmopolitan and which would distinguish them from non-cosmopolitan characteristics. It is possible to define this aspect of cosmopolitanism as the 'cosmopolitan disposition' and assert that there should also be identifiable 'carriers' of such cosmopolitan dispositions. Although the term 'disposition' is gaining currency in the cosmopolitanism field (e.g. Featherstone 2002: 1; Vertovec and Cohen 2002: 14), it is through Bourdieu's (1977) concept of the habitus that we develop our understanding of this term. Bourdieu understands the habitus to be a set of principles and procedures that come into play in people's relations with objects and others. It is a set of self-orienting, practical dispositions that incorporates structure into everyday practice. The habitus is formed in individuals through historically and socially situated conditions, and while a person's habitus will direct them toward particular choices, it does not amount to obedience to rules. In defining the habitus, in shorthand, as 'a system of dispositions' (Bourdieu 1977: 214), Bourdieu clarifies three aspects of what he means by disposition, with the most crucial component being that it is a 'predisposition, tendency, propensity or inclination' (Bourdieu 1977: 214). As we have specified, commentators commonly suggest that in terms of 'disposition', cosmopolitanism should be understood principally as an attitude of 'openness' toward others cultures (Hannerz 1996; Tomlinson 1999; Urry 2000a; Vertovec and Cohen 2002).

There are a couple of potential limitations associated with identifying and labelling cosmopolitanism as a 'disposition' and we suggest a modification which we believe offers greater suppleness to the idea of disposition, at least in this context. While Bourdieu goes to lengths to argue that a 'disposition' is socially located and structurally driven, while at the same time a set of flexible rules for application within unique settings, the concept is decidedly individualist at heart. Individuals – within their own social-structural locations – hold dispositions. In some ways this tells us little more than old-style values analysis. Values are always socially determined sets of propensities to judge certain things and situations in a particular way. Likewise, the idea of dispositions tells us that certain groups of people will have a propensity to see cultural things similarly. The idea of a disposition is also somewhat vague. Bourdieu's analytic scheme is elaborate and powerful, but his definition of disposition as predisposition, tendency, or inclination is decidedly vague and begs more questions than it answers. One of the major downsides of thinking about cosmopolitanism as a disposition is that dispositions are consistent and homological structures – they are 'whole' in that they are structured and patterned in consistent ways, and relatively *inflexible*. They encourage us to think about cosmopolitanism in a rather reductive way: as a perspective, state of mind, orientation, or habits of mind and life that are either held, or not held. This, we think, is only part of the story. In suggesting cosmopolitanism is a state of mind, Hannerz adds (crucially and insightfully) that 'to take a more processual view – [it is] a mode of managing meaning' (1990: 238). We need to move toward this concept that integrates individuals and their dispositions with objects and spaces and the performative accomplishment of the disposition, for cosmopolitan dispositions are always enacted or called for in particular spatio-temporal locations. This is a more processual, reflexive and dynamic view of what cosmopolitanism is and how it comes to possess efficacy and meaning in cultural life. Rather than seeing cosmopolitanism as just a disposition – with its structured sets of outlooks existing in particular fields – we need to think of cosmopolitanism as a more flexible application of a cultural outlook focused on strategically discerning and appreciating difference in relevant social settings. It is, then, a *disposition performed* in particular contexts and settings as required.

This suggests the idea that we can also imagine cosmopolitanism as a type of repertoire. Swidler's (2003) broad understanding of culture is that it is a repertoire or toolkit of habits, skills and styles from which people develop strategies of action. Repertoires are learned and acted out both to deal with emergent social situations. They can sometimes be strategic in nature (for example, to demonstrate one's breadth of cultural knowledge), or simply to act competently and successfully in any social situation (for example, to be able to order from a foreign menu or show respect through the performance of a simple local custom). Importantly, members of a culture have a common understanding of the range of options and actions afforded by the toolkit. If we think about cosmopolitanism not just as something that people either have or do not have as part of some consistently structured and applied set – as in a disposition – but as a sensibility that people sometimes draw upon and other times ignore then we think this is an improvement in conceptualizing the nature of 'being cosmopolitan'. In this model 'being cosmopolitan' refers to a set of outlooks and practices, including a disposition, increasingly available – yet not guaranteed – to individuals for the purposes of dealing with cultural diversity, hybridity and otherness. This is consistent with Lamont and Aksartova's (2002: 2) operationalization of ordinary cosmopolitanism as 'cultural repertoires... differently available to individuals across race and national context'. Like Lamont and Aksartova (2002), we think it advisable to focus on the grounding of such dispositions in everyday experiences: what people eat, watch, listen to, shop for and buy, and dream about. We see these repertoires as flexible, and sometimes contradictory. They are discursive, practical resources available to social actors to deal with emergent, everyday global agendas and issues, related to things like cultural diversity, the global, and otherness. Yet, we do not see such cosmopolitan values expressed fully, or at all times, and on all issues. Rather, 'cosmopolitanism' is a cultural discourse, underpinned by ideas about the 'good' and 'evil', sacred and profane, sides of globality – available to social actors (and some more than others), that is deployed intermittently. Consistent with Swidler's metaphor, it is sometimes taken from the 'toolkit' and other times ignored. The cosmopolitan impulse is restrained by personal, local and national anchors which alert people to the downsides of globality. Whatever ideals are understood, abstractly, we see a set of counter-discourses that inhibit their full expression. The advantage of this approach is that we do not claim cosmopolitanism to be an ever-expanding frontier of global community that people in all places and times increasingly adopt as if it were part of an evolutionary adaptation. Nor do we see cosmopolitanism as something fixed solely by social location. It is an increasingly prominent, available cultural discourse – and ideal – but one that conflicts with an array of other social and personal imperatives, and thus does not always blossom. Unlike Beck, who thinks we are compelled to be cosmopolitan (2006: 175ff.), we are alive to the possibility that people can deliberately withdraw from dialogue and refuse to engage with the other.

So, cosmopolitanism is a set of structurally grounded and locatable, discursive resources available to social actors which is variably deployed to deal with emergent agendas and issues, related to things like cultural diversity, the global, and otherness. It is a *cultural repertoire performed by individuals* to deal with objects, experiences and people and which is encouraged by particular contexts, fusions of circumstance and motive, and frames of interpretation. 'Globality' – in all its constitutive processes – provides the major context for the flowering of cosmopolitan subjectivities, including ways of seeing, acting and reflecting (attitudes, behaviours and values). Theoretically, cosmopolitanism is identified as a set of ideas, frames for interpretation, behavioural patterns, and knowledges that allow an individual to perform a cosmopolitan subjectivity. Such a form of selfhood is based around intercultural flexibility, openness, and symbolic efficacy. This movement from seeing cosmopolitanism as just a disposition to seeing it as a reflexively deployed cultural resource is an improvement, but again not the whole story. Although this theorization affords us flexibility in understanding the uptake and expression of cosmopolitan sensibilities, it does not yet account for time, objects and space particularly effectively. Cosmopolitanism is best understood when performed or identified in particular time-space settings. For example, Mica Nava (2002, 2007) shows how cosmopolitanism exists in department stores. Elijah Anderson (2004) develops the idea of a 'cosmopolitan canopy', usefully indicating the spatial dimension of everyday cosmopolitanism. Here Anderson suggests that some urban locations such as Reading Terminal Market in Philadelphia facilitate contact with cultural difference and that social interaction across the usual boundaries of class and race might be routinal components of everyday life. The emphasis on the expression of cosmopolitanism in spatial settings is a useful reminder of where and why cosmopolitanism manifests.

The cosmopolitan as an ideal type of symbolic specialist

What subjective outlooks are associated with cosmopolitan selfhood? We characterize the cosmopolitan individual as an ideal type of symbolic specialist, someone in possession and command of the cultural knowledge and skill to discern, appreciate and *use* the field of cultural difference. The cosmopolitan possesses specialist knowledges, forms of appreciation and particular ways of seeing which equip them with skills to transform the existence of otherness – rendered through globality or other forms of intercultural exchange – into a particular ethical-aesthetic value that, in so being transformed, cultivates a type of cultural capital. This ability to see, understand, then transform otherness into a consumable (knowable, malleable, resource-giving) cultural object is a valuable skill in the globalizing world. Through access to discourses of connectivity, openness and inclusivity, the cosmopolitan cultivates a capacity to frame and then appropriate cultural otherness. As Hannerz (1996) says, cosmopolitanism is a way of seeing based upon a broad willingness to engage with otherness, framed through a desire to be open. But more than this, the cosmopolitan must feel empowered to identify otherness and to seek a relationship with it in order to enhance or bring otherness into oneself.

Skeggs (2004: 158–590) points out that to command such cultural resources and draw them into oneself for the purposes of building or enhancing self is a form of 'embodied entitled subjectivity'. Skeggs' (2004) emphasis on the mediative and transformative powers of the cosmopolitan vision as a type of *enablement* is valuable, for it captures the power relationship inherent in the relationship of cosmopolitanism to forms of otherness. Like our own sense of the cosmopolitan as an enhanced, 'ideal symbolic specialist', Skeggs understands that to be cosmopolitan is a way of seeing, and then a way of appropriating cultural difference, which in turn constitutes a type of cultural power. At once, it purports to suggest that otherness is valued, but at the same time it tends to value certain forms of otherness, frequently for the purpose of enhancing self, and through categories established via legitimated means of cultural authority. In this sense, it is an appropriation based upon certain moral attributions: it knows what is to be valued, it knows what is culturally useful and it knows what potential uses such resources could be put. On all these matters, Skeggs' particular application of Bourdieu's methodological-conceptual framework is extremely valuable, although we suggest that her understanding of cosmopolitanness as principally a type of middle-class subjectivity that goes hand-in-hand with the resources offered by an identity-obsessed consumer culture is restrictive. What about working-class cosmopolitanisms, and an ethic of valuing otherness which works independently of the market and propertized accumulative processes? Moreover, is it possible that consumption-based engagements with otherness actually have the capacity to initiate deeper cosmopolitan sentiments and act as pathways to a more critical form of cosmopolitanism? Later we address these questions, both conceptually and empirically. First, however, we must turn to consider more thoroughly how the recent literatures on cosmopolitanism conceive the attributes and characteristics of the cosmopolitan.

Dimensions of the cosmopolitan disposition: mobilities, competencies and openness

We begin by outlining three broad tenets of a cosmopolitan disposition: (i) corporeal and virtual mobility, (ii) cultural competencies based in 'code-switching' abilities, and (iii) the endorsement of values of cultural inclusivity. On the basis of existing literatures we propose that these are traits and practices likely to be possessed by more cosmopolitan individuals, who are structurally enabled by various cultural, economic and social processes that foster their adoption and expression of cosmopolitan values. Individuals might possess some aspects of these traits, and they may surface or find expression in some cultural settings more than others. We see these three aspects of the cosmopolitan disposition as components of an ideal-type which can be identified by the peak concept of 'cultural openness'.

Mobilities

It is generally agreed that cosmopolitanism is partly defined through various sorts of mobilities (Beck 2006; Hannerz 1990; Urry 2000a, 2007). In this sense, the association between globalization and cosmopolitanism is most immediately identifiable. International transportation networks, principally air travel, make it relatively easy for people to voyage globally for the purpose or work and leisure, affording exposure to other geographies and cultures. However, travel alone – particularly in its regulated or 'fordist' form – is clearly not enough to constitute a cosmopolitan identity, although transnational connections of various types certainly help. Along with simply being mobile, the cosmopolitan is likely to find delight in the exhibition of such differences and contrasts (Hannerz 1990: 240). Indeed, such an awareness of difference can have critical transformative possibilities, cultivating one's sense that national or local spaces and cultures can be transcended (Appadurai 1996: 6), and allowing the development of (at least some) intercultural interpretive skills (Vertovec and Cohen 2002: 7). Szerszynski and Urry (2002: 470) point out that such mobilities are as much imaginative and virtual as they are corporeal. Television, internet and mobile telecommunications allow engagement with other cultures via mass-mediated imagery, access to an extraordinary number of globally focused visual flows, and virtual travel of extensive kinds. Szerszynski and Urry's (2002: 477) empirical research demonstrates the high levels of cultural competence in recognizing 'globality' as it is represented in such media forms, and how this is linked to the expression of a general – perhaps banal or spectral – cosmopolitan awareness. In their elite form, such globally mobile individuals are the 'cosmocrats' or even 'cosmoprats' (see Vertovec and Cohen 2002: 6–7), while in their popular form they are likely consumers of mass-media travel TV shows and magazines which encourage the fantasy of travel and exotic interaction. These latter mobile individuals are likely to fit into Hannerz's (1990: 241) rather depthless 'home plus' category of cultural immersion. Nevertheless, sociologists should not completely ignore the possibilities of such apparently banal cosmopolitan experiences. For example, Nava (2002) shows how an activity such as shopping can promote virtual mobilities, engagement in aestheticized settings and cross-cultural sensitivities, through cultivating one's sense of other worlds, exotic engagements, and alternative styles, while going hand in hand with the development of commercial, capitalist interests.

Cultural-symbolic competencies

The second tenet of cosmopolitanness involves highly developed cultural-symbolic competencies, subsuming the crucial cosmopolitan skill of code-switching. We take this to refer to an individual's ability to know, command and enact a variety of cultural knowledges and repertoires – to switch cultural codes as required as part of cultivating a sense of intercultural mastery that one possesses, but is not necessarily possessed by (Hannerz 1990: 240). Chaney's (2002) description of shifting aesthetic and cultural economies and associated privileging of forms of cultural citizenship, suggest the skilful, contextualized and self-aware deployment of cross-cultural symbols is a feature of the cosmopolitan disposition. This may well be for the purpose of situationally demonstrating one's own distinction, but equally it may be for demonstrating respect for others, cultivating one's moral worth, or gaining self-confidence in one's own status, as we discussed in Chapter 4. Chaney (2002: 130) defines the cosmopolitan citizen as having heterogeneous tastes, a cultivated indifference to the local, and the ability to transcend local cultures. Drawing on the work of Waldron (1992), Hall (2002) usefully analyses the conditions of identity formation and political belonging under such conditions, arguing persuasively that identities do not require singular, intact cultural attachments for their formation and expression. Although individuals require embeddedness in order to generate an identity position from which to look beyond, Hall argues that the contemporary world encourages, and sometimes demands, that individuals hold multiple affiliations and perceive from many standpoints. In this respect, cosmopolitanism requires an individual to draw upon a variety of discursive meanings, and to command and enact multiple cultural vocabularies, discourses and repertoires. Côté's (1996) 'identity capital' thesis develops a similar idea, arguing that in late-modern culture individuals have the potential to develop situated, contextual modes of self-presentation that are reflexive and self-monitoring, allowing ease of forms of 'cultural mobility' through time and space. Côté's thesis connects to the literature on omnivorous cultural consumption that developed after, and partly in response to, the work of Bourdieu, and emphasizes cultural and aesthetic flexibility, a dehierarchicalized space for cultural consumption, and even the value of cultural experimentation as markers of the omnivorous consumer (Peterson and Kern 1996; Van Eijck 2000). Emmison's (2003) empirical research into the social groundings of such forms of omnivorousness also emphasizes the possibility of cultural mobility. Emmison uses DiMaggio's (1987) reference to cultural code-switching, and Bernstein's (1972) research into class and modes of speech, to argue that an important cultural asset is the assemblage of an 'elaborated' cultural code that demonstrates familiarity and competence with multiple cultural forms and objects.

Inclusivity

The final tenet which we see as an essential platform for the cosmopolitan disposition is the inclusive valuing of other – possibly hybrid

– cultural forms whose origin is outside one's home culture. The cosmopolitan citizen must be receptive to the cultural outputs of others, and indeed willing to become engaged with them. This involves a conscious attempt to be familiar with people, objects and places that sit outside one's local or national settings. At one level, we might identify tourists with an interest in exotic places as potentially cosmopolitan. Such a disposition is a positive step in possessing cosmopolitan traits. Alone though it is not enough, for some travellers to culturally exotic destinations are merely in search of the above mentioned 'home-plus' experiences: 'India is home plus servants, Africa is home plus elephants and lions' (Hannerz 1990: 241). The reflexive cosmopolitan is likely to loathe such tourists and touristic experiences, having a deeper desire to be a participant in foreign cultures, with access to the backstage. Yet, this privileged participation may also be akin to a type of cross-cultural *flâneurie*: a dialectic of mastery and surrender (Hannerz 1990) that means any immersion is only temporary, and contingent. Ultimate autonomy is a required status of the cosmopolitan dilettante, and exit strategies which alleviate anxieties must be at hand.

Openness

Moving beyond these three principles towards a more general facet of cosmopolitanness, we suggest that one may see cosmopolitanism as defined by an attitude of openness, which in a broad sense encompasses all three principles. However vague and analytically blunt the term, it is possible to see how 'openness' to other's cultural forms, practices and experiences is central to all of the dimensions of cosmopolitanism outlined above. Accordingly, the idea of cultural 'openness' has been a wellspring for general conceptions of cosmopolitanness as an outlook or disposition. The available literature on what constitutes a cosmopolitan disposition frequently summarizes the core attitude as one of cultural 'openness' (Hannerz 1990; Tomlinson 1999; Szerszynski and Urry 2002; Vertovec and Cohen 2002). For example, Hannerz (1990: 239) defines the cosmopolitan as having 'an intellectual and aesthetic stance of openness toward divergent cultural experiences' and a 'willingness to engage with the other'. Szerszynski and Urry concur with this idea, adding that this disposition of cosmopolitan openness is exhibited 'towards people, places and experiences from other cultures' (2002: 468). However, as Skrbis *et al.* (2004: 127) point out, the notion of cosmopolitan openness is 'vague and diffuse', having little analytic value in helping to understand who and what is cosmopolitan. How one could empirically identify and measure such openness is not so clear. This is one of the most pressing problems in progressing sociological investigations of 'actually existing' cosmopolitanism (Calhoun 2002b; Robbins 1998). The latter section of this chapter explores and weighs up available empirical evidence. It uses primary and secondary sources, both qualitative and quantitative, to stack the theoretical visions up against the practices and perceptions of social actors. In doing so, we propose a typology of cosmopolitan styles which taps into key aspects of cosmopolitan imagination and action.

Cosmopolitanism: some fundamental types

In constructing the typology that follows we are drawing upon interview work we conducted in and around a major Australian city.[2] Before progressing, we feel it is worthwhile pointing out major features of the qualitative research methodology because this is relevant to the way our theoretical argument develops. Our research dealt with no particular social class, but investigated the 'vast middle' where we expect to find a variety of forms of everyday or ordinary cosmopolitanism. Our participants were neither global elites (Kanter 1995), nor the globally dispossessed (Pollock et al. 2000), but they represented a spectrum of class locations that could most accurately be described as gravitating towards, and oscillating around, a broadly defined middle class. We began by recognizing the intertwining of cosmopolitanism and globalization and our aim was empirically to investigate ways in which ordinary people engage with globalization. We encapsulate the object of our study under the rubric of cosmopolitan 'dispositions' yet we do not claim to be interviewing cosmopolitans, or talking directly about cosmopolitanism with our participants. Our focus on dispositions is consistent with Hannerz's (1990: 238) suggestion that cosmopolitanism is 'a perspective, a state of mind' involving particular competencies, modes of managing meanings, and varieties of mobilities. Furthermore, like Lamont and Aksartova (2002), we too focus on the grounding of such dispositions in everyday experiences.

We should like to make a few remarks that are methodologically and theoretically relevant. We found evidence which suggests that globally-derived cosmopolitan openness is counterbalanced by various allegiances, anxieties and self-interests. This situation resembles the dilemma

---

[2]Skrbis and Woodward (2007) provide a somewhat different approach to analysing themes from the same data.

highlighted by Simmel in his account of experiencing the *fin de siècle* city of modernity. In his famous essay on the metropolis and mental life, Simmel (2002) shows how people experience joy and stimulation through immersing themselves in cultural difference, and how this situation also creates anxieties about its corrosive effects. In the context of our study, we similarly identified strong enthusiasm for some elements of the cosmopolitan value of openness and the participants were generally enthusiastic about engagements that emphasized consumptive, aesthetic and self-developmental exchanges with others. Accompanying this positive discourse of engagement was a counter-discourse of fear, exclusion, global homogeneity, and suspicion of global others. Thus we found the expression of participants' awareness of both the potential benefits and costs of living in a globalized world, but overall there was not a strong commitment to either.

This discursive to-ing and fro-ing, which could be seen as having semblances of what Savage *et al.* (2005: 191) call 'global reflexivity', may in part be due to the nature of focus group methodology. Focus groups are known to generate a particular style and range of responses whereby participants may focus on a proposition, and then find its antithesis. For example, in the context of a focus group, a contribution like 'we can travel more widely now' is frequently rapidly counterbalanced by another of 'the world is becoming all the same'. Yet, what the focus group methodology affords is the opportunity to 'hear' major features of the cultural terrain: in this case, the meta-narratives and binary discourses which constitute the dominant positions available to people in understanding globalization. What is notable are the ways in which participants imagined and discursively articulated the possibilities for such openness within a discursive framework of cosmopolitanism. In the section that follows we outline a typology of cosmopolitan engagement based around the idea of particular styles of engagement with globality, cultural difference and ethics of hospitality and critical recognition.

Type 1: the sampling style of cosmopolitanism

The first category of cosmopolitanism we propose is perhaps best captured by the idea of 'sampling'. To sample something implies engagement and contact, but only as a form of temporary, fleeting connection as opposed to something that might be engaged with strategically as a particular way of learning about other cultures, transforming or enhancing self. Sampling styles of cosmopolitanism engage with cultural otherness on the terms of the user, frequently as a consumer, and are often about symbolic appropriation of cultural otherness in order to show mastery, or demonstrate competency via breadth of cultural tastes, and engage with what might be identified as a contemporary norm of taste (Peterson 2005). This is most likely to be a discrete cultural transaction based on exchange for the sake of personal enjoyment, frequently around ideas of play and leisure. The cross-cultural contact is likely to be carried out in particular time-space settings where the rules of engagement are known and also rather restrictive in that they culturally delimit the style of engagement one might have with cultural otherness. A good example from our research is Steve, who along with his partner, have been corresponding over the internet with motorcycle riders around the world, discussing a range of aspects of motorcycle culture as well as the possibility of reciprocal tourism based around biking expeditions. Now, this is admittedly a rather simple form of cosmopolitanism – focused on a domain of leisure and within a rather restricted field, but in important senses it fits with some 'building-block' aspects of the disposition based around the desire and capacity to engage with others outside the boundaries of the nation. As well as building friendships, Steve takes advantage of the commercial possibilities afforded by the internet in building his own motorcycle from scratch:

> I'm saving $7500 on importing a Harley frame instead of buying it local. It would cost me $11000 in Australia, but I can get it for $3500 landed here in Australia.

Another characteristic of this style of cosmopolitan engagement is that otherness is primarily a field which serves to expand the range of personal choice available to individuals. Globality means that there is now a vast 'supermarket' of goods, images and services that can be sampled locally or, for that matter, irrespective of location. This lets consumers 'pick and choose', according to their own preferences and desires, products from around the world. While this may evoke a sense of participatory 'cosmo-multiculturalism' (Hage 1997), complete with the indulgence of fantasies of authenticity, the open cosmopolitan culture fosters an individual's accumulation of transnational symbols, and his or her experience of another culture, such as food, and way of life. An important consideration here is that such consumption is also a form of symbolic accumulation that accrues consumer capital differentially. While the empirical links between consumption practices and forms of ethical cosmopolitanism are unmapped, the theoretical territory for its interpretation is powerfully clear. According to Hage (1998), working broadly within Bourdieu's framework, such practices always involve a position of symbolic power and dominance. He sees this ability to 'pick and choose' as a form of appropriation by a dominant culture through means of symbolic manipulation. In this way, such forms of cross-cultural engagement are politically charged and result in contradictory tendencies. On the one hand they are about experiencing and consuming difference and potentially positive in their potential to construct forms of ethical cosmopolitanism, and on the other they are a form of appropriation whereby cultural difference is consumed, subsumed and ultimately dominated. A participant in our research outlines this global 'supermarket of choice' vividly and enthusiastically:

> I think that how I shop is to buy the best from every country. So whatever that country is famous for I'd get it. That's a way that globalization has allowed, because you know the wine in whatever country in Europe is the best and you'd go and get that. Oysters in New Zealand are the best so you'd get that.

An important element of this style of cosmopolitanism is its surface nature. It may be described as 'accidental' in that most people will be exposed through global media to various types of cultural difference without their actually seeking this out, but it also reveals an unreflexive engagement with the other. Cosmopolitans of the sampling kind tend to exhibit an awareness of interconnections and may seek out possibilities for connections with others outside their own cultural milieu, but they are most likely to be associations with known others or like-minded individuals, such as relatives or family located abroad, or associated with mainstream news media and culture industries. To some extent, again, this is all about the facilitating and enabling infrastructure of globality and less about what such infrastructures might mean for collectivities, ethics and politics which are at the heart of the cosmopolitan ethos. Additionally, internet, telecommunications, satellite links and related technologies allow personal relationships to be maintained despite distances, and for people to keep in touch with home while abroad. For example, one of our respondents reports: 'My friends are always travelling and working overseas, and with the new technology it just makes it so much easier to keep in contact with them. With email we can see pictures and we don't really miss out on each other's lives'. Another participant in our research reinforces this understanding, emphasizing the potential of new communication possibilities, reductions in price with increases in scope, but in a way that is almost suggestive of being a bystander, rather than someone actually immersed in such changes:

> There's so many new ways to communicate, you've got sms. The internet has just made the world so much more accessible & smaller in the sense that now we're reaching more people and we're communicating faster. Phone calls are cheaper, you've got video and satellite links, and all sorts of crazy technology bringing people together.

The downside of this sampling style of cosmopolitan engagement is that it has little robustness – it is a brittle form of engagement in the extreme. It is a weak form of cosmopolitanism in that threats to selfhood, one's own socio-economic position, safety or security, and broader threats to national well-being seem to rapidly smother the expression of cosmopolitan sentiments. Here, we find that anxieties about the negative potentiality of globality turn cosmopolitanism in on itself. The dialectic of cosmopolitan openness is always counterbalanced by a counter-discourse of threat and cultural loss never far from the surface. For example, consider the exchange between three research participants regarding security and conflict:

> Karen: Terrorism and all the things that are on the news at the moment. It is bringing it closer to home. If we weren't so integrated, if we still lived on farms with cows and stuff like that we'd be safer. Obviously we wouldn't have as much knowledge and stuff like that but it is posing a greater risk to us...
>
> Jim: I have to agree with you, because originally you probably had millions of little clans that didn't even know each other, and as it becomes more globalized they all become joined together into big clusters and you do get problems like that. As a country, we can possibly make ourselves a target for things like that...
>
> Karina: So does it create more tension and conflict?
>
> Jim: Instead of little groups saying my group's better than your group, it's big things and it affects a lot more people.

The question is whether this cultural sampling, being a surface engagement, is really a form of cosmopolitanism at all. We suggest it is. Admittedly, it lacks any apparent critical engagement, is almost purely self-enhancing and presumably results in no change or even substantial challenge to core aspects of selfhood. What is more, as the last extract reveals, it has a very brittle foundation which is vulnerable to threats to one's self-interest, or the self-interest of the national collective. Yet it does demonstrate a willingness to act outside the boundaries of the nation and to seek novel cultural experiences. In this sense, it is a nascent form of cosmopolitanism: a type of sampling that is perhaps – but not yet identifiable as such – a pathway to, or building-block of, deeper cosmopolitan attitudes.

Type 2: the immersive style of cosmopolitanism

The second category of cosmopolitanism we propose is represented by the term immersive. This is a type of cultural engagement and exchange that is deeper, more strategic and desiring than the sampling variety. More than merely accidental, or circumstantially induced, it reflects a conscious pattern of action which is based on learning and cultivating engagements for the purpose of change, self-knowledge or improvement. As such, it should be understood as the cultivation of multicultural capital. This type of immersive style may be characterized as strategic in nature, in that cosmopolitan objects and experiences are things looked for and 'visualized' as a matter of routine cultural practice. An example from our research is Jim, a part-time 'dj' and musician, who illustrates very effectively how globality opens up opportunities for the exploration of cultural difference, at least in a mainstream form, in terms of musical styles and tastes. Moreover, this is a style of consumption that is self-enhancing – it rests upon the cultivation and expansion of one's usual set of cultural preferences. While the larger question is how domains of commerce and cultural expression are gateways for the development of deeper ethical forms of cosmopolitanism, this example amounts to a form of cultural cosmopolitanism – a desire to immerse oneself in the array of musical output from around the world and to be a participant in a global musical scene:

> Well I'm always searching for new artists from all parts of the world. Music is something that isn't really boxed in by all these laws and culturalism (*sic*) and so on. You can listen to music without anyone saying you can't go to that country. It's something that isn't bound by anything else so music is pretty much freely spread throughout the world.

In this style of cosmopolitan engagement, the individual can become a type of cultural aficionado and expert. S/he can cultivate and learn hybrid, culturally strange styles, sometimes to establish status within particular social reference groups or networks, but also for the pleasure gained by cultivating aspects of the self. But along with this possibly voracious desire for cultural novelty, this style of engagement reflects a deeper and more culturally skilled engagement with otherness. It shows some desire and willingness to be challenged and learn from different cultural experiences, and perhaps most importantly it shows some implicit value preference for the de-hierarchization of culture. In seeking out new, marginal and geographically dispersed forms of culture, it necessarily eschews the idea that local is best, that the limits of one's cultural consumption rest within the nation or region, and that 'culture' is something most frequently produced by educated middle-classes in the urban regions of advanced, western nations. On a broader canvas, it acknowledges the potential of cultural immersion and exchange to enhance self:

> I reckon it's a very good thing. How else are we going to gain knowledge of broader aspects, not just your own culture, you want to understand other people's cultures, how they live and all that. As well with new technologies and new ideas, and things like that come in. So, my view is it's a good thing.

The immersive style of cosmopolitanism also has a spatial dimension. The street, the local setting becomes a site for reconciling rigidity – in the sense of cultural sameness, formality and rationalization – with alterity, meaning strangeness and difference (Sennett 2002). To be immersed one may be 'plunged into a crowd of people who cannot be recognized, you are dislodged from your own subjective categories of difference' (Sennett 2002: 43). This involves an engagement with sites, people and objects unknown, or of such different magnitude and quality that the senses are heightened and aroused. In this immersive style of cosmopolitanism, such experience does not lead to fear and anxiety. The immersion in such a cultural puzzle is both disorienting and highly attractive – there is delight in such difference. Such a situation might occur in an exotic city far away from one's local environment, but this is not necessarily so. As Sennett (2002: 43) points out: 'The cosmopolitan adds the quality of a bringer of freedom through a kind of dislocation wrought by virtue of experiencing the stranger'. One of our research participants, Karen, lives in a suburb nearby a cluster of African migrant families. She displays both an attitude of openness and optimism about cultural integration, learning and sharing in the context of shared suburban space, and a concern about the capacity of immigrants to integrate. As such, the following quote shows the dialectic of cultural openness and hospitality, and the surfacing of its potential opposite, cultural anxiety:

> A large group of Sudanese have recently moved in close to me. I live at [Suburb]. It was quite noticeable, they were all different families and when they did come I was happy about the fact that we were all becoming intertwined because I'm really interested to learn about their culture. It made me interested to see their way of life. The mothers and the ladies aren't allowed to learn English so therefore can't communicate with me in the park, but the husbands and the males in the family are going out and going to school, it's like they've come here and we'd love to embrace their culture, but they're limiting it. So globalization in that respect I think all the channels are being opened but things aren't being let go of which are inhibiting the full integration of it'.

Type 3: the reflexive style of cosmopolitanism

As we suggested earlier in the chapter, the notion that there can be 'banal' or 'spectral' versions of the cosmopolitan attitude as well as 'authentic' or 'organic' versions is useful as a preliminary distinction. The danger with such a distinction is that too often the conclusion is reached that all consumptive or commercially-mediated forms of cosmopolitanism are necessarily banal, and therefore depthless. We must differentiate between these mundane forms and 'reflexive' cosmopolitanism.

The reflexive cosmopolitan shows a genuine commitment to living and thinking beyond the local or nation and is more likely to *act* in cosmopolitan ways that are ethically directed. If consumption or leisure forms the basis of the cosmopolitan action, it is combined with an ethical or political ethos which renders such consumption meaningful in terms of valuing cultural difference. One of our research participants, Philip, talks about his first travel experience in Malaysia. What might have been interpreted by someone else as repulsive, disgusting or difficult travel experiences are recast as revelatory, stimulating and thought-provoking:

> Well I grew up in [Town], and we had all cane farms around and a pretty spare population. My first trip overseas was to Malaysia, it was just people everywhere and fish and markets and prawns, open

sewerage drains. It was totally different and it made me appreciate just the space that we have here. I enjoyed Malaysia, I enjoyed the culture, but because I'd grown up and seen a bit of Australia I went here with my eyes open to see as much of that culture as I could. I spent most of the time wandering the kampongs trying to get as much exposure as I could.

Ideally, the reflexive cosmopolitan feels little or no ethical and political commitment to local and national contexts and in fact is likely to show an irony, almost bordering on suspicion, toward their own national myths and discourses. This demonstrates a broad willingness to step outside stable, privileged and established power categories of selfhood. The following comment from one of our research participants, Charmaigne, is exceptional within our data, but best sums up the idea that globalization can foster genuine cosmopolitan mixing through the removal of boundaries and by putting humanity ahead of national interest:

I think globalization is a positive thing. Sooner or later it makes everyone look at themselves. They have to, because you're removing boundaries. My vision of globalization is the whole world as a human race living on the planet and you're all starting to interact and you have your little tiffs about your ideas, but sooner or later you all have to live on the same planet. So my view is that globalization is a positive step towards that.

Similarly, the following comment by Valerie, concerning Australia's refusal to sign the Kyoto Protocol illustrates the capacity of the reflexive cosmopolitan style for critique based upon a universal ethic which values international cooperation and integration over the perceived self-interests of national politics:

Should Australia be bound by international conventions?

Valerie: To a certain extent, yes and no. With the environment, how many countries have signed the agreement and it's only Australia and America that say no to it and simply keep on polluting the air and saying no to it. I think the Australian government should sign the agreement.

The fact that we can identify three schematic types representing variations of the cosmopolitan disposition tells us nothing about the prevalence or distribution of such schemas, nor their consistency in terms of how and when such dispositions come into play on an everyday basis. In fact, we know that when it comes to the prevalence of these three types, we are likely to see an inverse frequency of occurrence for each (Woodward *et al.* 2008) That is, across a population, more people are likely to exhibit type 1 cosmopolitanism than type 2; and in turn type 3, the reflexive variety, is the least frequently occurring type of cosmopolitanism.

In terms of what these everyday reactions can tell us about forms of ordinary cosmopolitanism, we can suggest that cosmopolitanism, as it is imagined and practised in everyday settings, should not be seen as a soon-to-arrive superior system of social organization, but a possibility, and one substantially undercut by a range of everyday attitudes and beliefs about the possibilities and problems associated with globality. By their nature, these 'ordinary' forms of cosmopolitanism are not necessarily banal or depthless, but represent the gradual and sometimes discrepant infiltration and uptake of aspects of cosmopolitanism into the practices and outlooks of everyday citizens. These types of thinking and feeling cosmopolitan (*cf.* Cheah and Robbins 1998) are visible in more modest and mundane ways. Thus we suggest it is wise to work from the principle that the extent of such cosmopolitan change, its degree and ultimate effects, are something of an open and ongoing question.

6
The Cosmopolitan Symbolic Universe and Communities of Sentiment

Introduction

This chapter investigates a fundamental dilemma related to the structural composition of contemporary cultural cosmopolitanism. The argument we develop here combines perspectives on global networks with research into cultural consumption and social status. These are distinct, important ways of dealing with cosmopolitanness, but they are infrequently considered together as part of the same structural network. Theories of global object networks fail to consider questions of reception and consumption by audiences and users; researchers into cultural consumption generally ignore the nature of the global flows which disseminate and enrol consumers. The nature of the contemporary global architecture is that there are increasingly diffuse networks of human and non-human innovators, carriers and icons of exotic and polyethnic cosmopolitan difference. This is a fact of contemporary global life, which we understand to be a form of globally spatialized, material-symbolic exchange. Yet, this diffusion, whilst putatively global and potentially cosmopolitan in nature, can frequently have the unintended consequence of promoting social status systems and cultural relations founded on *uncosmopolitan* values (or, to use the language of Chapter 4, spectral cosmopolitan values) such as cultural appropriation and status-based social exclusion. Moreover, this material-symbolic engagement with cosmopolitan difference could also be rather mundane, engaged in routinely, without any great reflexive consciousness or capacity to destabilize current organizations of cultural power, or interpreted unproblematically as just one component of a person's environment. The point we make is that the diffusion of putative cosmopolitan objects does not guarantee their interpretation and use within cosmopolitan frames of social action. This key dilemma frames the diffusion of cosmopolitan values and objects.

The massive, powerful distributive capacity of capitalist networks has been frequently noted by both admirers and critics of capitalism. But the power of these globally networked exchanges to build cosmopolitan cultures is contradicted by the development of status systems, sometimes based on exclusion and appropriation, which delimit the uptake and expression of cosmopolitan values. The raw materials of cosmopolitan culture propagate in large part through the networked exchange of material and visual symbols which afford and construct the idea of global cultural exchange and cross-fertilization. However, the very system which spreads cosmopolitan objects also works in other ways to delimit their adoption. In earlier centuries, the driving force of cross-border contact was frequently associated with war, or religious conversion. Now, in the contemporary global cultural economy, the limits of the development and spread of cosmopolitanism are inextricably linked to the distributive powers of commerce and economic and technological exchange, which have a capacity to annihilate time and space in disseminating a range of goods associated with cultural difference. Moreover, the ultimate limits to the development of cosmopolitanism lie within the unequally distributed cultural capacities of individuals and groups to claim or reject putative objects of cosmopolitanism.

It is capitalism, insofar as capitalism can be understood as a social system based upon commodity, image and idea production, circulation and exchange, which is the motor force of cross-cultural exchange. Appadurai (1986: 27) has highlighted the global 'commodity ecumene, that is, a transcultural network or relationships linking producers, distributors and consumers of a particular commodity or set of commodities'. At the level of economic distribution, capitalism and cosmopolitanism are not mutually exclusive or antagonistic facets of the modern social order. In fact, it is capitalism – including the socially networked activities of commerce and exchange that are based upon the flow and movement of commodities between producers and consumers – which provides much of the impetus for the spread of cosmopolitan values, objects and outlooks. We live in an era of the 'global cultural economy'. Cosmopolitanism is an increasingly salient cultural possibility. Moreover, it is a possibility hardwired into the contemporary global culture industry, where culture is thoroughly part of the economic base and what are produced are objects of difference and image (Lash and Lury 2007).

Yet, while these systems of production, distribution and exchange offer a potential for an expanding universe of symbolic and material cosmopolitanism, in no way does they guarantee that people are becoming more cosmopolitan. There are some major hurdles to overcome here which render this account of a 'master-pathway' for generating cosmopolitanism questionable. While capitalism and economic exchange are largely responsible for the geographic spread of objects and ideas, the distribution of objects and ideas is by no means equal, nor are their implications and effects unproblematic. The heterogeneous nature of the cosmopolitan global economy may mean that it is increasingly possible for individuals to transcend the outputs and terrain of a distinctly 'national' or 'local' culture and, as a consequence, that the hegemonic cultural structure of the nation-bounded cultural-economy is challenged, or at least diluted. However, this does not preclude the likelihood that there are multiple forms of identification that neutralize or are in conflict with cosmopolitan identifications, nor does the mere fact of distribution tell us anything about the attribution of *cosmopolitan meanings*. Even if it was accepted that the global cultural economy multiplies and proliferates cosmopolitanness, we do not claim that the implications of this reality are trivial or neutral. The way 'cosmopolitanness' can be turned into status-loaded forms of cultural capital means that the unintended consequence of the cosmopolitan symbolic field can in fact be exclusionary; behind the exoticism and difference of particular commodities, relationships of symbolic exploitation and economic domination still exist. Moreover, what is a cosmopolitan object for some, is mundane for others, or has little meaning or implication beyond aspects of expressive consumer identities.

We can say, therefore, that in the contemporary global cultural economy there is an emergent (though incomplete and partial) compatibility between system and subjectivity. By this we mean that there is a mutual compatibility between the development of globally networked systems of economic production and the cultivation of cosmopolitan individual's habits and styles of consumption. Consumers of cosmopolitan difference are enrolled into networks of global economic exchange, empowered by discourses of choice and exoticism, and perform their status as consumers of cosmopolitan objects. Having established global commodity networks and circuits over the last few centuries, capitalist systems of exchange have succeeded in laying the ground for their own expansion. Given the possibility of wider and more diverse consumption possibilities, individuals then begin to change their own habits and expectations, which in turn serve independently to stimulate further cosmopolitanization of cultural consumption fields such as food, music, fashion or even religion and spirituality. Simmel (1904) noted this type of compatibility between 'civilization' and the seeking of novelty: as social systems complexify, that which is novel becomes recognized as a means for symbolic differentiation. Moreover, there is a *constantly unfolding demand for novelty* amongst particular social groups, whether they be young people, the middle classes, avant-gardists or capitalists, who for varying reasons desire newness and difference, and can identify it within the cultural outputs of others. But it is not just the 'demand' side of individual consumption where novelty and difference are an important currency. Fernand Braudel notes the power that the fashion dynamic has to energize social and economic evolution:

> Perhaps if the door is to be opened to innovation, the source of all progress, there must be first some restlessness which may express itself in such trifles as dress, the shape of shoes and hairstyles (Braudel 1992: 333).

The argument we make here is that there is now an emerging confluence between global networks of capitalist exchange and the potential growth of cosmopolitan habits in a range of everyday fields. Indeed, on the 'demand' side, shifting and complexifying status systems, fluid forms of identity which increasingly embrace cultural difference and the search for novelty in consumption habits, all point to continued demand for cosmopolitan goods. On the 'supply' side, producers are increasingly aware that cultural difference, exoticism and novelty offer powerful framing devices for their goods in globally networked markets. Thus, the sourcing of objectified cosmopolitan difference becomes a means of social differentiation, status and exclusion, and is driven by a master process of cultural appropriation.

A further key point of this chapter is that cultural meanings are inevitably fused with the economic process of global expansion forming what we call a 'cosmoscape' – spaces, practices, objects and images which afford and construct networks which make cosmopolitan engagements and hence cosmopolitan subjectivities possible. Contemporary global capitalism is a complex set of networked flows of things and people. We argue that to study such networks of objects and things as merely economic is fallacious, for objects always have symbolic qualities. As things from somewhere else, potentially cosmopolitan objects, whether they be a motor vehicle, an item of fruit, a fashion object, a movie or a piece of music, carry interpretable markers of cultural origin and difference. They have a performative character. Not only do they signify cosmopolitan difference, but more importantly they are (or can be) interpreted by particular consumer audiences as affording cosmopolitan difference. If we move from seeing capitalism as about abstract commodities that are simply produced, distributed and sold to passive consumers, to see it as being about symbols and objectified meanings, we can grasp how the modern economy of signs, brands, flows and emotions is perfectly placed to proliferate a culture of cosmopolitan experience. This global field of apparent cosmopolitanness is not given, but has to be reconstructed symbolically and performatively. It is represented, performed and interpreted as having cosmopolitan qualities, emphasizing interconnectedness and post-national orientations in a range of everyday fields. Yet there must be an active process of interpreting cultural difference, a frame which identifies the character of otherness as applicable. For this to happen, the elements of social location, cultural capital, symbolic competencies and personal motivation must be fused.

This chapter will elaborate the symbolic and representational qualities and characteristics of cosmopolitan things in various fields, drawing upon examples from the fields of music, food and urban experience. The chapter develops the idea that there will be human and non-human carriers of cosmopolitanism, especially prevalent in creative occupations and fields, who perform various iconic iterations of the ideal cosmopolitan identity. Important questions will no doubt remain about the links between such symbols of cosmopolitanism and the development of deep ethical principles of hospitality and cross-cultural generosity. Moreover, the way such consumption of cosmopolitan icons is both determined by social structural location and becomes a form of cultural capital that sometimes operates in a perverse way to exclude rather than include will remain a live issue. Despite these serious questions, the Chapter maintains that there is a fundamental link between contemporary capitalism and the potential development of forms of cultural cosmopolitanism.

Cosmoscapes and commodity networks

As well as constituting the architecture of global flows, cosmoscapes offer a performative frame for commodities, transforming things through a variety of practices, discourses and images into cosmopolitan objects. Objects themselves have no *a priori*, objective cosmopolitan quality.

Things may be from 'here' or 'there', but to be perceived as cosmopolitan they must always be interpreted as having the quality of cultural difference, where particular material-symbolic markers are identified as signalling and affording cosmopolitanism. Such a capacity to define and claim the cosmopolitanness of particular objects relates to forms of cultural capital and the ability to interpret, categorize and label, as we discussed in Chapter 5.

The movement and flow of objects around the globe is one of the defining features of economic globalization, but an inherent feature of such flows is the way these objects carry with them elements of 'global consciousness' (Robertson 1992). As symbolic materializations of other people, distant lands and cultures they constitute the architecture of an increasingly cosmopolitan array. This development signals a regime of capitalism which unites consumers and producers across large distances, alters established patterns of production and consumption and shifts the material and symbolic constitution of status hierarchies by providing a whole new range of resources for social imagination and differentiation.

What circulates, and what performs cosmopolitanness, in the global symbolic economy? Appadurai's (1990, 1996) work has been an important breakthrough for the development of a field of study that both specifies the broad brush rhetorics of literatures on economic globalization, and suggests the cultural basis of the exchange of material goods. In elaborating a cultural specification of Marxian theories of the commodity, Appadurai (1990) suggests a commodity is anything that is *exchanged*. Taking a processual view of commodity exchange, he focuses on objects as they go into and out of their commodity status – objects are 'candidates' (1996: 13) for being commodities, but do not remain simply and forever 'in' or 'out' of a commodity status. Part of his fundamental point is that objects cycle through circuits of exchange; they are susceptible to paths and diversions (1990: 16) as they transfer through hands, become visible, and cross borders. Such movements subject cultural objects to continuous shifts of definition and meaning as they go across and within unique cultural systems. As a result, we can say that objects which flow through societies via commodity exchange are really no longer simple 'commodities' at all, but objectified containers of meaning amenable to reconstruction and reinterpretation by groups. As Foster (2006: 287) notes, 'commodities in motion engage desires and stimulate the imagination in the construction of both personhood and place'. The relevant task is one of tracing the networks of actors, objects and images which create value and relationships. This opens the possibility for certain social groups to interpret and define particular objects as having cosmopolitan values.

Building on his analyses of object processes and cultural meaning in later work, Appadurai (1996) broadened his theoretical vision beyond the commodity and exchange systems to suggest that the global economy is constituted by a number of interrelated and overlapping dimensions founded on a series of networked 'scapes'. Scapes should not be seen as precise descriptions of the content or processes of global networks, but rather as heuristics for thinking about the 'form and feel' of such networks. Appadurai's approach is significant for two reasons. First, his is a post 'world-system' approach to the global economy, which theorizes global capitalism as complex, fluid and disjunctural. He argues that the global economy can no longer be captured by theories of global development that originate within a traditional Marxist perspective (Appadurai 1996: 32), for these seem unable to capture the interplay of emergent and fluid actors, objects and networks, and the overlapping of structure and culture, representation and imagination. The second fundamental advance Appadurai makes is his insistence on the cultural basis of global capitalism – it is a 'global *cultural* economy'. The 'economy' is not something that can be extricated from cultural movements and flows, specifically electronic media and migration. Nor can the global economy be separated from the work of representation and imagination which constructs a field for actors to make their actions meaningful in a global context. Global 'mediascapes' present and disseminate information, but the importance of these media is not just in creating 'consumable' forms of entertainment or information, but in providing the cultural material necessary for the *imagining* of globality and its associated capacity to enable or facilitate flows, movement and exchange. Appadurai (1996: 35) comments that the media provide 'large and complex repertoires of images, narratives, and ethnoscapes to viewers throughout the world, in which the world of commodities and the word of news and politics are profoundly mixed'. This process blurs the lines between what is realistic and what is fictional and optimizes the capacity of actors to 'deploy their imaginations' (Appadurai 1996: 5) in imagining the future of their own cultural circumstances. As well as imaginative mobility, physical capacity for mobility is also enhanced. Whether by choice and privilege or by intolerable circumstances and disadvantage, more people are routinely mobile, resulting inevitably in changing entrenched notions of neighbourhood, city and nation as they integrate into new environments:

> the warp of these stabilities is everywhere shot through with the woof of human motion, as more persons and groups deal with the realities of having to move or the fantasies of wanting to move... And as international capital shifts its needs, as production and technology generate different needs, as nation-states shift their policies on refugee populations, these moving groups can never afford to let their imaginations rest too long, even if they wish to (Appadurai 1996: 33-4).

Appadurai (1996) places significant emphasis upon *the idea of the imaginary*, a capacity to imagine other people, environments and settings, and one's own actions beyond one's immediate locality. Such an imaginary domain, where one is encouraged to think about social action beyond the fixity of current surroundings is constructed, nurtured and ultimately provoked by the existence of a field of globality. The collective imagination is increasingly global in orientation and creates a 'community of sentiment' (1996: 8) where discourses that emerge from media fields both construct new mythologies of the global and afford individuals and groups the capacity to navigate through such fields. In the case of migrants, for example, a critical aspect of movement, integration and adaptation relates to the consumption of mass media images, scripts, models and narratives (1996: 6) which provide cultural resources for individual and collective action.

Alexander (2006b), writing on the idea of global civil society, takes a broadly similar approach to Appadurai, arguing that globalization is as much a collective representation – an imaginary sphere – as it is a factual, materialist one. Alexander (2006a) theorizes the civil sphere as a plurality of institutional, discursive, symbolic structures that guide styles of communication and obligation among its members. While recognizing that the nascent global sphere is relatively undeveloped in a formal, institutional way, Alexander (2006b) notes the robust nature of the communicative elements of the global civil sphere. His Durkheimian approach suggests that understandings of global events and processes never really rely on fact, but are represented by and interpretable through a range of performances and objects which rely on drawing from known, potent discourses for their efficacy. Here, we can highlight especially both 'factual' and 'fictional' mass media – television, news networks, movies, music, branded goods and even novels

– which create a worldwide material culture that is increasingly more commonly shared. This global civil representational sphere relies not on government, but *governmentality* – modes of self-monitored conduct – the rationale and basis of which is in turn structured by sets of shared images, objects and symbolically-coded discourses. One's own actions and perspectives must more frequently be accounted for in the context of global rather than local or national life. Alexander (2006b: 523) comments:

> It is within this symbolic and institutionally constructed sea of global public opinion that there emerges the world stage, on which transpire polls, demonstrations, social movements, scandals, corruptions, terrorism, electoral triumphs, and tragedies, performances that palpably create the very sense that there is a supra-national life.

In a similar line of argument, Szerszynski and Urry (2006) put useful emphasis on the visual, ocular nature of globality in creating a field of cosmopolitanism, but also pay similar attention to the visual and iconic elements in forming globality. Global cultural difference must be sighted in various ways (e.g. 'us', 'not us', 'all of us') and in turn imagined through symbols and visual media. The starting point for such imaginings can be seen in McLuhan's (1962) idea of the global village, while the process is perhaps best highlighted by Williams' (1974) idea of 'televisual flow', where the distinctions between home and away, local and global, fixed and fluid seem less relevant as they are structured by the continuous, instantaneous flow of global visual media. A product of this gradual, but radical, intensification and compression of global relations is that it is now possible for most citizens of a nation to think, feel and act beyond the boundaries of that national space, even if such global meanderings are frequently carried out from the comfort of their lounge rooms. This heightened potential for virtual, imaginary, or corporeal global mobility has opened up the traditionally fixed sphere of social citizenship – from being a citizen of a nation-state, to being a citizen of the globe.

Szerszynski and Urry (2006) point to various sorts of mobility which enable and support visual mobility, constructing a symbolically mediated 'cartographic citizenship' which is an important element in forming the emergent culture of cosmopolitanism. First, are the hard, 'material' movements of physical travellers, including tourists but also migrants and refugees. Tourism and travel is the largest industry in the world:

the cost of travel has decreased relative to incomes over time, and people travel more frequently and a significant percentage of citizens in western nations undertake long-distance journeys (see Szerszynski and Urry 2006). On top of all this, Szerszynski and Urry (2006) point out that there is a whole range of media and technology that enable both virtual and imaginative travel. Virtual travel includes communicative devices which facilitate international contact, such as postcards, letters, telephones and emails. Imaginative travel is enabled through television, magazines and the internet.

Szerszynski and Urry (2002) apply the banal/authentic distinction to a discussion of globalism in a study of the reception and uptake of cosmopolitan ethics in everyday media programming. They argue that a 'publically screened' form of cosmopolitanism has been well established in a variety of media, and that such discourses are well understood by a wide section of the population. It is now possible – perhaps even desirable – to spend entire evenings in the televised company of cooks, gardeners, designers and travel show hosts, all equally eager to divulge the mysteries of technique and the satisfactions of sophisticated consumption. Flicking across the channels reveals 'Pho' or 'Tajine' or the *al fresco* possibilities of Balinese-inspired gardens or the colours and tastes of the Mediterranean or the world's travel hotspots.

A telling example of cosmopolitan media can be found in the recently founded magazine and website *Monocle*. Launched by *Wallpaper* magazine and founder Tyler Brûlé (see Vertovec and Cohen 2002: 7, for a brief discussion of various cosmopolitan media, including *Wallpaper*), *Monocle* is an instruction manual for budding cosmopolitans and a global guide for those already part of the club. A genuinely interesting example of such a magazine, *Monocle* is based in London and put together by an international team of journalists and writers, aided of course by an even larger array of advertisers, photographers, web content developers, art and photography directors. *Monocle* is aimed at high-end global consumers (the consumptive cosmopolitans) but it is also aimed at intellectual cosmopolitans – those with a desire, curiosity and openness not only for global goods, but also for narratives of globality and innovations which make it easier or more pleasurable to be mobile. A perusal of the advertising material in *Monocle* can tell us something about the expected readership and experience of reading the magazine and of the contemporary ethic of cosmopolitanism more broadly. First, we can see that *Monocle* advertises a fairly standard collection of high-end global brands such as Cartier, Boss, Louis Vuitton, Mont Blanc, and Gucci. In the March 2008 edition it also had advertisements for international banks such as HSBC ('The world's local bank') and UBS, and a large colour advertisement for the 'Dellis Cay' private residences in the Caribbean. There are also numerous advertisements for household and design goods and fashion products.

The March 2008 edition of *Monocle* also had a range of unusual, unexpected and high-quality stories about particular fields of consumption or consumption experiences designed to appeal to connoisseurs of the exotic and rare, who have a hunger for knowledge about things new or unusual. For example, there are detailed stories on particular brands of the Chinese spirit 'bai jiu' (the magazine advises 'it's still the drink that most businessmen turn to when they want to toast their latest deal'); an emerging European nut distribution company and commentary on the global market for nuts; a report on luxury shopping mall developments in China; the Danish 'anti-fashion brand SNS Herning' who now produce high-quality knitwear for top-line fashion designers; and a story on the travel destination of Santa Cruz, Tenerife, which the magazine suggests is charming, architecturally interesting and as yet largely undiscovered by most tourists. Along with this range of consumptive cosmopolitan stories are a number of informative, investigative pieces into various human and political aspects of the global cosmopolitan network. These include in-depth stories on: the guards who patrol the Russian-Finland border trying to stop people and drug traffickers; the apparent 'steady stream' of African businessmen moving into China ('10000 of them now live in Guangzhou'); a story on the way plane-spotters are an increasingly important local weapon to the global terror threat; a profile on the Afghani ambassador to Washington; and a story on the editor of China's newspaper 'The People's Daily'. It provides a genuinely cosmopolitan array of content, a glossy and artfully constructed series of images and includes an ongoing manga comic series attached at the back of each edition which manages to cross the low-high culture divide and presumably to provide some fantasy reading after one has finished the more serious reading related to assembling the self and to understanding the global environment.

Monocle is a magazine produced by a cosmopolitan array of workers that remains just a small step ahead of its cosmopolitan audience. It perfectly illustrates the dilemma of the global cosmoscapes. *Monocle* presents genuinely interesting and unlikely stories which construct and reflect an inquisitive, ethical outlook that searches for and values cultural difference. In this sense, it manages to represent both consumptive and ethical strands of cosmopolitanism. On the other hand, it is clear that *Monocle*'s readership is intended to be the well-resourced, globally-mobile connoisseurs, or at least the aspirants to such a tribe. These are not the gauche consumers of all and sundry global brands and everyday tourist destinations – they are assumed to seek out the rare, unusual and exceptional. As such, *Monocle* empowers those seeking fine cosmopolitan distinctions and shows these readers who, what and where should become their cultural property; this is what is at stake. It assumes and encourages a readership to become educated and knowledgeable global actors one or two levels above the tourist pages of other glossy magazines, or the travel pages of global newspapers such as *London Times* or *The New York Times*. The key question is, will such forms of consumption foster genuine cosmopolitan outlooks that extend beyond the realm of the commodity, or is such a process inherently about the unequal 'propertizing' of cultural difference? As Skeggs (2004: 158) comments:

> The intellectual cosmopolitans learn to know themselves through traveling through the cultures of others, turning them into objects of distanced contemplation for oneself. The intellectual cosmopolitans learn to know themselves through the cultures of others. This then is the aesthetic/prosthetic self, shopping, sizing-up the value of what is available, participating in the art-culture system of otherness, where others become a resource – in the propertizing of the self.

In his critique of the class basis of cosmopolitanism, Calhoun cautions on this matter: 'food, tourism, music, literature and clothes are all easy faces of cosmopolitanism, but they are not hard tests for the relationship between local solidarity and international civil society' (Calhoun 2002b: 105). While we agree with Calhoun's sentiment to the extent that resolving this matter becomes an empirical matter for further research, we also note the persistent materialist tendency to presume consumption behaviours are insignificant. Szerszynski and Urry (2002) suggest that the selling of these mundane forms of cosmopolitan style may go hand-in-hand with more fundamental and progressive social-structural changes. Rather than being mere surface features, and apparently trivial aspects of globalization, they do, in fact, have an important symbolic value and are the harbingers of wider social changes. On the side of leisure and lifestyle we have travel shows and newspapers based around food, adventure and dimensions of luxury and discovery; on the political and economic side, daily news devotes itself to international events, traumas and dramas which can either suggest to us we need to cocoon and insulate ourselves further from the world, or can also encourage us to take actions which confirm our own investment in the global meaning of social action.

The experience of the Scottish author Thomas Carlyle in nineteenth-century London illustrates a rather extreme example of this 'cocooning' response to the aural qualities of the emergent cosmopolitanism of a global city (Holme 2002; New York Times 1886; Ellison and Woodward 2005). For reasons of convenience and economy, Carlyle chose to live in Cheyne Row in Chelsea, then a moderately-priced row house facing an increasingly populous and lively thoroughfare. Almost at once Carlyle began to record his annoyance with the level of noise penetrating the walls of his house. The problem, though, was not, as we might expect, one of volume, so much as of diversity. Amongst the usual sources of domestic annoyance, including the noise made by his neighbour's Cochin China Fowl, Carlyle singles out Black minstrels, Italian organ grinders and an exuberantly expressive Irish family as unwanted intrusive noise of the city. The peculiar and unwonted worldliness of these sounds and their stubborn refusal to remain fixed to their habitual (cultural) origins abroad provoked Carlyle to action. He directed that a room be constructed deep within his house fashioned of materials that would absorb all such disturbances. From here, exempt from the polluting arena of worldly sound, Carlyle imagined a space amenable to the projection and amplification of his respiration, the scratch of his pen, and the occasional digestive gurgle. As it turned out, the room proved to be the very noisiest in the entire house and was completely lacking in ventilation, and Carlyle abandoned it with disgust. Sometimes cosmopolitan cultural 'noise' can have the opposite effect!

Szerszynski and Urry (2006) also point to the role of iconic events and media spectacles – globally presented and reported – which help to present cultural difference, while at the same time fostering a sense of global identification and belonging. Citing Anderson's (1983) work on collective belonging, they suggest that post-national identifications of global citizenship can be fostered through the global imagery and narratives found in diverse media. Such representations point to the ways people can empathize with or become curious about culturally different experiences. Global media spectacles are an important way of communicating such collective belonging by identifying the local as only one of multiple sites of belonging, for example: the apartheid rupturing speeches of Nelson Mandela; the funeral of Princess Diana; the terrorist attacks in America, 2001, or London, 2005; the Asian Tsunami of 2004 and Hurricane Katrina which destroyed large parts of New Orleans in 2005. Szerszynski and Urry (2006) cite the 'Earthrise' photograph, taken by astronaut Will Anders in 1968, as an iconic representation of the earth, illustrating the ultimate connectedness of the earth's people and their co-reliance on a relatively small piece of rock that exists on the edge of the blackness of space. Featured on Christmas Day in the New York Times, 'Earthrise' was accompanied by the words of poet Archibald MacLeish, who wrote that the photo allows people to 'see ourselves as riders on the Earth together, brothers on that bright loveliness in the eternal cold – brothers who know now that they are truly brothers' (MacLeish, in Szerszynski and Urry 2006: 121).

Likewise, sounds can also foster and afford cosmopolitan outlooks. Alex Ross (2007) shows that cross-cultural forms and styles have been central to the development of the western musical canon. He points out, for example, that 'Debussy fell in love with Javanese and Vietnamese ensembles at the Paris Universal Exhibition of 1889' (Ross 2007: 516). Classical music, he says, changes its meaning as it traverses the globe, suggesting the cosmopolitanization of accepted styles: 'It now connotes any ancient practice that has persisted into the modern era – the ritual opera of China, the imperial court music of Japanese *gagaku*, the *radif* or "order" of Persian melodies, the great classical traditions of India, and the polyrhythmic drumming of West African tribes... All this activity renews the folkish projects of Bartók, Janácek, the young Stravinsky, and de Falla – the quest for the real, the "dance of the earth"' (Ross 2007: 519). In the field of popular contemporary music, Regev (2007b) argues that there is a relational property to the global consumption and production of music, such that the a taste for cultural otherness in turn creates demands for such differences, ending with a mix-up of styles, practices and influences: 'cultural elements from alien cultures are thus inserted, integrated and absorbed into the producer's own ethno-national culture. Consequently, consumers of home-made cultural products and art works become inadvertently open to experiences from other ethno-national cultures' (Regev 2007b: 126). Such a process inevitably leads to the mixing of styles of production and consumption, and to the increasingly irrelevance of national borders and styles. What we have, according to Regev, is a type of global bank of sounds: 'current world culture can be portrayed as a bank of visual, sonic and textual stylistic elements and techniques of expression, from which every local producer at the national level can draw materials for her own use, and in which every producer – once gaining some publicity – deposits certain variants and nuances of such elements' (Regev 2007b: 126).

The Asianization of music, especially British pop and dance music, has been an important trend in the last decade or so. This ranges, for example, from the relatively formal and experimental such as Sheila Chandra; to the electro samples and dance of Asian Dub Foundation, Transglobal Underground, and Fun-da-mental; the electro-dance of Talvin Singh and the global sounds of Thievery Corporation. Hesmondhalgh (2000) has written about Transglobal Underground's lyrical rhetoric of global unity, their references to oriental spirituality and primitivism and their multicultural and visual exoticism. This so-called 'Asian beat' or 'Asian Kool' (Sharma 2003) movement challenges the dominance of the white-pop tradition in the UK, represented by pop singers like Cliff Richard or Elton John, British bands like Oasis and The Jam, or contemporary electro composers such as Richard D. James (Aphex Twin). This movement brings Asian youth in as producers of popular musical culture. According to Sharma (2003: 411), it has generated a respected Asian elite of cultural producers, who are 'seen to represent a kind of elite avant-garde in commercial culture: fashionably and effortlessly fusing translatable elements from the "East" with a "modern" Western way of being'. Talvin Singh, the British performer and entrepreneur who combines classical Indian instrumentation with ambient and danceable electronic styles might be the best example here.

Such sonic and visual cultural production, insofar as it affords ideas of trans-national interconnectedness, can assist in the development of cosmopolitan viewpoints. At least, it can possibly represent new ways of being with the cultural other, or – through the pleasurable practices of listening or dancing – engender a new respect for other cultures. But we also need to treat such claims with a degree of methodological reflexivity and have due regard for questions of the everyday reception and use of such imagery and objects. First, we need to countenance the possibility of moral indifference to these forms of cosmopolitan representation (Stevenson 2003: 116). Stevenson (2003) summarizes these debates effectively. He points to Tester's (1995, 1999) argument that the world awash with sounds and images from 'elsewhere' actually creates a blasé attitude amongst media audiences. In the case of news and visual media, audiences may view these images, but see them as an unpleasant window into other people's worlds which can thankfully be quickly shut off to protect one's comfort and emotional balance. Rather than being a cosmopolitan 'bridge', they are an ambivalent 'door' which can be closed to protect those offended (disgusted) by the consumption of visual unpleasantries. Using the example of global charities, Stevenson admits that such events putatively tap into latent cosmopolitan attitudes, potentially helping people to see their connections and responsibilities to others. Yet, there is rarely a deep engagement with the systematic causes of inequality of cultural difference, one's own moral responsibility and a deeper ethic of solidarity based upon a complex understanding of hospitality and responsibility. As Bauman (1998) puts it, too often these events constitute 'carnivals of charity'. The result, a kind of televisual 'post-emotional' society (Meštrović 1997) of synthetic emotions and packaged and performed sentiment, fails to generate the deep emotional bonds necessary to effect change.

In a sociological study of identification and place in the global era, research by Savage *et al.* (2005) reveals that among a sample of Northern English Anglophone respondents there is considerable fluidity in many peoples' identifications and that there were moderately high levels of mobility (roughly 48 per cent of the sample). However, there were very few respondents (less than 5 per cent) who could be classified as genuinely cosmopolitan (2005: 197), and only another 13 per cent who could be said to have some frame of comparative identity (2005: 191). The respondents were reasonably regular travellers, may have lived overseas for a period of time, have family and friends overseas, and perhaps were involved in hobbies that afforded global contacts – in many ways, making them perfect candidates for a flowering cosmopolitanism. Yet none of these things guaranteed becoming cosmopolitan, at least in the way contemporary theory discusses such attributes. Indeed, often the nature of contacts reconfirmed the idea of a home based predominantly in white, Northern England. Thus, global reflexivity of various types 'does not, on the whole, disrupt people's sense of located identity' (Savage *et al.* 2005: 202). They conclude that even when it does occur, cosmopolitanness 'does not seep into people's lives because of the pervasive power of global idioms and cues, but rather depends on particular, indeed local and personal, circumstances' (2005: 202). Becoming cosmopolitan was more likely to eventuate from exposure to exceptional circumstances or events which quite radically challenge or alter people's orientations. Along similar lines, research by Skrbis and Woodward (2007) and Woodward *et al.* (2008) shows that while many people are likely to endorse and feel positive about a range of aspects of the global field like personal consumption choices, food, media and tourism, these feelings are also counterbalanced by strongly felt discourses of loss of national and local cultural identity, risk and violence, notions of home, comfort and ease. Because such factors are structurally located in categories related to social location and individual biography, they mitigate the development of widespread and fully formed cosmopolitan outlooks. In the next section we take a closer look at the intersection of social status with circuits of globality.

Global commodities: *bonnes à penser*

The exchange of economic goods involves the exchange of ideas. As commodities, goods are reducible to quantities of money. But, goods are much more, and as symbolic things, goods circulate a variety of meanings. Claude Levi-Strauss (1966) enunciated this principle in his famous dictum of *bonnes à penser* when he said that things were never simply good for eating or being used as utilities, but that all utilities were to be valued because they were in fact 'good to think' with. Thus, objects help us to locate, mediate and also challenge cultural categories. They afford this function because humans are constantly searching for signs of social and cultural status in others and themselves through their material environment, and also because objects are flexible in their meanings. A can of Coca-Cola may be a mundane symbol of American cultural saturation and homogenization in one cultural context, a glamorous symbol of the everyday exotic, or simply one variety of black, sweet sticky drink in another (Miller 1998). Likewise, Long and Villareal (2000) show that a maize husk can have a multiplicity of different meanings, it can 'have value for US consumers as an artifact of "traditional ethnic cuisine"; for Mexican peasants as a flexible currency for securing harvest labour; and for Mexican migrants in the United States as flexible reminders of home' (Foster 2006: 290).

Exchange and cultural diffusion

What constitutes this frame for interpreting cultural objects? We must look to economic exchange as the engine for this process. This focus on exchange should lead us to consider both the social and material forces that 'produce' global objects, and also the discourses and practices that frame them as exotic, different or 'other'. Fernand Braudel's (1992) studies of material life are instructive here in grounding the links between economic and cultural systems. Primarily conceived as a study of the historical intricacies of material life, Braudel also provides a useful account of some of the structural conditions for the diffusion of cultural difference. It is in this way that his work is helpful for understanding an important feature of the economic networks which diffuse cosmopolitan objects.

Braudel notes that there are always a number of distinct elements to historical forms of capitalism. First and most recognizably, there is a market economy, which is the fundamental feature of capitalism. This consists, in the first instance, of systems of production and exchange involving factories, workshops, small businesses, markets and market places, financial institutions and arrangements, and so on. It is the 'traditional economy' amenable to the language of economics. Opposed to these grounded forms of institutional capitalism, there is a stratospheric tier to capitalism, constituted by the discussions of elite financiers, institutional cooperation and arrangements made by the upper rank of capitalists. These are actors who dream, act and organize on behalf of capitalist activity. But (and this is Braudel's main concern) there is also a zone of intermediate, prosaic, everyday activity lying beneath the formal arrangements of the market economy which plays a crucial role in constituting capitalist activity. Here, Braudel's analysis mixes culture and economy as he shows via historical methods how human activities of economic exchange are always culturally laden. The everyday fact of the emerging global economy of the sixteenth to nineteenth centuries was its constitution as a system of exchanging ideas and cultural difference, for circulating the goods and commodities from one economic zone to another and so gradually transforming the cultural make-up of all trading partners in the process. Braudel's historical examples reveal the structural and institutional factors responsible for the widespread circulation of objects, accounting for the infusion of the material into the everyday and showing how cultural practices and objects materially and visually constitute global cultural differences (if not global solidarity).

Braudel shows that the limits to material-cultural circulation primarily rest on the capacity of the means of transport technologies to eliminate the tyranny of distance. Just as digital transfer is much more efficient than physical means, airplanes are faster at transporting goods over long distances than trucks, trains and horses. But, even more so in the contemporary era, satellite television and the internet circulate symbolic goods and images instantaneously. Settlements are important as critical spatio-geographic aggregators – of consumer demand, specialization of labour, production and distribution. As the focal point of exchange networks, they also afford reciprocity of cultural perspectives. As well as the capacity to transport and deliver objects there must be a growing dissatisfaction with what one has and a growing desire for more, for the novel, exotic or better, and for greater speed of cultural transmission. Braudel analyses a range of objects in this light, but one of the most prosaic he discusses is salt. An ultra-common commodity, salt is essential for humans and animals, and for preserving a variety of foods. Because of this, exploration and trade over distances depended on the availability of salt and there emerged a huge industry in mining and trading salt. In an important way, something as simple as the availability and trade of salt played a role in allowing the mobility of cultural meanings. Braudel also shows how fashion plays a similar role in the process of cultural exchange. As it circulates ever more widely, fashion objects carry innovation, novelty and difference as their trademarks, but they also speak to *changing desires for difference*, for the taste in something culturally novel, the *joie de vivre* and energy of a culture. When lack of contentedness with one's current material life was provoked through an increasing awareness of the different, exotic and plain better or more interesting, one was forced to confront and overcome the 'ceiling of the possible' (1992: 435). In the case of fashion, when the phantasms of aspirant social classes were stimulated, the economy was also kicked into action. Braudel quotes seventeenth-century dramatist Thomas Dekker, who highlights how fashion is underpinned by the process of aestheticized cultural exchange:

> His codpiece is with Denmark, the collar, his Duble and the belly in France, the wing and narrow sleeve in Italy: the short waste hangs over a Dutch Botchenstall in Ultrich: his huge slopes speak Spanish: Polonia give him the Bootes (Braudel 1992: 321).

Status changes and the demand for culturally novel goods and experiences

In the modern economy, Marx and Engels envisaged capitalism as having an increasingly cosmopolitan character, both in terms of its production and consumption. It has been commonplace to dwell on the productivist implications of Marx and Engels' comment and see capitalist production as requiring for the sake of increasing profits a global reach that one might take to be indicative of a surface cosmopolitanism. Yet, their comments on consumption are prophetic. They point to the growth of 'new wants' that fix on things outside of local and national boundaries; the intellectual creation of nations becoming 'common property'; and the development of a 'world literature'. Marx saw this as an inevitable result of the bourgeois class's search for profits and the mechanical laws of capitalism that require continual exploitation of land and labour. The result is that 'national one-sidedness and narrow-mindedness become more and more impossible' (Marx and Engels 1948).

Interestingly, Marx and Engels' conclusion about the apparently increasing impossibility of cultural narrowness and insularity was echoed nearly 150 years later by Peterson and Kern (1996), scholars who have made one of the most provocative findings in the literatures on cultural consumption for the last few decades. Peterson and Kern (1996: 906) show that the modern economy, infused by markers of cultural practices on matters of social status and honour, has increasingly made insularity and cultural narrowness an outdated set of habits. What was once required for the expansion of the capitalist economy – cross-cultural contacts – is now a fundamental principle of the modern status economy. Part of their conclusion is that standards of 'good taste' now involve knowledge and consideration of cultural goods produced outside one's own national culture. Indeed, in some circles, cultural difference becomes a highly positive status marker. As Peterson (1997: 87) puts it: being high status now does not require snobbishness but means having cosmopolitan 'omnivorous' tastes. Being attuned to the cultural outputs of others requires a sense of inclusivity and the appreciation of cultural difference. However, we cannot uncritically accept that 'inclusivity' and 'appreciating difference' are unproblematic cultural stances. To reiterate Skeggs' (2004: 158) argument, such attitudes are based on relationships of 'ownership and entitlement' whereby certain groups, by virtue of their capacity to define the meaning of cultural objects and peoples, are able to value and propertize cultural difference in exclusionary ways.

A Weberian model of status honour is instructive for understanding the character of the fundamental change Petersen and Kern address. Weber showed that social action happens in part through the effective deployment of symbols of status. He outlines three principles of social stratification, one of which relates to status honour. One of the dimensions of this type of status relates to the way people are stratified according to their consumption of goods or their 'style of life'. Through the skilful use and display of objects and the masterful deployment of modes of interaction within particular social settings, individuals are able to demonstrate and achieve social honour. Within sociological studies of consumption and class Weber's schema has been thoroughly explored, including earlier key works by Veblen, Simmel, Warner and, perhaps most importantly, Bourdieu. Bourdieu's (1984) analysis of cultural tastes links cultural consumption preferences and styles of consuming to patterns of social class in relational linear fashion, relative to preconceived hierarchically ordered categories of cultural goods, along a low to high culture spectrum. Recent scholarship has gone well beyond Bourdieu's original conceptualization of the taste hierarchy, but retained his core ideas of classification and status, cultural capital and social stratification. His work has been applied outside the French context in a range of studies which have developed the nexus linking class and taste, as well as introducing further complexities such as the contrast between omnivorous and univorous taste structures, or the relative influence of social networks compared with education as formative influences on cultural competency (DiMaggio 1987; Lamont 1992; Peterson 1992; Bryson 1996; Erickson 1996; Peterson and Kern 1996; Relish 1997).

Chaney (2002) has recently described how shifting aesthetic and cultural economies, coupled with the rising importance of cultural citizenship, have generated the possibility of deploying cosmopolitan symbols as signs of distinction, at least for select groups within a population. He defines the cosmopolitan cultural citizen as having heterogeneous tastes, and the ability to transcend native culture by adopting a learned indifference to local goods (Chaney 2002: 158). Cosmopolitans are geographically and culturally mobile, and must have the capacity to interpret cosmopolitanism, and especially distinguish it from the comfort and familiarity of the local. As Hall (2002: 26) has put it, cosmopolitanism requires the ability to draw upon and enact vocabularies and discourses from a variety of cultural repertoires. The cosmopolitan has the technical and intellectual resources or 'capital' to gain employment across national boundaries, and typically has an ability to traverse, consume, appreciate and empathize with cultural symbols and practices that originate outside their home country.

Because of their capacity for various types of cultural mobility, we could think of the cosmopolitan as similar to the cultural omnivore identified in recent literature on aesthetic tastes. The cultural omnivore has an ability to appreciate and discern rules and repertoires associated with cultural symbols or forms that originate across cultural boundaries (Peterson 1992; Peterson and Kern 1996). These consumers, assumed to be part of a new middle class, have an openness and 'desire to participate in or "sample" other social and cultural worlds' (Wynne and O'Connor 1998: 858). Whether they are best understood as a class, a category or even 'tribe' of cosmopolitan consumers who actively and conspicuously consume global cultural goods, or whether such consumption is merely circumstantial, ordinary or 'unreflexive', is something further empirical research could usefully address (see for example, Edmunds and Turner 2001). Whatever the conclusion, the patterns of consumption of these emerging omnivores suggest some affinities between them and what we could term 'cosmopolitan consumers'. We elaborate this discussion below.

It is from Peterson's research on cultural consumption that the groundwork has emerged for an understanding of the emergence of the omnivorous, cosmopolitan consumer. For example, Peterson (1990) asserts that the World Music genre, defined as incorporating music of non-Western origin, is likely to be the preferred music of the affluent baby-boomers, and predicts that it may replace classical music as the music of the intellectual classes into the twenty-first century. Van Eijck (2000: 216) speculates that one attraction of these forms of music 'lies in the musical experiment and the juxtaposition of diverse musical elements'. But more than this, such cosmopolitan omnivorousness becomes a symbol of social status and of one's moral worth. More broadly, it is a particular type of cultural capital that demonstrates one is able to appreciate the cultural products and practices of others, suggesting openness and flexibility, which are 'important resources in a society that requires social and geographical mobility, "employability", and "social networking"' (Van Eijck 2000: 221). Such a credential is an important emergent form of capital, argue Peterson and Kern (1996: 906):

> While snobbish exclusion was an effective marker of status in a relatively homogeneous and circumscribed WASP-ish world that could enforce its dominance over all others by force if necessary, omnivorous inclusion seems better adapted to an increasingly global world managed by those who make their way, in part, by showing respect for the cultural expressions of others.

The research into omnivorous cultural consumers teaches us some important lessons about the cosmopolitan consumer. It also raises questions about how a cosmopolitan mode of cultural consumption might be different to the omnivore model. First, we must understand that the identification of these cultural omnivores has almost exclusively taken place in western, developed nations, principally in North

America, Europe and Australia (see Peterson 2005). Is this a product of the fact that research into these patterns has only been conducted by scholars in these parts of the world because it reflects patterns of cultural consumption in those nations or, alternately, is omnivorousness associated with elites in many different cultures? Peterson (2005) notes that non-western nations have their own art-music traditions which could lend themselves to cosmopolitan interpretations within those countries, but is cosmopolitanism an exclusively western cultural vision? Moreover, the Anglocentric nature of such patterns, even if they are only related to where such research is undertaken, may tell us something important about the flows of cultural goods into these western nations. Is it the case that exotic goods of cultural difference predominantly flow from the less developed world to the west? Do underdeveloped nations serve as a source of cosmopolitan cultural stock, from which culturally privileged consumers source new forms of status distinctions, whether it be music, art, food, clothing or religion?

Additionally, there are other questions to ask about the usefulness of the omnivore pattern for conceptualizing the cosmopolitan consumer. First, measurements of omnivorousness have primarily been undertaken through the dimensions of breadth and volume of a particular domain of consumption, related to a hierarchy structured along the low-high dimension. The first thing we should notice is that researchers actually reproduce the character and structure of traditional taste models in their inquiries into this new omnivorous pattern. Committed predominantly to survey methodologies, research has been undertaken in ways which are likely only to partially challenge traditional conceptualizations of taste portfolios. Necessarily using only simple measures, such a model is an unlikely way of furthering understanding of cosmopolitan consumers. In addition, research by Warde *et al.* (2007) has drawn attention to possible multiple types of omnivores. They argue that, to date, 'the social and aesthetic meanings associated with omnivorousness remain to be unravelled because almost all existing work has been based upon inference and interpretation from survey data, and one can only get so far in understanding individual's thoughts and actions using such a method' (Warde *et al.* 2007: 144). Interviewing a sample of omnivores, they find that while extensive engagement with multiple cultural forms is becoming more normal among educated professionals, that there exists a range of styles of engagement with such consumption practices. That is, there is not one omnivore type, but different ways of being an omnivore, constituting sets of possible orientations for engaging with the global cosmoscape. Importantly, each type brings a different rationale and unique set of reasonings associated with their consumption, sometimes dealing with cultural difference in deep, reflexive ways and other times treating it routinely and uninterestingly. This suggests that not all consumers of cosmopolitan otherness will be actual cosmopolitans. The other aspect of the omnivore concept is that studies have most frequently been carried out using music as the field of inquiry (Peterson 2005), though there are now more complex interrelational studies emerging.

Finally, the omnivore concept cannot be said to be analogous to cosmopolitanism because as a rather narrowly defined and operationalized concept it really fails to get at the *ways* people consume, and especially the ethical or political aspects of their consumption. Though variety and curiosity – the hallmarks of the omnivorous disposition – may negate snobbery, such traits can also be associated with connoisseurship, cultural possession and mastery and a desire for the exceptional and rare which are the basis of subtle processes of cultural differentiation and exclusion. The variability of such expressions is likely to be found in matters of audience and context, but overall, the study by Warde *et al.* (1999) found that dining variety gave the middle classes opportunities for demonstrating competence, staking claims of exclusivity, sophistication or refinement, and for making connections with others. All up, a broad repertoire of culinary experience is a significant symbolic token, useful for intra-group differentiation. Based on their data, Warde *et al.* (1999: 123) comment:

> Possibly the trick of contemporary status competition is to appear to honour the populist ethic of equivalence among cultural preferences while still laying claim to cultural refinement and superiority by implicitly marking some genres as exceptionally worthy. The appeal of ethnic cuisines other than one's own is almost certainly symbolic too, linking specialized knowledge with a cosmopolitan orientation.

If the consumption of modern culture was predominantly Enlightenment ('fine', 'cultivated', learned') culture, and if high-modern culture is predominantly driven by the low/high-brow hierarchy ('elites', 'schooling', rigid hierarchies), then the basis of late modern culture is founded upon the breakdown of such hierarchies, at least in terms of the variety and breadth of cultural consumption evident in people's stated preferences and practices (Lash 1990). These practices include the incorporation of cultural outputs of 'others', the valuing of non-western goods, the valuing of experiencing other cultural forms, and the valuing of marginalized cultural goods. This all points to the development of a 'cosmopolitan omnivorousness'. The domain of aesthetics and popular culture has thus been the wellspring for popular expressions of everyday cosmopolitanism and at least at some level, one cannot deny the positive effect associated with the increased visibility of cultural differences in cultural domains like food, music and spirituality. For this, in part, we need to look to the practices of late-modern consumption, based in identity construction and cultural reflexivity, and the capacity of capitalist networks in harnessing and disseminating the cultural goods of 'others'. Yet the downside of this increased availability of cultural possibilities is that they become incorporated into systems of honour, taste and status. More than this, in doing so they become the basis for nuanced cultural knowledges and strategies amongst particular social groups, which hold the possibility of exclusionary practices. Perhaps even worse, they become a taken-for-granted part of people's consumption portfolios, where cultural difference has been included, appropriated, bounded, cleaned-up or contained, then effectively subjugated and incorporated into the mainstream. We can only hope that such incorporations change both the 'consumer' *and* the 'consumed', mainstream and marginalized.

Conclusion: Cosmopolitanism as an Intellectual and Political Project

Cosmopolitanism is an intellectual and political project that makes the promise of a global civil society. In its mature, ideal – yet to be realized – form it is richly interwoven in the social fabric, deeply felt by members, and an inclusive, ethically-based practical response to the social fact of globality. As a principle of social solidarity cosmopolitanism asks members reflexively to reconsider local loyalties as the primary basis for social and cultural interaction. It is founded upon the development of shared connections, material linkages and ethical reflexivities which seek inspiration beyond the local and national, or the restricted and parochial. The result of such developments leads to the acknowledgement of, engagement with and possibly incorporation of social groups previously considered to represent the other.

It is difficult to foresee how the development of such a cosmopolitan society will proceed (Alexander 2006a: 552). We used a discussion of the European project to illustrate how the cosmopolitan project is always embedded in tensions between national and supranational, local and universal, vision and constraints. The same can be said for our analysis of cosmopolitanism as a cultural disposition; tensions structure such outlooks and practices in ways which mean the progression to a mature cosmopolitan culture is inhibited. In some ways, our analysis points to sobering conclusions, suggesting that the necessary conditions and scenarios for such an arrangement are so highly differentiated, socially maldistributed and inevitably fractured, that an institutionally and morally developed cosmopolitan sphere would struggle to take a significant hold across a national population, let alone the globe. Indeed, throughout this work we have identified that issue that competing tensions structure the instigation of a cosmopolitan sphere of meaning. Cosmopolitanism always relies on the identification of the parochial, circumscribed and the local for it to become meaningful. These are the generative binary opposites of cosmopolitanism and their existence suggests reaching for a cosmopolitan sphere will be a social and political struggle. Yet while objects, ideas and images circulate to increasing numbers of people across the globe the possibility of a cosmopolitan sphere seems to live on. And, admittedly, even a mature cosmopolitan culture would not be homogeneously inclusive and just, but would be founded upon the restless interplay of dynamics which sometimes erode, and sometime promote, such values and practices. In this way, developing a cosmopolitan culture must always be seen as originating within the struggles articulated in local and national contexts, suffused by the logics and limits of the nation state and national civil culture.

The fact that the dream of cosmopolitan culture has been around so long attests to its power to excite the social consciousness. As a cultural ideal, however imperfectly realized, it nevertheless continues to structure patterns of engagement with cultural difference and global mobilities of various types. As a cultural ideal it also confronts scholarly imaginations and is currently an important topic in academic circles in the humanities and social sciences. Indeed, scholars analysing its contemporary expressions cannot remove themselves from their own immersion in the array of everyday cosmopolitan fields, and their budding cosmopolitan desires and fantasies frequently seep into their analyses and diagnoses. Paradoxically, over-investing the concept with hope and idealism leads to deflating real chances of its having widespread cultural efficacy; an unrealistic, soft approach to the question of cosmopolitan virtues would hold little hope of bringing forth the political and ethical changes necessary for its long-term, deep manifestation. Running against such idealism, in this book we have tried to adopt an approach informed by classical sociological themes, infused with various elements of political, ethical and cultural realism as they are played out in contemporary social settings. Moreover, we have tried to use a range of sociological concepts – frequently of the classical genre, but also relatively recent ideas that facilitate thinking around classical issues of 'the social' – to frame our understanding of various elements of the cosmopolitan project. We have thus conceived our frame of reference as 'the social', believing that diagnosis of an emergent cosmopolitan condition does not necessarily involve throwing out classical ways of thinking about the apparent new times of the global civil sphere.

Conclusion: Cosmopolitanism as an Intellectual and Political Project

Toward this goal of making classical theories of the social work to explain the nascent cosmopolitan sphere, we have identified much that is of value in the ideas of Simmel, Weber and Durkheim. Our argument has been that these authors have much to say about development and change in the sphere of 'the social', pretty much regardless of historical era. In the case of Simmel we have taken his focus on different forms of sociation enabled by the growth of population nodes such as cities. Urban settings are ordered, sanctioned spaces for observation of the other within socially controlled settings, where identity differentiation becomes increasingly possible, and abstract, widespread and efficient forms of exchange drive the spatial aggregation of citizens. Such economic exchanges bring together individuals who once would not have faced each other, but now do so through the often flattening medium of economic currency and through particular identifiable consumption zones. The possibility, at least, of attention to – and the embrace of – difference becomes possible in such settings. Furthermore, Simmel's capacity to understand flexible, ironic forms of attachment – for example, through the identification of social types such as the stranger or the flâneur – clearly identifies one of the enduring characteristics of being cosmopolitan in the contemporary world. For these social types, alterity and belonging, difference and indifference, are understood as dialogically related, inseparable states that are spatially inscribed and continuously performed.

From Weber, we have sought inspiration from his capacity to link political and ethical outlooks to matters of lifestyle. Furthermore, borrowing from Turner (2006), we have developed the idea of a critical recognition ethics into a framework that we call imaginative realism. Here, we contrast the qualities of the concepts 'imaginative' and 'utopian', believing that identifying cosmopolitan bonds with utopias is politically and sociologically naïve. We have argued that, at least in part, what is more likely is that cosmopolitan bonds emerge from social actors' capacity to be intrigued by, empathize with and reflexively observe cultural others: engagements where imagining the reflexive possibilities offered such contacts becomes activated. Moreover, we have argued that such imaginative capacities must be grounded in and spring from real locales, hence our companion principle of realism.

From Durkheim, we have taken inspiration from his emphasis on the nature of social bonds as arising from moral sentiments. Surely, a key component of the cosmopolitan ethic is the capacity individuals have to imagine bonds with others, to honour commitments which bind them to fellow humans and to realize the idea that each individual is called to a higher social purpose through their associations with others. For Durkheim, it was apparent that such bonds did not end at the borders of the nation state, but required a form of moral universalism which transcended the potentially dangerous loyalties of nationalism. Thus one of our key arguments has been that classical sociology, because of its attempt to understand the general conditions that define *fin-de-siècle* social change, can provide enduring, important tools for the description and analysis of any emergent cosmopolitan condition.

In understanding cosmopolitanism as emerging from bonds of solidaristic sentiments and the imagination we have also been careful to acknowledge the hard, real and socially-spatially located origins of such cosmopolitan bonds. We have been critical of the view that emergent cosmopolitanism requires an associated clearing-away of the symbolic and legislative power of the nation state, as if the nation state somehow is an impediment to the development of cosmopolitan cultures. Our argument has been that the nation state is the enabler and supporter of cosmopolitanism more than its natural adversary, as reductive conceptions intent can frequently suggest.

On the establishment of a cosmopolitan civil sphere, we have also acknowledged the real difficulties individuals face in establishing bonds with strangers. It is, perhaps, a universal psychological reality – no doubt a result of our species' evolutionary history – that most of us display stronger feelings of empathy with and recognition of those who are close, familiar and recognizable than towards the abstract, the distant, strangers and humanity. We are 'hot' animals, not 'cold'; we tend to be emotional rather than ironic. However, cosmopolitanism asks us to face up to rapid changes in this regard and effectively requires individuals to turn such processes on their head. The effective expression of mature cosmopolitan sentiments is caught up in this dialectical tension between local and non-local, familiar and foreign, concrete and abstract. As we have pointed out, in sharp contrast to the attraction of the local and familiar, much scholarship in the cosmopolitan tradition privileges the abstract and the universal over locally defined realities. The solution, we have suggested, is with the argument of Appiah (2005) and Calhoun (2003b), who see cosmopolitanism not as a disparaging dismissal of the local, singular and familiar; rather, the local, singular and familiar are necessary preconditions of an effective cosmopolitanism. In this way, we argue cosmopolitanism is something that is identifiable as a set of practices and outlooks, which spring from citizens who are enabled and capable of making such imaginative leaps beyond their local settings. These cosmopolitan sentiments are likely to emerge most fully from citizens of a state which understands its role as a *governmental mechanism*, rather than as having claims to particular truths. That is, a secular, rather than confessional, state is not alone a sufficient condition for cosmopolitan flowerings, but it is likely to be able to play the enabling role that cosmopolitanism requires.

In various chapters in the book we have advanced the argument that cosmopolitanism could profitably be seen as a type of assemblage or complex where various ethical, cultural and political requirements exist which bring the cosmopolitan subject into being. For a starting point, we have used Max Weber's work to see how far an interpretive sociology might be able to throw light on the construction of the cosmopolitan social actor. Taking inspiration from Weber, we maintain a sociology of cosmopolitanism must be a moral science. What Weber usefully reminds us is that we should see the idea of cosmopolitanism as a system of ethics derived from the analysis and evaluation of the actions of self and of other. We add to this a sense of the ethical personage as historically located to emphasize that the ethical figure of the cosmopolitan is a political and cultural fiction: an entity that does not stand outside of place and history, but is constructed by it. We suggest that this particular type of person – the cosmopolitan – is the ironist, an individual who is 'cold' rather than 'hot' in terms of loyalties, and who finds ambiguity and uncertainty challenging and interesting.

But, additionally and crucially, what we have tried to do is to highlight the various means and mechanisms though which the cosmopolitan subject comes into being. For example, we discuss the role of the secular democratic state in allowing its citizens to adopt ironic, flexible and open attitudes toward the other, of not foreclosing questions of cultural purity and order. As for the cultivation of cosmopolitanness, a basic distinction we have developed concerns the link between *cosmopolitans* and *cosmopolitanism*, that is, between the subject and identity status of the cosmopolitan individual and the historical, political and material circumstances which give rise to the formation of these individuals.

Thinking of this form of self or lifestyle in Weberian terms as a 'status', we argued that cosmopolitanism is not simply assumed, but is a form of self or person that is slowly constructed, over hundreds of years, in specific historical settings. By following Weber, we can see that there is unlikely to be a one-way relationship between political and economic structures and forms of personal comportment, with the former driving the latter, as some recent literatures have implied. Rather, these forms of ethics can be seen as ways in which political groups make sense of themselves and are able to generate an 'ideological' justification of their own value. This form of self can then feed back reflexively into developing political structures: the cosmopolitan and cosmopolitanism exist in a mutually nourishing relationship. Along similar lines, we have pointed out how there is a confluence in the way economic relationships and exchange networks coexist with forms of subjectivity. For example, producers are increasingly aware that markers of cosmopolitan difference attach a desirable cachet to the goods they produce, while consumers increasingly see that sourcing the best and newest from around the world is not only possible, but effective in establishing their social status, as well as meeting desires for novelty. In this way, there is a dialogic relationship between production and consumption, subject and object; the structure of cosmopolitan networks is by no means one way, but depends on the recursive interplay of each dimension.

A significant part of the book investigates the ways social actors are incorporated into, and respond to, the emergent cosmopolitan universe. There are a number of important aspects of this process which we have investigated. One of our chief contributions in this area of cosmopolitan research has been to advance the idea, working from Appadurai's insights, that there are emergent cosmoscapes. We have defined these as spaces, practices, objects and images which afford and construct networks within which cosmopolitan engagements become possible. In other words, these networks of people and things constitute the raw materials which, under the right political and cultural conditions, allow for the surfacing of cosmopolitical agendas and practices and, indeed, provide the frameworks for their interpretation as evidence of 'cosmopolitanization'. As part of the expression of cosmopolitan sentiments within spheres of everyday life, we have made the case that there should be identifiable carriers of the cosmopolitan: humans and non-humans alike, which act as symbolic containers of cultural difference which we can track and map, talk and listen to, observe and interpret. These are mobile, portable symbolic tokens of cosmopolitan sentiments, interacted with and observed by social actors and social scientists alike in everyday settings.

An important dimension of these cosmoscapes is that they are the sites where economic processes fuse with political legitimacies and cultural practices. That is, such features of economic globalization need first to be sanctioned and allowed for by the structures which nation states have created and to which they submit themselves: in short, global neo-liberalism. Cosmoscapes can only emerge if the political conditions are favourable. This theoretical articulation of cosmopolitanism as being expressed in and through different spheres is something we have emphasized. Here, we should also like to emphasize that cosmopolitanism can be seen as a type of assemblage, of political, cultural, material and human actors. The networked relationships between such structures build up over time, through recursive relationships of exchange, so that there are slow accretions of 'cosmopolitan' spaces and arrangements.

Furthermore, we have also drawn attention to the question of how individuals interpret and deal with such cosmoscapes. After all, cosmoscapes only exist because actors – including researchers such as ourselves – interpret the flow of things and people through a cosmopolitan lens. And, we cannot necessarily assume that the existence of a cosmoscape leads to the widespread adoption of fully development cosmopolitan ethics and practices. While we have been careful to warn against individualizing imperatives in theories of cosmopolitanism, on the other hand there can not be a cosmopolitan sphere without aggregates of individual cosmopolitans, among other things. Our question has been: if there is a forest of putative cosmopolitan symbols which manifests fields of objectified, visualized cultural difference, in what ways do actors relate to such material-symbolic constructs?

To be a useful sociological concept, we have argued that cosmopolitanism must be observable in objects, settings and spaces, and indeed written into bodies, their movements and practices. Attendant to this, we have also attempted to alert readers to questions of method and measurement in relation to the concept. Even when we try to pin the key concept down, we end with a rather eclectic mix of indicators. This remains something empirical researchers need to grapple with. Moreover, even if we agree upon matters of definition and measurement, yet more serious problems emerge. We have urged scholars to take a critical, realist look at this imaginative and practical capacity, since we cannot assume these forms exist in any ideal way. Like any major social shift, the deep cosmopolitanization of culture is slow, discrepant and highly variable in terms of its uptake. What may on the surface look like cosmopolitanism may in fact through unintended consequences translate into its exact opposites. Thus, the networks of people and things we have called cosmoscapes are apparently real, but they may in fact promote *uncosmopolitan* values. What this means is that the objectual, material constitution of cosmopolitan objects in things like food, music, dress or habits is susceptible (and, indeed, by its very nature open) to acts of interpretation which render the objects neutral, or even *un*cosmopolitan in nature. This is what empirical research on cultural consumption, and also research into social difference and globality, has recently illustrated. By and large, people use global things for their own purposes, including identity construction, community belonging and status claims. Sometimes these facets of everyday life are exclusionary and boundary drawing, as much as they are inclusive and de-hierarchical. Hence cosmoscapes are a regular feature of modern everyday life, but they do not guarantee reflexive outcomes or genuinely transformative engagements that we associate with mature forms of cosmopolitan engagement.

One of our key conclusions here is that there may not be ideal types of cosmopolitans or a pure type of cosmopolitanism, but merely fleeting, unstable and transient manifestations of it. There are cosmopolitanisms, but there are also spaces and times where cosmopolitans can flourish, and those where they can not. There are times and spaces where cosmopolitan frames, performances and interpretations seem relevant and real, and others where they will struggle to take hold. This mutability and ephemerality occurs as much historically as it can through different parts of the same city on the same day. One of our conclusions is thus that cosmopolitanism is less an unfolding global certainty, and more an aspirational ideal: a process that certain social groups bring to life for their own purposes in particular spacetime contexts. In this section of the work, we have emphasized the idea that cosmopolitan settings, objects and practices emerge not through absolute and concrete time-spaces, but through the energy objects and people can bring to manifest cosmopolitanism. Along a type of behavioural and attitudinal spectrum, we argue that this desire is expressed through certain 'styles' of engaging with cosmopolitan things, which we characterize as sampling, immersive and reflexive. These styles bring their own ways of constructing, dealing with and engaging cosmopolitan difference; they are the networks of human and non-human structures – economic and cultural – which compose modern cosmopolitanism.

The inherent difficulty in theorizing cosmopolitanization processes is that the concept itself carries such normative weight and such political promise, that the sheer hope for a fairer, more equitable and de-hierarchized global culture that cosmopolitanism promises can in fact become a dead weight on its own progress. Certainly, the excitement the concept has recently generated attests to its capacity to generate theoretical innovation in the humanities and social sciences. While we have been enthusiastic embracers of this push, in this book,

Conclusion: Cosmopolitanism as an Intellectual and Political Project 157

as something of a counter to this in-built idealism, we have tried to thrust the idea back into line with some of the most enduring threads in social and cultural theory. While acknowledging the deep and tangled roots of the cosmopolitan impulse, we have tried to combine it with some of the most insightful work from more recent strands of research, including work from the field of cultural consumption and materiality studies, transnationalism and belonging research, and theories of the politico-ethical actor. Theories of contemporary cosmopolitanism deserve serious treatment. We have maintained that this does not involve throwing out the best of modernist social theory, but incorporating it into a meaningful analysis of social change. In forging links between the classical and contemporary traditions of social theory we hope to have shed some light on the cosmopolitan condition.

Cosmopolitanism is a new type of social solidarity; one where strangers are recognized and incorporated, where one's own assumptions and stories are comparable to all others, and where a variety of dimensions of social statuses are opened up, instead of closed off. The key dimension of this solidarity remains a feeling of belonging, of attachment and a spirit of collective goodwill. Yet because cosmopolitanism asks social actors radically to expand their circles of belonging and inclusion, change does not happen quickly or easily across the social spectrum. Certainly, we have emphasized that cosmopolitanism is not just about 'feelings' or 'attitudes', but the structures, networks and materials which allow such dispositions to seem appropriate or advantageous or prestigious in specific spaces and times, and which consequently make it likely to be adopted in a widespread manner. Our line of inquiry suggests that the world is not at the stage where it can be said to have a cosmopolitan culture, but that we have a culture that is cosmopolitanizing. Its uptake and accretion is naturally gradual, but it is also uncertain and driven by contradictory, binarizing forces. One the one hand we see increased mobilities, fluidities and spaces for contact across zones that were once separated; but on the other we find anxieties, exclusions and challenges to such forms of belonging which defuse the accretion of cosmopolitan assemblages. To be cosmopolitan will not involve breaking down these dialectical processes, but understanding they in fact are the very forces which construct the possibility – imperfect as it is – of a cosmopolitan culture.

References

Agamben, G. 1998. *Homo Sacer: Sovereign Power and Bare Life*, Stanford: Stanford University Press.
Agamben, G. 2005. *State of Exception*, Chicago: Chicago University Press.
Ahmed, S. 2000. *Strange Encounters: Embodied Others in Post-Coloniality*, London: Routledge.
Alexander, J.C. 1987. 'The Centrality of the Classics', in Giddens, A. and Turner, J. (eds) *Social Theory Today*, Stanford: Stanford University Press.
Alexander, J.C. 2006a. *The Civil Sphere*, Oxford: Oxford University Press.
Alexander, J.C. 2006b. 'Global Civil Society', *Theory, Culture and Society*, 23(2–3): 521–4.
Anderson, B. 1983. *Imagined Communities: Reflections on the Origin and Spread of Nationalism*, New York: Verso.
Anderson, E. 2004. 'The Cosmopolitan Canopy', *Annals of the American Academy of Political and Social Science*, 595(1): 14–31.
Appadurai, A. 1986. 'Introduction: Commodities and the Politics of Value', in Appadurai, A. (ed.) *The Social Life of Things: Commodities in Cultural Perspective*, Cambridge: Cambridge University Press.
Appadurai, A. 1990. 'Disjuncture and Difference in the Global Cultural Economy', in Featherstone, M. (ed.) *Global Culture: Nationalism, Globalization and Modernity*, London: Sage.
Appadurai, A. 1993. 'Patriotism and Its Futures', *Public Culture*, 5: 411–29.
Appadurai, A. 1996. *Modernity at Large: Cultural Dimensions of Globalization*, Minnesota: University of Minnesota Press.
Appiah, K.A. 1996. 'Cosmopolitan Patriots', in Cohen, J. (ed.) *For Love of Country*, Boston: Beacon Press.
Appiah, K.A. 2005. *The Ethics of Identity*, Princeton: Princeton University Press.
Archibugi, D. 2000. 'Cosmopolitical Democracy', *New Left Review*, 4: 137–50.
Archibugi, D. and Held, D. (eds) 1995. 'Editors' Introduction', in *Cosmopolitan Democracy: An Agenda for a New World Order*, Cambridge: Polity.
Archibugi, D. and Held, D. (eds) 1995. *Cosmopolitan Democracy: An Agenda for a New World Order*, Cambridge: Polity.
Arnold, M. 1965. *Culture and Anarchy*, Ann Arbor: University of Michigan Press.
Bader, V. 1999. 'Religious Pluralism', *Political Theory*, 27: 597–634.
Barber, B. 1996. 'Constitutional Faith', in Cohen, J. (ed.) *For Love of Country*. Boston: Beacon Press.
Bauböck, R. 2002. 'Political Community Beyond the Sovereign State, Supranational Federalism, and Transnational Minorities', in Vertovec, S. and Cohen, R. (eds) *Conceiving Cosmopolitanism – Theory, Context, Practice*, Oxford: Oxford University Press.
Bauman, Z. 1991. *Modernity and Ambivalence*, Oxford: Polity Press.
Bauman, Z. 1996. 'From Pilgrim to Tourist – Or a Short History of Identity', in Hall, S. and du Gay, P. (eds) *Questions of Cultural Identity*, London: Sage.

Bauman, Z. 1997. 'The Making and Unmaking of Strangers', in Werbner P. and Modood T. (eds) *Debating Cultural Hybridity: Multi-cultural Identities and the Politics of Anti-Racism*, London: Zed Books.
Bauman, Z. 1998. *Work, Consumerism and the New Poor*, Buckingham: Open University Press.
Bauman, Z. 2004. *Europe: An Unfinished Business*, Cambridge: Polity.
Baumeister, R.F. and Leary, M.R. 1995. 'The Need to Belong: Desire for Interpersonal Attachments as a Fundamental Human Motivation', *Psychological Bulletin*, 117(3): 497–529.
Beck, U. 2000. 'The Cosmopolitan Perspective: Sociology and the Second Age of Modernity', *The British Journal of Sociology*, 51(1): 79–105.
Beck, U. 2002a. 'The Terrorist Threat: World Risk Society Revisited', *Theory, Culture and Society*, 19(4): 39–55.
Beck, U. 2002b. 'Cosmopolitan Society and Its Enemies', *Theory, Culture and Society*, 19(1–2): 17–44.
Beck, U. 2002c. 'The Cosmopolitan Perspective: Sociology of the Second Age of Modernity', in Vertovec, S. and Cohen, R. (eds) *Conceiving Cosmopolitanism – Theory, Context, Practice*, Oxford: Oxford University Press.
Beck, U. 2006. *The Cosmopolitan Vision*, Cambridge: Polity.
Beck, U. and Grande, E. 2007. 'Cosmopolitanism: Europe's Way out of Crisis', *European Journal of Social Theory*, 10(1): 67–85.
Beck, U. and Sznaider, N. 2006. 'Unpacking Cosmopolitanism for the Social Sciences: a Research Agenda', *The British Journal of Sociology*, 57(1): 1–23.
Benjamin, W. 1973. *Charles Baudelaire*, London: New Left Books.
Bernstein, B. 1972. *Class, Codes and Control*, London: Paladin.
Billig, M. 1995. *Banal Nationalism*, London: Sage.
Boli, J. and Thomas, G.M. 1999. 'INGOs and the Organization of World Culture', in *Constructing World Culture: International Nongovernmental Organisations Since 1875*, Stanford: Stanford University Press.
Bourdieu, P. 1977. *Outline of a Theory of Practice*, Cambridge: Cambridge University Press.
Bourdieu, P. 1984. *Distinction: A Social Critique of the Judgement of Taste*, London: Routledge.
Braudel, F. 1992. *Civilisation and Capitalism, 15th–18th Century*, Berkeley: University of California Press.
Brennan, T. 1997. *At Home in the World: Cosmopolitanism Now*, Cambridge, MA: Harvard University Press.
Brennan, T. 2001. 'Cosmopolitanism and Internationalism', *New Left Review*, 7: 75–84.
Brubaker, R. 2004. 'In the Name of the Nation: Reflections on Nationalism and Patriotism', *Citizenship Studies*, 8(2): 115–27.
Bryson, B. 1996. 'Anything but Heavy Metal: Symbolic Exclusion and Musical Dislikes', *American Sociological Review*, 61: 884–99.
Burke, E. 1985. *Reflections on the Revolution in France and Other Writings*, London: Oxford University Press.
Buss, D.M. 1990. 'The Evolution of Anxiety and Social Exclusion', *Journal of Social and Clinical Psychology*, 42: 459–91.
Calhoun, C. 2002a. 'Imagining Solidarity: Cosmopolitanism, Constitutional Patriotism, and the Public Sphere', *Public Culture*, 14(1): 147–71.

160 References

Calhoun, C. 2002b. 'The Class Consciousness of Frequent Travellers: Towards a Critique of Actually Existing Cosmopolitanism', in Vertovec, S. and Cohen, R. (eds) *Conceiving Cosmopolitanism – Theory, Context, Practice*, Oxford: Oxford University Press.
Calhoun, C. 2003a. '"Belonging" in the Cosmopolitan Imaginary', *Ethnicities*, 3(4): 531–68.
Calhoun, C. 2003b. 'Social Solidarity as a Problem for Cosmopolitan Democracy', paper prepared for the Yale University conference on *Identities, Affiliations, and Allegiances*, October 3–4. Available at http://www.yale.net/polisci/info/conferences/calhoun1.doc. Accessed 28 September 2008.
Calhoun, C. 2007. *Nations Matter: Citizenship, Solidarity and the Cosmopolitan Dream*, London: Routledge.
Calhoun, C., Gerteis, J., Moody, J., Pfaff, S. and Virk, I. 2002. *The Classical Social Theory Reader*, Cambridge, MA: Blackwell.
Castells, M. 2000. *The Rise of the Network Society*, Oxford: Blackwell.
Chaney, D. 2002. 'Cosmopolitan Art and Cultural Citizenship', *Theory, Culture and Society*, 19(1–2): 157–74.
Cheah, P. 2006. 'Cosmopolitanism', *Theory, Culture and Society*, 23(2–3): 486–96.
Cheah, P. and Robbins, B. (eds) 1998. *Cosmopolitics: Thinking and Feeling Beyond the Nation*, Minneapolis: University of Minnesota Press.
Chernilo, D. 2006. 'Social Theory's Methodological Nationalism', *European Journal of Social Theory*, 9(1): 5–22.
Chernilo, D. 2007. 'A Quest for Universalism: Re-assessing the Nature of Classical Social Theory's Cosmopolitanism', *European Journal of Social Theory*, 10(1): 17–35.
Chernilo, D. 2008. 'Classical Sociology and the Nation-State', *Journal of Classical Sociology*, 8(1): 27–43.
Chossudovsky, M. 1998. *The Globalization of Poverty: Impacts of IMF and World Bank Reform*, London: Pluto.
Cook, D. 2004. *Adorno, Habermas and the Search for a Rational Society*, London: Routledge.
Côté, J. 1996. 'Sociological Perspectives on Identity Formation: The Culture-Identity Link and Identity Capital', *Journal of Adolescence*, 19: 417–28.
Davidson, J. 1998. *Courtesans and Fishcakes: the Consuming Passions of Classical Athens*, New York: St Martin's Press.
Delanty, G. 2000. *Citizenship in a Global Age*, Buckingham: Open University Press.
Delanty, G. 2006. 'The Cosmopolitan Imagination: Critical Cosmopolitanism and Social Theory', *The British Journal of Sociology*, 57(1): 25–47.
Delanty, G. and Rumford, C. 2005. *Rethinking Europe: Social Theory and the Implications of Europeanization*, London and New York: Routledge.
Deleuze, G. 1992. 'The Society of Control', *October*, 59: 3–7.
Deleuze, G. and Guattari, F. 1987. *A Thousand Plateaus: Capitalism and Schizophrenia*, Minneapolis: University of Minnesota Press.
Derrida, J. 1994. 'Of the Humanities and the Philosophical Discipline. The Right of Philosophy from the Cosmopolitical Point of View', *Surfaces* 4(1) http://www.pum.umontreal.ca/revues/surfaces/vol4/derridaa.html. Accessed 10 September 2008.
Derrida, J. 2001. *On Cosmopolitanism and Forgiveness*, London: Routledge.

Dickens, C. 1956. *Bleak House*, Boston: Houghton Mifflin.
Diken, B. 1998. *Strangers, Ambivalence and Social Theory*, Aldershot: Ashgate.
Dilthey, W. 1989. *Introduction to the Human Sciences*, Princeton: Princeton University Press.
DiMaggio, P. 1987. 'Classification in Art', *American Sociological Review*, 52: 440–55.
Dryzek, J.S. 2006. *Deliberative Global Politics: Discourse and Democracy in a Divided World*, Cambridge: Polity.
Durkheim, E. 1973. 'Individualism and the Intellectuals', in Bellah, R. (ed.) *On Morality and Society*, Chicago: University of Chicago Press.
Durkheim, E. 1992. *Professional Ethics and Civic Morals*, London: Routledge.
Durkheim, E. 2002. *Suicide: A Study in Sociology*, London: Routledge.
Durkheim, E. and Mauss, M. 1998. 'Between Sociology and Anthropology I: Note on the Notion of Civilization', in Rundell, J. and Mennell, S. (eds) *Classical Readings in Culture and Civilization*, London: Routledge.
Dye, T.R. 1963. 'The Local-Cosmopolitan Dimension and the Study of Urban Politics', *Social Forces*, 41: 239–46.
Edmunds, J. and Turner, B.S. 2001. 'The Re-invention of a National Identity? Women and "Cosmopolitan" Englishness', *Ethnicities*, 1(1): 83–108.
Elias, N. 1994. *The Established and the Outsiders*, London: Sage.
Elias, N. 1996. *The Germans: Power Struggles and the Development of Habitus in the Nineteenth and Twentieth Centuries*, Cambridge: Polity.
Ellison, D. and Woodward, I. (eds) 2005. *Sites of Cosmopolitanism: Citizenship, Aesthetics, Culture*, Brisbane: Griffith University Centre for Public Culture and Ideas.
Emmison, M. 2003. 'Social Class and Cultural Mobility: Reconfiguring the Cultural Omnivore Thesis', *Journal of Sociology*, 39(3): 211–30.
Erickson, B.H. 1996. 'Culture, Class, and Connections', *American Journal of Sociology*, 102(1): 217–51.
Featherstone, M. 2002. 'Cosmopolis: An Introduction', *Theory, Culture and Society*, 19(1–2): 1–16.
Fine, R. 2003. 'Taking the "Ism" out of Cosmopolitanism', *European Journal of Social Theory*, 6(4): 451–70.
Fine, R. 2007. *Cosmopolitanism*, London: Routledge.
Foster, R.J. 2006. 'Tracking Globalization. Commodities and Value in Motion', in Tilley, C., Keane, W., Küchler, S., Rowlands, M. and Spyer, P. (eds) *Handbook of Material Culture*, London: Sage.
Foucault, M. 1977. *Discipline and Punish: The Birth of the Prison*, New York: Allen Lane.
Foucault, M. 1986. *The Care of the Self*, London: Pantheon.
Foucault, M. 1988. 'The Ethic of Care of the Self as a Practice of Freedom', in Bernauer, J. and Rasmussen, D. (eds) *The Final Foucault*, Boston, MA: MIT Press.
Fraser, N. 2007. 'Transnationalizing the Public Sphere: On the Legitimacy and Efficacy of Public Opinion in a Post-Westphalian World', *Theory, Culture and Society*, 24(4): 7–30.
Frisby, D. 1991. 'The Aesthetics of Modern Life: Simmel's Interpretation', *Theory Culture and Society*, 8: 73–93.
Frisby, D. and Featherstone, M. (eds) 1997. *Simmel on Culture*, London: Sage.
Funder, A. 2002. *Stasiland*, Melbourne: Text.

162 References

Giddens, A. 1990. *The Consequences of Modernity*, Cambridge: Polity.
Giddens, A. 1991. *Modernity and Self-identity: Self and Society in the Late Modern Age*, Cambridge: Blackwell.
Giddens, A. 2000. *Runaway World: How Globalization is Reshaping Our Lives*, London: Routledge.
Goody, J. 2004. *Islam in Europe*, Cambridge: Polity.
Guibernau, M. 2004. *Catalan Nationalism, Francoism, Transition and the Democracy*, London: Routledge.
Habermas, J. 1989. *The Structural Transformation of the Public Sphere: An Inquiry into a Category of Bourgeois Society*, Cambridge: Polity.
Habermas, J. 1996. *Between Facts and Norms: Contributions to a Discourse Theory of Law and Democracy*, Cambridge: Polity.
Habermas, J. 1998. *The Inclusion of the Other: Studies in Political Theory*, Cambridge, MA: MIT Press.
Habermas, J. 2001a. 'Why Europe Needs a Constitution', *New Left Review*, 11: 5–26.
Habermas, J. 2001b. *The Postnational Constellation: Political Essays*, Cambridge: Polity.
Habermas, J. 2006. *Time of Transitions*, Cambridge: Polity.
Hage, G. 1997. 'At Home in the Entrails of the West: Multiculturalism, Ethnic Food and Migrant Home-building', in Grace, H., Hage, G., Johnson, L., Langsworth, J. and Symonds, M. (eds) *Home/World: Space, Community and Marginality in Sydney's West*, Annandale: Pluto Press.
Hage, G. 1998. *White Nation. Fantasies of White Supremacy in a Multicultural Society*, Annandale: Pluto Press.
Haggerty, K. and Ericson, R.V. 2000. 'The Surveillant Assemblage', *The British Journal of Sociology*, 51(4): 506–22.
Hall, S. 2002. 'Political Belonging in a World of Multiple Identities', in Vertovec, S. and Cohen, R. (eds) *Conceiving Cosmopolitanism – Theory, Context, Practice*, Oxford: Oxford University Press.
Hannerz, U. 1990. 'Cosmopolitans and Locals in World Culture', *Theory, Culture, and Society*, 7: 237–51.
Hannerz, U. 1992. *Cultural Complexity*, New York: Columbia University Press.
Hannerz, U. 1996. *Transnational Connections*, London: Routledge
Hayden, P. 2005. *Cosmopolitan Global Ethics*, Aldershot: Ashgate.
Hebdige, D. 1990. *Subculture: The Meaning of Style*, London: Routledge.
Held, D. 1995. *Democracy and the Global Order: From the Nation-State to Cosmopolitan Governance*, Cambridge: Polity.
Held, D. 1996. *Models of Democracy*, Cambridge: Polity.
Held, D. 2002. 'Culture and Political Community: National, Global and Cosmopolitan', in Vertovec, S. and Cohen, R. (eds) *Conceiving Cosmopolitanism – Theory, Context, Practice*, Oxford: Oxford University Press.
Held, D., McGrew, A., Goldblatt, D. and Perraton, J. 1999. *Global Transformations: Politics, Economics and Culture*, Cambridge: Polity.
Hesmondhalgh, D. 2000. 'International Times: Fusions, Exoticism and Antiracism in Electronic Dance Music', in Born, G. and Hesmondhalgh, D. (eds) *Western Music and its Others: Difference, Representation and Appropriation in Music*, Berkeley: University of California Press.
Himmelfarb, G. 1996. 'The Illusions of Cosmopolitanism', in Nussbaum, M.C. and Cohen, J. (eds) *Patriotism and Cosmopolitanism*, Boston: Beacon Press.

Hirst, P. and Held, D. 2002. 'Globalisation, the Argument of Our Time', http://www.opendemocracy.net/debates/article-7-28-637.jsp. Accessed 12 November 2003.

Hirst, P.Q. and Thompson, G. 1999. *Globalization in Question*, Cambridge: Polity.

Hodgson, M.G.S. 1974. *The Venture of Islam: Conscience and History in World Civilization, 3 vols*, Chicago: University of Chicago Press.

Hollinger, D.A. 1995. *Postethnic America: Beyond Multiculturalism*, New York: Basic Books.

Holme, T. 2002. *The Carlyles at Home*, London: Persephone Books.

Holton, R.J. 2002. 'Cosmopolitanism or Cosmopolitanisms? The Universal Races Congress of 1911', *Global Networks*, 2(2): 153–70.

Holton, R.J. and Phillips, T. 2001. 'Popular Attitudes to Globalisation', *Different Globalisations*, 20(2): 5–21.

Hornblower, S. 2002. *The Greek World, 479–323 B.C.*, London: Routledge.

Huntington, S. 1996. *The Clash of Civilizations and the Remaking of World Order*, New York: Simon & Schuster.

Hutchings, K. and Dannreuther, R. (eds) 1999. *Cosmopolitan Citizenship*, New York: St. Martin's Press.

Isin, E.F. and Wood, P.K. 1999. *Citizenship and Identity*, London: Sage.

Kagan, R. 2003. *Paradise and Power: America and Europe in the New World Order*, Atlantic Books: London.

Kanter, R.M. 1995. *World Class: Thriving Locally in the Global Economy*, New York: Simon & Shuster.

Keating, M. 1988. *State and Regional Nationalism: Territorial Politics and the European State*, Hemel Hempstead: Harvester Wheatsheaf.

Keating, M. 2001. *Nations against the State: The New Politics of Nationalism in Quebec, Catalonia and Scotland*, London: Palgrave.

Kennedy, M.D. 2006. 'Calhoun's Critical Sociology of Cosmopolitanism, Solidarity and Public Space', *Thesis Eleven*, 84: 73–89.

Kirwan-Taylor, H. 2002. 'The Cosmocrats', *Harpers and Queen*, October: 188–91.

Knorr-Cetina, K. 1997. 'Sociality with Objects: Social Relations in Postsocial Knowledge Societies', *Theory, Culture and Society*, 14(4): 1–30.

Koehler, J.O. 1999. *Stasi: the Untold Story of the East German Secret Police*, Boulder, CO: Westview.

Lamont, M. and Aksartova, S. 2002. 'Ordinary Cosmopolitanisms: Strategies for Bridging Racial Boundaries among Working Class Men', *Theory, Culture and Society*, 19(4): 1–25.

Lamont, M. 1992. *Money, Morals, and Manners: The Culture of the French and American Upper-Middle Class*, Chicago: University of Chicago Press.

Lasch, C. 1995. *The Revolt of the Elites and the Betrayal of Democracy*, New York: Norton.

Lash, S. 1990. *Sociology of Postmodernism*, London: Routledge.

Lash, S. and Lury, C. 2007. *Global Culture Industry: The Mediation of Things*, Cambridge: Polity.

Latour, B. 1993. *We Have Never Been Modern*, Hemel Hempstead: Harvester Wheatsheaf.

Latour, B. 2001. 'Gabriel Tarde and the End of the Social', in Joyce, P. (ed.) *The Social in Question: New Bearings in History and the Social Sciences*, London: Routledge.

References

Latour, B. 2004a. *Politics of Nature: How to Bring the Sciences into Democracy*, Cambridge, MA: Harvard University Press.
Latour, B. 2004b. 'Whose Cosmos, which Cosmopolitics? Comments on the Peace Terms of Ulrich Beck', *Common Knowledge*, 103: 450–62.
Levi-Strauss, C. 1966. *The Savage Mind*, London: University of Chicago Press.
Long, N. and Villareal, M. 2000. 'Small Product, Big Issues: Value Contestations and Cultural Identities in Cross-Border Commodity Networks', *Development and Change*, 29: 725–50.
Lyotard, J-F. 1984. *The Postmodern Condition: A Report on Knowledge*, Manchester: Manchester University Press.
Malcomson, S.L. 1998. 'The Varieties of Cosmopolitan Experience', in Cheah, P. and Robbins, B. (eds) *Cosmopolitics: Thinking and Feeling Beyond the Nation*, Minneapolis: University of Minnesota Press.
Mann, M. 1993. *Sources of Social Power*, Cambridge: Cambridge University Press.
Marotta, V. 2000. 'The Stranger and Social Theory', *Thesis Eleven*, 62: 121–34.
Marx, K. 1993. *Grundrisse: Foundations of the Critique of Political Economy*, Harmondsworth: Penguin.
Marx, K. and Engels, F. 1948. *The Communist Manifesto*, New York: Labour News Co.
Mauss, M. 1973. 'Techniques of the Body', *Economy and Society*, 2(1): 70–88.
McCrone, D. 2001. *Understanding Scotland: The Sociology of a Stateless Nation*, London: Routledge.
McLuhan, M. 1962. *The Gutenberg Galaxy*, London: Routledge & Kegan Paul.
Meijer, R. 1999 (ed.) *Cosmopolitanism, Identity and Authenticity in the Middle East*, Richmond: Curzon.
Melucci, A. 1989. *Nomads of the Present: Social Movements and Individual Needs in Contemporary Society*, Philadelphia: Temple University Press.
Merton, R.K. 1957. *Social Theory and Social Structure*, Glencoe: Free Press.
Meštrović, S.G. 1997. *Postemotional Society*, London: Sage.
Meyer, J. 1951. 'The Stranger and the City', *American Journal of Sociology*, 56(5): 476–83.
Meyer, J.W., Boli, J., Thomas, G.M. and Ramirez, F.O. 1997. 'World Society and the Nation-State', *American Journal of Sociology*, 103(1): 144–81.
Mignolo, W.C. 2000. 'The Many Faces of Cosmo-polis: Border Thinking and Critical Cosmopolitanism', *Public Culture*, 12(3): 721–48.
Miller, D. 1998. *Material Culture and Mass Consumption*, Oxford: Blackwell.
Monbiot, G. 2000. *Captive State: The Corporate Takeover of Britain*, London: Macmillan.
Monocle, 11: March 2008.
Nash, K. 2003. 'Cosmopolitan Political Community: Why Does it Feel So Right?', *Constellations*, 10(4): 506–18.
Nava, M. 1998. 'The Cosmopolitanism of Commerce and the Allure of Difference: Selfridges, the Russian Ballet and the Tango 1911–1914', *International Journal of Cultural Studies*, 1(2): 163–96.
Nava, M. 2002. 'Cosmopolitan Modernity: Everyday Imaginaries and the Register of Difference', *Theory, Culture and Society*, 19(1–2): 81–99.
Nava, M. 2007. *Visceral Cosmopolitanism: Gender, Culture and the Normalisation of Difference*, Oxford: Berg.

Nelkin, D. and Andrews, L. 2003. 'Surveillance Creep in the Genetic Age', in Lyon, D. (ed.) *Surveillance as Social Sorting: Privacy, Risk and Digital Discrimination*, London: Routledge.
New York Times 1886. 'Carlyle's Soundproof Room' February 24.
Nussbaum, M.C. 1994. 'Patriotism and Cosmopolitanism', *Boston Review*, 19(5): 3–34.
Nussbaum, M.C. 1996. 'Patriotism and Cosmopolitanism', in Cohen, J. (ed.) *For Love of Country*, Boston: Beacon Press.
Nussbaum, M.C. and Cohen, J. (eds) 1996. *For Love of Country: Debating the Limits of Patriotism*, Boston: Beacon Press.
Oakeshott, M. 1993. 'The History of Political Thought', in Letwin, S.R. (ed.) *Morality and Politics in Modern Europe*, New Haven: Yale University Press.
Oestreich, G. 1982. *Neostoicism and the Early Modern State*, Cambridge: Cambridge University Press.
Ong, A. 1998. *Flexible Citizenship: The Cultural Logics of Transnationality*, Durham: Duke University Press.
Park, R.E. 1928. 'Human Migration and the Marginal Man', in *The Collected Papers of Robert Ezra Park, Volume 1*, New York: Arno Press.
Parsons, T. 1937. *The Structure of Social Action*, New York: McGraw Hill.
Parsons, T. 1951. *The Social System*, New York: Free Press.
Parsons, T. 1971. *The System of Modern Societies*, Englewood Cliffs: Prentice Hall.
Parsons, T., Bales, R.F., Olds, J., Zelditch, M. and Slater, P.E. 1955. *Family, Socialization and Interaction Process*, New York: Free Press.
Peterson, R.A. 1990. 'Audience and Industry Origins of the Crisis in Classical Music Programming: Towards World Music', in Pankratz, D.B. and Morris, V.B. (eds) *The Future of the Arts*, New York: Praeger.
Peterson, R.A. 1992. 'Understanding Audience Segmentation: from Elite and Mass to Omnivore and Univore', *Poetics*, 21: 243–58.
Peterson, R.A. 1997. 'The Rise and Fall of Highbrow Snobbery as a Status Marker', *Poetics*, 25: 75–92.
Peterson, R.A. 2005. 'Problems in Comparative Research: The Example of Omnivorousness', *Poetics*, 33(5–6): 257–82.
Peterson, R.A. and Kern, R.M. 1996. 'Changing Highbrow Taste: from Snob to Omnivore', *American Sociological Review*, 61: 900–7.
Pieterse, J.N. 2006. 'Emancipatory Cosmopolitanism: Towards an Agenda', *Development and Change*, 37(6), 1247–57.
Pollock, S., Bhabha, H.K., Breckenridge, C.A. and Chakrabarty, D. 2000. 'Cosmopolitanisms', *Public Culture*, 12(3): 577–90.
Putnam, R. 2000. *Bowling Alone*, New York: Simon and Shuster.
Rabinow, P. 1986. 'Representation Are Social Facts', in Clifford, J. and Marcus, G.E. (eds) *Writing Culture: the Poetics and Politics of Ethnography*, Berkeley: University of California Press.
Rawls, J. 1993. *Political Liberalism*, New York: Columbia University Press.
Rawls, J. 1999. *The Law of Peoples*, Cambridge: Harvard University Press.
Regev, M. 2007a. 'Cultural Uniqueness and Aesthetic Cosmopolitanism', *European Journal of Social Theory*, 10(1): 123–38.
Regev, M. 2007b. 'Ethno-National Pop-Rock Music: Aesthetic Cosmopolitanism Made from Within', *Cultural Sociology*, 1(3): 317–41.

Relish, M. 1997. 'It's Not All Education: Network Measures as Sources of Cultural Competency', *Poetics*, 25: 121–39.
Rifkin, J. 2004. *The European Dream: How Europe's Vision of the Future is Quietly Eclipsing the American Dream*, Cambridge: Polity.
Ritzer, G. 2004. *The McDonaldization of Society*, Thousand Oaks: Pine Forge.
Robbins, B. 1998. 'Introduction Part I: Actually Existing Cosmopolitanism', in Cheah, P. and Robbins, B. (eds) *Cosmopolitics: Thinking and Feelings Beyond the Nation*, Minneapolis: University of Minnesota Press.
Robertson, R. 1992. *Globalization: Social Theory and Global Culture*, London: Sage.
Robinson, J.P. and Zill, N. 1997. 'Matters of Culture', *American Demographics*, 19: 48–52.
Robinson, J.P., Shaver, P.R. and Wrightsman, L.S. 1993. *Measures of Political Attitudes, Volume 2*, Sydney: Academic Press.
Ross, A. 2007. *The Rest is Noise: Listening to the Twentieth Century*, New York: Farrar, Straus and Giroux.
Roudometof, V. 2005. 'Transnationalism, Cosmopolitanism and Globalization'. *Current Sociology*, 35(1): 113–35.
Said, E. 1979. 'Zionism from the Standpoint of Its Victims', *Social Text*, 1: 7–58.
Savage, M., Bagnall, G. and Longhurst, B. 2005. *Globalization and Belonging*, London: Sage.
Scheffler, S. 2001. *Boundaries and Allegiances: Problems of Justice and Responsibility in Liberal Thought*, Oxford: Oxford University Press.
Schmitt, C. 1996. *The Concept of the Political*, Chicago: University of Chicago Press.
Schuetz, A. 1944. 'The Stranger: An Essay in Social Psychology', *American Journal of Sociology*, 49(6): 499–507.
Sennett, R. 2002. 'Cosmopolitanism and the Social Experience of Cities', in Vertovec, S. and Cohen, R. (eds) *Conceiving Cosmopolitanism – Theory, Context, Practice*, Oxford: Oxford University Press.
Shah, N. 2006. 'Cosmopolitanizing and Decosmopolitanizing Globalization: Metaphorical Re-description and Transformations of Political Community', *Globalizations*, 3(3): 393–411.
Sharma, S. 2003. 'The Sounds of Alterity', in Bull, M. and Back, L. (eds) *The Auditory Culture Reader*, Oxford: Berg.
Shils, E.A. and Young, M. 1975. 'The Meaning of the Coronation', in Shils, E.A. (ed.) *Center and Periphery: Essays in Macrosociology*, Chicago: University of Chicago Press.
Simmel, G. 1904. 'Fashion', *The American Journal of Sociology*, LXII(6): 541–58.
Simmel, G. 1949. 'The Sociology of Sociability', *American Journal of Sociology*, 55(3): 254–61.
Simmel, G. 1964. 'The Stranger', in Wolff, K.W. (ed.) *The Sociology of Georg Simmel*, New York: The Free Press.
Simmel, G. 1991a. 'The Problem of Style', *Theory Culture and Society*, 8(3): 63–71.
Simmel, G. 1991b. 'The Berlin Trade Exhibition', *Theory Culture and Society* 8(3): 119–23.
Simmel, G. 2002. 'The Metropolis and Mental Life', in Bridge, G. and Watson, S. (eds) *The Blackwell City Reader*, Oxford: Blackwell.
Simmel, G. 2004. *The Philosophy of Money*, London: Routledge.
Skeggs, B. 2004. *Class, Self, Culture*, London: Routledge.

Skrbis, Z. and Woodward, I. 2007. 'The Ambivalence of Ordinary Cosmopolitanism: Investigating the Limits of Cosmopolitan Openness', *Sociological Review*, 55(4): 730–47.
Skrbis, Z., Kendall G. and Woodward, I. 2004. 'Locating Cosmopolitanism: Between Humanist Ideal and Grounded Social Category', *Theory, Culture and Society*, 21(6): 115–36.
Smith, A.D. 1983. 'Nationalism and Classical Social Theory', *The British Journal of Sociology*, 34(1): 19–38.
Smith, P. 2001. *Cultural Theory: An Introduction*, Oxford: Blackwell.
Soysal, Y.N. 1994. *Limits of Citizenship: Migrants and Postnational Membership in Europe*, Chicago: University of Chicago Press.
Stalder, F. and Lyon, D. 2003. 'Electronic Identity Cards and Social Classification', in Lyon, D. (ed.) *Surveillance as Social Sorting: Privacy, Risk and Digital Discrimination*, London: Routledge.
Stevenson, N. 2003. *Cultural Citizenship. Cosmopolitan Questions*, Buckingham: Open University Press.
Stevenson, N. 2006. 'European Cosmopolitan Solidarity: Questions of Citizenship, Difference and Post-Materialism', *European Journal of Social Theory*, 9(4): 485–500.
Stichweh, R. 1997. 'The Stranger – On the Sociology of Indifference', *Thesis Eleven*, 51: 1–16.
Stiglitz, J. 2003. *Globalization and Its Discontents*, Harmondsworth: Penguin.
Swidler, A. 2003. *Talk of Love: How Culture Matters*, Chicago: University of Chicago Press.
Szerszynski, B. and Urry, J. 2002. 'Cultures of Cosmopolitanism', *Sociological Review*, 50(4): 461–81.
Szerszynski, B. and Urry, J. 2006. 'Visuality, Mobility and the Cosmopolitan: Inhabiting the World from Afar', *The British Journal of Sociology*, 57(1): 113–31.
Tabboni, S. 1995. 'The Stranger and Modernity: From Equality of Rights to Recognition of Difference', *Thesis Eleven*, 43: 17–27.
Tajfel, H. 1981. *Human Groups and Social Categories*, Cambridge: Cambridge University Press.
Tarde, G. 1907. *Social Laws: An Outline of Sociology*, London: Macmillan.
Taylor, C. 1994. 'The Politics of Recognition', in Gutmann, A. (ed.) *Multiculturalism: Examining the Politics of Recognition*, Princeton: Princeton University Press.
Tester, K. 1995. 'Moral Solidarity and the Technological Reproduction of Images', *Media, Culture and Society*, 17: 469–82.
Tester, K. 1999. 'The Moral Consequentiality of Television', *European Journal of Social Theory*, 2(4): 469–83.
Tomlinson, J. 1999. *Globalization and Culture*, Cambridge: Polity.
Torpey, J. 2000. *The Invention of the Passport: Surveillance, Citizenship and the State*, Cambridge: Cambridge University Press.
Toulmin, S. 1990. *Cosmopolis: The Hidden Agenda of Modernity*, Chicago: University of Chicago Press.
Turner, B. 1999. *Classical Sociology*, London: Sage.
Turner, B. 2000a. 'Cosmopolitan Virtue: Loyalty and the City', in Isin, E.F. (ed.) *Democracy, Citizenship and the Global City*, London: Routledge.

168 References

Turner, B. 2000b. 'Liberal Citizenship and Cosmopolitan Virtue', in Vandenberg, A. (ed.) *Citizenship and Democracy in a Global Era*, London: Macmillan.
Turner, B. 2002. 'Cosmopolitan Virtue, Globalization and Patriotism', *Theory, Culture and Society*, 19(1): 45–64.
Turner, B. 2006. 'Classical Sociology and Cosmopolitanism: A Critical Defence of the Social', *The British Journal of Sociology*, 57(1): 133–51.
Turner, S. 1986. *The Search for a Methodology of Social Science*, Dordrecht: Reidel.
Turner, S. 2004. 'The Maturity of Social Theory', in Camic, C. and Joas, H. (eds) *The Dialogical Turn: New Roles for Sociology in the Postdisciplinary Age*, Lanham, MD.: Rowman and Littlefield.
Urry, J. 2000a. *Sociology Beyond Societies: Mobilities for the Twenty-First Century*, London: Routledge.
Urry, J. 2000b. 'The Media and Cosmopolitanism', paper presented at Transnational America Conference, Munich. Department of Sociology, Lancaster University, at: http://www.com.lancs.ac.uk/sociology/soc056ju.html. Accessed 21 August 2003.
Urry, J. 2007. *Mobilities*, Cambridge: Polity.
van der Veer, P. 2002. 'Colonial Cosmopolitanism', in Vertovec, S. and Cohen, R. (eds) *Conceiving Cosmopolitanism – Theory, Context, Practice*, Oxford: Oxford University Press.
Van Eijck, K. 2000. 'Richard A. Peterson and the Culture of Consumption', *Poetics*, 28(2/3): 207–24.
Veblen, T. 1991. *The Theory of the Leisure Class*, Fairfield, NJ: A.M. Kelley.
Vertovec, S. and Cohen, R. (eds) 2002. *Conceiving Cosmopolitanism – Theory, Context, Practice*, Oxford: Oxford University Press.
Waldron, J. 1992. 'Minority Cultures and the Cosmopolitan Alternative', *University of Michigan Journal of Law Reform*, 25(3): 751–93.
Wallerstein, I. 1979. *The Capitalist World-Economy*, Cambridge: Cambridge University Press.
Wallerstein, I. 1991. 'The National and the Universal: Can There Be Such a Thing as World Culture?' in *Geopolitics and Geoculture: Essays on the Changing World-System*, Cambridge: Cambridge University Press.
Warde, A., Martens, L. and Olsen, W. 1999. 'Consumption and the Problem of Variety: Cultural Omnivorousness, Social Distinction and Dining Out', *Sociology*, 33(1): 105–27.
Warde, A., Wright, D. and Gayo-Cal, M. 2007. 'Understanding Cultural Omnivorousness: Or, the Myth of the Cultural Omnivore', *Cultural Sociology*, 1(2): 143–64.
Weber, M. 1948a. 'Class, Status, Party', in Gerth, H. and Mills, C. (eds) *From Max Weber: Essays in Sociology*, London: Routledge and Kegan Paul.
Weber, M. 1948b. 'Politics as a Vocation', in Gerth, H. and Mills, C. (eds) *From Max Weber: Essays in Sociology*, London: Routledge and Kegan Paul.
Weber, M. 1968. *Economy and Society*, Totowa, NJ: Bedminster.
Weber, M. 2001. *The Protestant Ethic and the Spirit of Capitalism*, London: Routledge.
Werbner, P. 1999. 'Global Pathways: Working Class Cosmopolitans and the Creation of Transnational Ethnic Worlds', *Social Anthropology*, 7(1): 17–35.
White, G.W. 2000. *Nationalism and Territory: Constructing Group Identity in Southeastern Europe*, Lenham: Rowman and Littlefield Publishers.

White, S.K. 1980. 'Reason and Authority in Habermas: A Critique of the Critics', *American Political Science Review*, 74(4): 1007–17.
Whyte, I.D. 2002. *Landscape and History Since 1500*, New York: Reaktion Books.
Wickham, G. and Kendall, G. 2008. 'Critical Discourse Analysis, Description, Explanation, Causes: Foucault's Inspiration Versus Weber's Perspiration'/ 'Kritische Diskursanalyse, Beschreibung, Erklärung, Gründe: Foucaultsche Aussichten – Webersche Einsichten', *Historical Social Research/Historische Sozialforschung*, 33(1): 142–61.
Williams, R. 1974. *Television: Technology and Cultural Form*, London: Routledge.
Wimmer, A. and Schiller, N.G. 2003. 'Methodological Nationalism, the Social Sciences, and the Study of Migration: An Essay in Historical Epistemology', *The International Migration Review*, 37(3): 576–610.
Wood, M.M. 1934. *The Stranger: A Study of Social Relationships*, New York: Columbia University Press.
Woodward, I. 2007. *Understanding Material Culture*, London: Sage.
Woodward, I., Skrbis, Z. and Bean, C. 2008. 'Attitudes Toward Globalization and Cosmopolitanism: Cultural Diversity, Personal Consumption and the National Economy', *The British Journal of Sociology*, 59(1): 207–26.
Wynne, D. and O'Connor, J. 1998. 'Consumption and the Postmodern City', *Urban Studies*, 35(5–6): 841–64.
Zubaida, S. 2002. 'Middle Eastern Experiences of Cosmopolitanism', in Vertovec, S. and Cohen, R. (eds) *Conceiving Cosmopolitanism – Theory, Context, Practice*, Oxford: Oxford University Press.

Index

Agamben, G., 8, 86–7, 93
Ahmed, S., 92
  see also stranger
Aksartova, S., 17, 19, 23, 100, 102, 107, 114
  see also cultural repertoires, ordinary cosmopolitanism, working class
Alexander, J.C., 27, 131–2, 149
  see also civil sphere, global civil society
Anderson, B., 136
Anderson, E., 108
Andrews, L., 87
Appadurai, A., 3, 9, 13, 27, 111, 125, 129–31, 154
  see also cultural economy, cosmoscapes, imaginary, scapes
Appiah, K.A., 4, 21, 34–7, 43, 50, 152
  see also rooted cosmopolitanism
Archibugi, D., 5, 12, 44–6
Arnold, M., 82, 95
Asian beat, 138

Bader, V., 21
Bagnall, G., 93, 102, 115, 139
Bales, R.F., 60
Barber, B., 36–7
Bauböck, R., 22
Bauman, Z., 13, 51–2, 84, 92, 94, 139
  see also postmodernity, the stranger
Baumeister, R.F., 34
Beck, U., 6–7, 13–15, 18–21, 27, 36, 40–4, 47, 50–80, 85, 96–7, 101, 108, 110
  see also cosmopolitan realism, methodological nationalism, risk
belonging, 4–5, 13–32, 33–53, 54–64, 82–103, 112–36, 151, 156–7
belongingness hypothesis, 34
Benjamin, W., 91, 95–6
Berlin Trade Exhibition, 91

Berlin Wall, 31, 35, 55, 83, 86
Bernstein, B., 112
Bhabha, H.K., 12–17, 40, 101, 114
  see also cosmopolitan virtue
Billig, M., 24
biometrics, 87–8
  see also technology
Boli, J., 12, 57
bonnes à penser, 140
Bourdieu, P., 1, 11, 22, 105–6, 110–17, 144
  see also cultural capital, cosmopolitan disposition, habitus
Braudel, F., 127, 140–2
  see also commodity exchange networks, fashion, salt
Breckenridge, C.A., 12–17, 40, 101, 114
  see also cosmopolitan virtue
Brennan, T., 18, 46
Brubaker, R., 42
Bryson, B., 144
Burke, E., 42
Buss, D.M., 34

Calhoun, C., 4–5, 15–16, 20, 25, 27, 35–8, 41–51, 84, 114, 135, 152
  see also frequent travellers
Carlyle, Thomas, 136
Castells, M., 2
Chakrabarty, D., 12–17, 40, 101, 114
  see also cosmopolitan virtue
Chaney, D., 25, 111–12, 144
  see also cultural citizenship
Cheah, P., 19, 29, 37, 44, 100, 123
Chernilo, D., 39–40, 42, 100
Chossudovsky, M., 2
citizenship, 3, 8, 12–13, 18, 20, 25, 28, 36, 38, 46, 50, 72–3, 78, 84, 98, 112, 132, 136
  cultural, 25, 112
  global, 84, 136
  world, 38

170

city, 24, 65–7, 74, 91–101, 115–16, 120, 136
civil sphere, 131, 150, 152
class, 8, 16–17, 23–6, 34–8, 77–8, 83–6, 109–35, 142–7
classical sociology, 56–75, 91, 152
climate change, 31
code-switching, 110–12
Cohen, J., 12
Cohen, R., 14, 20, 22, 104–6, 111, 113, 133
colonialism, 2, 65–6
commodity exchange networks, 129
communicative action, 48–51
Cook, D., 51
cosmopolitan
 citizenship, 36
 competencies, 9–10, 104, 110–11, 128
 consumption, 3, 8, 23–6, 84, 90–2, 97, 105, 110–57
 democracy, 3, 12, 44–6
 discourses, 25
 disposition, 14, 22–4, 105–6, 110–13, 122
 ideal, 37, 52
 ethics, 70, 80–1, 133
 hermeneutics, 69
 imagination, 36, 61, 114
 individual, 9, 101, 104, 109, 126, 153
 law, 3, 55, 74–6
 morals, 3, 6–7, 11, 21–2, 26, 29–30, 34, 39, 41, 60–2, 70–3, 76–98, 105, 110, 112, 138–9, 145, 149, 152–3
 objects, 8–11, 103–48, 150, 154–6
 outlook, 23, 42, 44, 50, 57, 61, 80, 86, 101–2, 135, 137
 practices, 18–19, 39, 102
 project, 5–6, 35–53, 149–50
 realism, 42, 53
 repertoires, 11, 23, 25–6, 32, 107, 111–12, 130, 144
 society, 15, 19, 149
 subjectivity, 99–100, 108
 universalism, 19, 29–31, 37–8, 42, 45, 53, 57, 61, 152
 virtue, 40, 83, 96, 150
 vs local, 17–18, 24, 37, 39, 93
cosmopolitanism,
 accidental, 10, 104, 117, 119
 actually existing, 10, 17, 100, 114
 and code-switching, 110–12
 and Europe, 6, 28–31, 35–6, 51–3, 54–75, 86, 146, 149
 and non-humans, 9–10, 101, 103, 124, 128, 154, 156
 and novelty, 8, 120, 127, 142, 154
 and objectualization, 101
 and observability, 100–2
 and propertizing the self, 135
 as symbolic specialist, 109
 attribution of, 5, 14, 18, 105, 110, 126
 authentic, 24, 95, 97–8, 116, 121, 133
 banal, 10, 23–4, 44, 90, 97–100, 104, 111, 121, 123, 133
 carriers of, 9–10, 101, 105, 124, 128, 154
 constitutional, 22, 44, 48–9
 cultural, 18, 24, 119, 124, 128
 extreme, 53
 identification of, 15, 101–23, 151
 immersive, 11, 119–20, 156
 indeterminacy of, 14
 indicators of, 11, 18, 24, 101–2, 155
 intellectual, 16, 18, 22, 25–6, 113, 135, 144
 multidimensionality of, 99, 110–13
 mundane, 17, 24–5, 121–6, 135
 ordinary, 19, 24, 26, 100, 107, 114, 123, 145
 performative character of, 9, 104–6, 128
 political, 54–73
 reflexive, 121–3
 rooted, 37–8, 45, 94
 sampling, 104, 115–19, 164
 strategic, 104, 107, 115, 119
 styles of, 11, 25, 77, 114–23, 144, 146, 156
 survey measures of, 102
 Wal-Mart, 44
 working class, 17, 23, 110

cosmopolitanisms, 17, 19, 110
cosmopolitanization, 3, 9–10, 30, 36, 39, 44, 50, 79–80, 89, 101, 127, 137, 154–6
cosmoscapes, 9–10, 128, 142, 154–6
Côté, J., 112, 144
  see also cultural mobility, identity capital
critical recognition ethics, 30, 54, 69–70, 151
cultural appropriation, 8–9, 124, 127
cultural capital, 9, 16, 26, 103–4, 109, 119, 126, 128–9, 144–5
cultural competencies, 10, 104, 110
cultural economy, 8, 125–6, 130
cultural mobility, 112, 144
cultural omnivore, 26, 144–5
cultural repertoires, 19, 25, 105, 107–8, 144

D'Alembert, 37
Dannreuther, R., 12
Davidson, J., 79
Delanty, G., 3, 29, 51, 103
  see also cosmopolitan democracy
Deleuze, G., 13, 85, 88
  see also societies of control
democracy, 3, 12, 20–1, 36, 44–51, 52, 54–5, 82
  cosmopolitan, 3, 12, 44–51
  global, 20
Derrida, J., 17, 84
Dickens, C., 38
Diken, B., 92
  see also strangers
Dilthey, W., 67
DiMaggio, P., 112, 144
Diogenes of Sinope, 4, 7, 31, 33, 34, 82
Dryzek, J.S., 44
Durkheim, E., 27, 30–1, 39–40, 47, 56, 60–4, 74, 131, 151–2
  see also suicide
Dye, T.R., 24

Edmunds, J., 26, 145
Elias, N., 64, 80–1, 92, 94–5
  see also ethics of the self

elite, 8, 16–17, 21, 25, 43, 57, 79, 81, 83–4, 90, 102, 111, 114, 138, 141, 146–7
Ellison, D., 136
emotions, 43, 47, 49, 128, 139, 152–3
  cold, 7, 43, 152–3
  hot, 30, 43, 47, 49, 74, 94–5, 152–3
Emmison, M., 112
Enlightenment, 31, 37, 43, 71, 82–4
Engels, F., 142–3
Erickson, B.H., 144
Ericson, R.V., 88
ethics, 1, 6–7, 30, 67, 69–70, 80–3, 95, 98, 115, 117, 133, 151, 153
  of the self, 83
  recognition, 30, 54, 69–70, 151
ethnicity, 9, 14–15, 21, 25, 38, 42, 44, 47–8, 53, 74, 124, 140, 147
Europe, 6, 28–31, 35–6, 51–3, 54–75, 86, 146, 149
European Constitution, 6, 46, 49, 53
European dream, 52–3
European Union (EU), 6, 28, 29, 36, 51–3, 55, 74
exclusion, 9, 26, 52, 64, 105, 115, 124–7, 143, 145, 147, 156–7
expatriates, 16–17

fashion, 38, 64, 73, 79, 97, 127, 134, 138, 142
Featherstone, M., 20, 22, 66, 105
Fine, R., 6, 35, 43, 46
Foster, R.J., 129, 140
Foucault, M., 7, 80–3, 86, 88
Fraser, N., 52, 69
frequent travellers, 16, 102
Frisby, D., 66, 90
Funder, A., 86

Gayo-Cal, M., 146, 147
  see also cultural omnivores
Gerteis, J., 27
Giddens, A., 2, 7, 23, 34, 68–9, 83
  see also reflexive cosmopolitanism
global,
  business elite, 16, 90
  capitalism, 44, 127, 130
  civil society, 46, 131, 149
  communications, 84, 111, 117

democracy, 20
networks, 8–9, 16, 124, 127, 130
politics, 54–5, 86
warming, 55, 85
globalization, 1–3, 14, 16, 23, 44, 52, 58, 59, 66, 67, 68, 79, 81, 85, 89, 96, 110, 114–15, 122, 129, 131, 135, 154
Goldblatt, D., 3
Goody, J., 31, 58
government, 2, 13–14, 19–22, 29, 46, 55, 76, 132, 153
international, 20, 55
governmentality, 132
Grande, E., 51
Guattari, F., 13, 85
Guibernau, M., 42, 43

Habermas, J., 4–5, 27, 36, 39, 43, 45–52, 69, 70, 76–7, 96
see also communicative action, constitutional cosmopolitanism, instrumental rationality, public sphere
habitus, 1, 22, 105–6
Hage, G., 116–17
Haggerty, K., 88
Hall, S., 13, 25, 112, 144
Hannerz, U., 13, 17–18, 22, 24, 37, 105–6, 109–14
see also expatriates, home-plus, mobility
Hayden, P., 54, 55
Hebdige, D., 24
see also mundane cosmopolitanism
Hegel, 33, 69, 82, 95
Held, D., 3, 5, 12, 13, 18, 20–1, 36, 39, 44–6
see also cosmopolitan democracy, cosmopolitan law
Hesmondhalgh, D., 138
Himmelfarb, G., 12
Hirst, P., 20–1
Hirst, P.Q., 2
Hobbes, 13, 31, 47, 52, 71, 72
Hodgson, M.G.S., 59
Hollinger, D.A., 19
Holme, T., 136
Holton, R.J., 12, 23

Hornblower, S., 52
human rights, 29–30, 71, 78
Huntington, S., 57
Hutchings, K., 12
hybridity, 19, 107

identity capital, 112
identity cards, 88–9
imaginary, 58, 131, 132
imaginative realism, 5, 36, 44, 53, 151
individualism, 62, 84, 90 92
extreme, 90
pathological, 89–90
interpretive sociology, 6, 67–8
irony, 7, 8, 30, 74, 76, 90, 92, 94, 96, 98, 122, 151–3
Isin, E.F., 47

Kagan, R., 13
Kant, I., 4, 13, 18, 19, 31, 40, 52, 61, 71, 73, 79, 82, 83, 97
see also Kantian universalism
Kanter, R.M., 16–17, 78, 84, 114
Keating, M., 43
Kendall, G., 69
Kern, R.M., 26, 112, 143–5
Kirwan-Taylor, H., 16
Knorr-Cetina, K., 101, 103
Koehler, J.O., 85

Lamont, M., 17, 19, 23, 100, 102, 107, 114, 144
see also cultural repertoires, ordinary cosmopolitanism, working class
Lasch, C., 8, 48, 51, 83–5, 89, 92, 95
Lash, S., 8, 96–8, 104, 125, 147
see also banal cosmopolitanism, postmodernism
Latour, B., 48, 61, 96–7
Leary, M.R., 34
Levi-Strauss, C., 140
liberalism, 48, 54–5, 84
lifestyle, 7–8, 76–98, 135, 151, 153
Long, N., 140
Longhurst, B., 93, 102, 115, 139
Lury, C., 125

174 Index

Lyon, D., 88
  see also surveillance, technology, terrorism
Lyotard, J-F., 7, 95

Malcomson, S.L., 17
  see also actually existing cosmopolitanism
Mann, M., 81, 89
Marotta, V., 94
Martens, L., 146–7
Marx, K., 27, 39, 40, 56, 77, 78, 91, 129, 130, 142, 143
Mauss, M., 1, 61, 78, 80
McCrone, D., 43
McDonaldization, 2, 57
McGrew, A., 3
McLuhan, M., 43, 132
media, 13–14, 22–5, 44, 56, 84, 85, 102, 111, 117, 130–3, 136, 138–9
  spectacles, 136
  visual, 130–3
Meijer, R., 15
Melucci, A., 13
Merton, R.K., 24
Meštrović, S.G., 139
methodological nationalism, 40, 42, 55, 56–65, 79, 80
Meyer, J., 94
Mignolo, W.C., 18
migrants, 16, 17, 40, 92–3, 131, 132, 140
migration, 92–3
Miller, D., 140
mobility, 3, 16–18, 26, 85, 93, 110, 130, 132, 139, 145
  cultural, 112, 144
  visual, 132
modernity, 12, 16, 40, 59, 62, 69, 75, 79–80, 87, 92–5, 115
  first, 59–75
  second, 59–75
Monbiot, G., 20
money, 32, 61, 63–7, 84, 140
Monocle, 133–5
Moody, J., 27
music, 9, 23, 25, 26, 66, 84, 85, 119, 127, 128, 131, 135, 137–8, 145–7, 148, 155

Nash, K., 43
nation state, 5, 6, 12–13, 19–21, 28–30, 33–53, 54–75, 78, 80, 83, 85, 95–6, 150–4
  confessional, 28–30, 72, 153
  democratic, 5, 16, 21, 28, 36, 46, 49, 52, 153
  erosion of, 13, 45
  homogeneity of, 21, 51, 57
  secular, 28–30, 82, 153
nationalism, 14, 24, 29, 30, 42–3, 53, 59, 72, 74, 79, 96, 152
Nava, M., 18, 19, 25, 108, 111
  see also cosmopolitan discourses, Selfridges
Nelkin, D., 87
networks, 8–9, 16, 32, 35, 45, 49, 110, 120, 124–40, 141, 144, 148, 154–7
  commodity exchange, 129
  nomads, 13
  novelty, 8, 120, 127, 142, 154
Nussbaum, M.C., 4, 12, 21, 27, 36, 37, 38, 41

Oakeshott, M., 73, 80
O'Connor, J., 26, 145
Oestreich, G., 72, 76
Olds, J., 60
Olsen, W., 146–7
omnivorousness, 26, 144–5
Ong, A., 98
openness, 11, 13, 18, 19, 22, 24, 25, 26, 33, 103–9, 110–14, 115, 118, 120, 121, 133, 144, 145
other, 1, 3, 8, 29, 30, 31, 67, 69, 70, 71, 90, 98, 99, 108, 113, 117, 149, 151, 153

Park, R.E., 94
Parsons, T., 31, 32, 47, 56, 60, 62, 74
particularist (particularism), 37, 45, 53
Perraton, J., 3
Peterson, R.A., 26, 112, 116, 143, 144, 145, 146, 147
  see also cultural omnivores, music
Pfaff, S., 27
Phillips, T., 23

Pieterse, J.N., 44
political lifestyle, 76–98
political realism, 54–5
politics, 15, 20, 21, 33–98, 117, 122, 130
Pollock, S., 12, 14, 15, 16, 17, 40, 101, 114
  see also cosmopolitan virtue
postmodernity, 21, 94, 97, 98
public sphere, 5, 44–5, 77
  international, 44
Putnam, R., 47

Rabinow, P., 18
Ramirez, F.O., 12, 57
rationality, 7–8, 48, 49, 51, 70, 71, 73, 83–5, 89, 95, 96
  hyper-, 83–5
  instrumental, 48, 51
Rawls, J., 21
recognition ethics, 30, 54, 69–70, 151
reflexivity, 6–7, 10–11, 19, 24–6, 36, 39, 50, 83, 104, 107, 108, 112, 113, 115, 117, 121–3, 124, 138, 139, 147, 148, 149, 151, 154, 156
refugees, 16, 17, 40, 89, 132
Regev, M., 25, 137, 138
relativism, 42, 53, 57, 70
religion, 21, 38, 47, 69, 71, 81, 82, 89, 127, 146
Relish, M., 144
Rifkin, J., 52, 53
  see also European dream
risk, 31, 34, 36, 62, 74, 79–80, 85, 140
Ritzer, G., 2, 96
  see also McDonaldization
Robbins, B., 10, 19, 29, 100, 114, 123
  see also actually existing cosmopolitanism
Robertson, R., 129
Robinson, J.P., 24
Ross, A., 137
  see also music
Roudometof, V., 42, 44
  see also cosmopolitan virtue
Rumford, C., 29, 51

Said, E., 13
Sarajevo, 15

Savage, M., 93, 102, 115, 139
  see also belonging
scapes, 9, 10, 13, 128–40, 154–6
Scheffler, S., 39
Schiller, N.G., 42
Schmitt, C., 42, 59, 72, 92, 95
Schuetz, A., 92, 94
  see also the stranger
Selfridges, 25
Sennett, R., 93, 120
September 11, 85, 88
Shah, N., 46
Sharma, S., 138
  see also music
Shaver, P.R., 24
Shils, E.A. 33, 47, 73, 79, 80
Simmel, G., 6, 27, 31, 32, 39, 62, 63–7, 74, 80, 90–6, 115, 127, 144, 151
  see also Berlin Trade Exhibition, city, money, stranger, style
Skeggs, B., 11, 109–10, 135, 143
  see also cultural appropriation, exclusion, intellectual cosmopolitanism
Skrbis, Z., 3, 12, 22, 40, 102, 113, 114, 139
  see also strategic cosmopolitanism
Slater, P.E., 60
Smith, A.D., 40, 135
Smith, P., 96
social order, 29, 35, 36, 47, 51, 60, 125
sociation, 89–98, 151
societies of control, 88–9
solidarity, 5, 6, 19, 25, 31, 36, 46, 47–50, 53, 135, 139, 141, 149, 157
  integrated, 50
sovereignty, 6, 43, 45, 46, 53, 72
Soysal, Y.N., 13
Stalder, F., 88
  see also surveillance, technology, terrorism
state of exception, 87, 96
status, 7–9, 26, 34, 38, 77–80, 91–7, 112, 113, 120, 124–9, 140, 142–8, 153, 154, 156, 157
Stevenson, N., 52, 138–9
  see also cultural citizenship

Index

Stichweh, R., 94
Stiglitz, J., 2
stranger, 4, 19, 92–4, 120, 151–2, 157
stratification, 78, 143–4
style, 11, 25, 77, 114–23, 144, 146, 156
  immersive, 119–21
  reflexive, 121–3
  sampling, 115–19
suicide, 62
surveillance, 8, 68, 85–8
surveillant assemblage, 88, 97
Swidler, A., 107–8
  see also cultural repertoires
symbolic economy, 129
symbolic specialist, 117
Sznaider, N., 13
Szerszynski, B., 44, 101, 102, 111, 113, 132, 133, 135, 136, 137
  see also indicators of cosmopolitanism, visual media, visual mobility

Tabboni, S., 94
Tajfel, H., 30, 34
Taliban, 30, 70, 71
Tarde, G., 61, 63, 90
Taylor, C., 21, 69
technology, 64, 83–98, 117, 133
  bad, 85–9
  biometrics, 87–8
  communications, 84, 111, 117
  identity cards, 88–9
  televisual flows, 132
  terrorism, 13, 86, 87, 88, 132
Tester, K., 138
Thomas, G.M., 12
Thompson, G., 2
Tomlinson, J., 13, 22, 106, 113
Torpey, J., 85
Toulmin, S., 7, 48, 51, 83, 89, 92, 95
tourism, 25, 104, 113, 116, 132, 134, 135, 139
travel, 2, 8, 14, 16, 18, 23, 31, 61, 84, 89, 101, 102, 110, 111, 113, 132, 133–5, 139

Turner, B., 21, 26, 27, 30, 31, 32, 43, 59, 60, 62, 67, 68, 69, 70, 74, 76, 90, 96, 100, 145, 151
  see also cosmopolitan hermeneutics, cosmopolitan virtue, recognition ethics
Turner, S., 28, 68, 69

uncosmopolitan, 3, 9, 15, 29, 124, 155, 156
United Nations, 23, 55
universalism, 19, 29, 31, 37, 38, 42, 45, 53, 57, 61, 152
  abstract, 38, 45, 53
  Kantian, 19, 31, 61
Urry, J., 3, 13, 18, 19, 22, 23, 24, 44, 101, 102, 106, 110, 111, 113, 132, 133, 135, 136, 137
  see also media, mobility, banal cosmopolitanism

Van der Veer, P., 20
Van Eijck, K., 26, 112, 145
Veblen, T., 91, 92, 95, 144
Verstehende Soziologie, 67–71
Vertovec, S., 14, 20, 22, 104, 105, 106, 111, 113, 133
Villareal, M., 140
Virk, I., 27

Waldron, J., 112
Wallerstein, I., 2, 57
  see also global capitalism
Warde, A., 146, 147
  see also cultural omnivores
Weber, M., 6–7, 27, 30, 38, 39, 40, 54, 57, 62, 63, 67–70, 71–80, 81, 83, 92, 95, 96, 143, 144, 151, 153
  see also interpretive sociology, status, stratification, *Verstehende Soziologie*
Werbner, P., 17, 20
  see also working class
Western view, 20
White, G.W., 33
  see also nationalism
White, S.K., 51
Whyte, I.D., 33
Wickham, G., 69

Williams, R., 132
Wimmer, A., 42
Wood, M.M., 94
　see also stranger
Wood, P.K., 47
Woodward, I., 22, 34, 102, 114, 123, 136, 139
　see also cosmopolitan consumption, cosmopolitan objects, strategic cosmopolitanism
world music, 26, 84, 145
Wright, D., 146, 147
　see also cultural omnivores
Wrightsman, L.S., 24
Wynne, D., 26, 144

Young, M., 33, 79

Zelditch, M., 60
Zill, N., 24
Zubaida, S., 20